Critical Issues

in

Labor Arbitration

PROCEEDINGS OF THE TENTH ANNUAL MEETING

NATIONAL ACADEMY OF ARBITRATORS

PHILADELPHIA, PENNSYLVANIA • January 31-February 2, 1957

Edited by

Jean T. McKelvey

*Professor, New York State School of Industrial and
Labor Relations, Cornell University*

BNA INCORPORATED • WASHINGTON, D. C.

1957

Printed in the United States of America
31

CONTENTS

iii

CONTENTS

EDITOR'S PREFACE

Organized in Chicago in 1947, the National Academy of Arbitrators celebrated its tenth anniversary at the annual meeting held in Philadelphia, January 31-February 2, 1957. This volume contains the proceedings of the decennial convention. It is the third such volume to be published for the Academy by The Bureau of National Affairs, Inc. Starting in 1955 the Academy published its proceedings under the title: ARBITRATION TODAY. The following year, 1956, the proceedings were issued under the title: MANAGEMENT RIGHTS AND THE ARBITRATION PROCESS.

In addition to the current volume, the Academy also is publishing this year, under separate cover, selected papers from its first seven annual meetings under the title: THE PROFESSION OF LABOR ARBITRATION. The completion of these four volumes makes available to all those interested in the arbitration process—industry, labor, practitioners, and students—a wealth of material on arbitration in labor-management relations covering such topics as theories, procedures, substantive issues, law, and professional ethics.

Reviewing the first decade of the Academy's history in his Presidential Address which introduces this volume, John Day Larkin notes that the Academy was created for the specific purpose of improving the process of arbitration. He goes on to trace the ways in which the Academy has endeavored to accomplish this goal through its activities and functions as a professional organization. But an organization, like an individual, must look ahead, as well as back. The challenge of the next decade is set forth by Ralph T. Seward who served as the first President of the Academy. Another past President, George W. Taylor, comments on the place of arbitrator in a free society in his dinner address: "The Effectuation of Arbitration by Collective Bargaining." This paper stirred memories of Dr. Taylor's earlier address to the Academy: "Effectuating the Labor Contract through Arbitration"* and served to tie the present to the past by indicating the reciprocal relationship between collective bargaining and arbitration.

---

* Published in *The Profession of Labor Arbitration*, ch. 2.

The other papers delivered at the tenth annual meeting, in a program arranged by Paul Guthrie, covered four areas of current interest in arbitration. One session dealt with procedures, addressing itself to the question: Can the drift toward technicalities in arbitration be halted? Two presented research findings on substantive issues: the arbitration of discharges and of incentive problems. A fourth session was devoted to a discussion of the proposed Uniform Arbitration Act. To assist the reader in following the debate on this Act the editor has placed in the Appendix the text of the revised Draft Act, and the Report of the Academy's Committee on Law and Legislation.

In preparing the volume for publication the editor wishes to acknowledge the cooperation of the speakers, who once again made her task an easy one. In addition, she wishes to express for the Academy its appreciation of the editorial encouragement and assistance of Mr. John D. Stewart, Vice-President of the Bureau of National Affairs, Inc. The Academy is also greatly indebted to Miss Sibyl Sills of the Sills Reporting Service who donated her time to make a stenographic transcript of the sessions.

In addition to the papers and committee reports found in this volume, there is one innovation which merits comment and explanation. This is the final chapter entitled: "The John Deere-UAW Permanent Arbitration System" by Harold W. Davey, which is the first of a projected series of research studies by members of the Academy on Umpire Systems in Mass Production Industries. In order to make these studies available upon their completion the decision has been made to publish them initially as chapters in the annual volumes. Ultimately it is the intention of the Board of Editors, under the Chairmanship of William H. Davis, to bring the separate chapters together and to issue them as a single volume which will for the first time describe, analyze and evaluate what has been the most striking development in the arbitration field in recent years: the growth of permanent arbitration systems in mass production industries. The Academy is proud that its members have served as arbitrators in so many of these situations and hopes to prod them to make available to others their own rich experience as practitioners. It is especially grateful to Professor Davey for completing his assignment in time for publication in the decennial volume.

Finally, the editor notes with sorrow the death of J. Noble Braden, Vice-President of the American Arbitration Association, on February 15, 1957, just two weeks after the close of the Academy meeting. Mr.

Braden attended this convention and the transcript bears witness to the many helpful remarks he made during the sessions. Had he lived, he planned to cooperate with the editor in providing additional material for this volume. His untimely death leaves all of us with a debt which can never be repaid.

Jean T. McKelvey

Ithaca, New York
March 26, 1957

INTRODUCTION: THE FIRST DECADE

Recently a college professor, who is not familiar with the arbitration process, asked me why the National Academy of Arbitrators came into being. Ten years after its founding, no one who is familiar with the field of labor-management arbitration raises such a question. But it is only fitting, after the experiences of this decade, that we briefly review the Academy's initial objectives in the light of its subsequent accomplishments.

In 1947 an article was published which severely criticized certain practitioners in the field of grievance arbitration. The author objected to what he termed the "big business" aspect of it. He implied that some who were engaged in labor-management arbitration were playing politics with their decisions and passing out awards on a "now-it's-your-turn" basis.[1] These comments, which have been reprinted in a current case book on labor law,[2] are still conveying to students of this subject the impression that many of those engaged in the arbitration of labor grievances are practicing without ethical standards.

Unfortunately there was just enough truth in some of the things this critic had to say in 1947 to cause certain arbitrators to take steps to remedy the situation. The National Academy of Arbitrators was created for the specific purpose of improving the arbitration process. In this venture it has had substantial cooperation from the parties to industrial disputes. Both management and labor representatives have contributed much to aid us in our study of the problems in which we all become involved.

While arbitration is ancient in origin, labor-management arbitration as we know it is a unique American institution. In fact, as a process for resolving disputes in the industrial relations field, it is essentially a development of the first half of the twentieth century. And its greatest usefulness has developed in the United States during the past fifteen years.

---

[1] 3 *Labor and the Nation*, No. 5, pp. 48-49.
[2] Handler and Hays, *Cases and Materials on Labor Law*, 2nd Ed., St. Paul, 1953, pp. 399-400.

During World War II, when many of us saw the War Labor Board inundated with unresolved disputes, which ranged from major wage issues to the most trivial grievances in industrial plants throughout the country, certain of those serving on the Board began to encourage the parties to collective agreements to introduce arbitration as a terminal step in the grievance procedure of their contracts. The Board even provided its own panel of arbitrators and managed to reduce its backlog of disputed cases by getting the parties to submit many of them to arbitration rather than take up the time of the entire Board. Often management was reluctant to accept this process as a substitute for its final decision-making in grievance matters. But with the counter-offer of the no-strike pledge for the duration of the agreement, more and more companies and unions began to find arbitration acceptable.

Also, since the War Labor Board was a temporary, emergency agency for handling unresolved disputes, some appropriate peacetime solution for deadlocked labor-management issues had to be worked out. Our very tradition of free enterprise, and free collective bargaining, suggested a solution by the parties themselves. The provision in the collective agreement for a grievance procedure ending in final and binding arbitration was a way of keeping petty issues at home, out of the hands of the government, and particularly out of the courts, while at the same time keeping production lines operating. In this way the parties were privileged to choose their own judge; one with special knowledge and competence in the industrial relations field.

It is significant that at the Labor-Management Conference of 1945 the committee on "Existing Collective Agreements" unanimously recommended the use of arbitration to resolve disputes over contract terms. And today this is a major factor in the maintenance of industrial peace.[3] Of approximately 100,000 collective bargaining agreements in the United States (according to our best information), more than 90% of them have some type of arbitration provision.

The most admirable aspect of this development is that it is something which labor and management have developed to serve them. As the late Herbert Syme said: "Labor arbitration is one of the great examples of American voluntarism."[4] It is outside the orbit of government. But it

[3] George W. Taylor, *Government Regulation of Industrial Disputes*, New York, 1948, p. 231.
[4] *Labor Law Journal*, March 1946, p. 142. See also A. N. Hand, "The Arbitration Movement in Historical Perspective," *Arbitration Journal*, N. S. 8: 170 (1953) for a similar view.

is not a substitute for litigation. It is a substitute for the strike and the lock-out. It is a process whereby the parties to collective agreements may resolve their differences and continue to live in peace and relative harmony, without resort to economic pressure and loss to all concerned. It is, in short, one aspect of the American democratic process.

Those of us who were engaged in the practice of labor-management arbitration ten years ago often felt that we were adrift on an uncharted sea. We were forever finding ourselves in out-of-the-way places, in the midst of local tensions. In such an atmosphere, the parties to the disputes we were called in to resolve were at once quick to curry favor with the impartial arbitrator, and equally quick to suspect his every move. If he decided the case in your favor, he was approvable for another such assignment; if he decided against you, he was forever expendable. And this was too often the parties' conclusion, regardless of the merits of the case.

Speaking of the situation in 1947, Bill Simkin has said: "Many of us in this 'lone wolf' type of work felt a need for a common meeting ground."[5] The only indication of what fellow arbitrators were doing in situations comparable to those confronting us was to be found in selected cases which were published in the *Labor Arbitration Reports* of The Bureau of National Affairs, or in the Prentice-Hall *Labor Law Service*. We not only read, with some chagrin, what our critics had to say; we often listened to the parties' complaints of some of the alleged questionable practices of those pretending to be arbitrators. It was the conviction of a dedicated group of professional men that the arbitration process could be preserved only if it were kept in professional hands and away from both the amateurs and the shysters. This led to two meetings in the summer of 1947 which resulted in the founding of the National Academy of Arbitrators.

The first of these meetings was a brief, informal gathering in Washington, D. C. This was followed by a meeting at the Stevens Hotel in Chicago, September 13, 1947, with forty-three qualified arbitrators, representing the several sections of the United States. From this meeting came the N.A.A. organization, its constitution, its by-laws and its first working committees.

---

[5] National Academy of Arbitrators, *Annual Report of the Membership Committee*, January 19, 1950.

The purposes and aims as initially stated are:

> To establish and foster high standards and competence among those engaged in the arbitration of industrial disputes on a professional basis; to adopt canons of ethics to govern the conduct of arbitrators; to promote the study and understanding of the arbitration of industrial disputes.

The Academy is not, and never was intended to be, an agency for the selection or appointment of arbitrators. From the first it was understood that the designation of arbitrators in particular situations, where the parties could not agree, and where the assistance of an outside agency might be required, should be left to the American Arbitration Association, the Federal Mediation and Conciliation Service, or the appropriate state agency. The purpose of the Academy was to strengthen the arbitration process in those particulars not already serviced by the appointive agencies. It was not the intent or the purpose to duplicate the functions of existing agencies, but rather to supplement their established activities. Such has continued to be the objective of this Academy.

Between the founders' meeting in 1947 and the first annual meeting in Chicago, January 16 and 17, 1948, the Membership Committee brought the list of charter members up to 105. From that time forward this committee has remained one of our most important, paying particular attention to the experience records and character references of those seeking membership in the Academy. While we may differ among ourselves as to the qualifications of individual applicants, we have generally agreed that the applicant should be of good moral character, as demonstrated by adherence to sound ethical standards in his arbitration practice, and that he should have substantial and current experience as a neutral arbitrator of labor-management disputes. It has been our purpose to foster the highest possible standards of integrity, competence, honor and character among those engaged in the arbitration of industrial disputes on a professional basis. Without standards of exceptional integrity this process cannot survive.

Approximately 250 arbitrators have been admitted to membership in the Academy. But it cannot be said that all of these have remained practitioners of the profession. Some have become public servants. Two are in the United States Senate. Others have become judges. One has become chancellor of a major university. One has become sheriff of Cook County, Illinois. And others have been advanced to responsible administrative positions in government, in industry and in the academic world. A few have retired. And our current roster lists fourteen deceased members.

To offset this loss to our ranks, we are adding from ten to twenty qualified members annually. This number will vary according to the number and quality of applications received.

There has been some criticism of our roster because certain members are no longer primarily engaged in the practice of arbitration. Indeed we now have members who, though qualified when admitted, have since accepted positions as advocates for labor or management in the industrial relations field and currently have little or no practice as neutral arbitrators. Once having established his qualifications and been admitted, one remains a member of the Academy, if he wishes, in spite of some change in occupational status. It has been said that arbitrators are expendable. But so also are those holding political office or administrative positions in government and industry. And some of our outstanding members have moved from active to inactive status as arbitrators and returned. The point of no return is when the Ethics Committee, upon the basis of substantial and conclusive evidence, finds that a member is conducting himself in a manner which may jeopardize the arbitration process and the Academy decides that the member's name should be expunged from our list. Thus far this drastic step has not been necessary.

At the January 1948 meeting, the Ethics Committee began its study of proper practices and procedures for arbitrators. It was only a matter of a few months thereafter that the American Arbitration Association set up a committee to restudy its rules and procedures. As the work of the two committees progressed, it became evident that one set of rules governing the conduct of arbitrators in labor-management disputes would be more appropriate than two. In the final stages of the preparation of the ethical standards, the Ethics Committee of the National Academy worked with the A.A.A. Committee. By cooperating with the A.A.A. and the Federal Mediation and Conciliation Service, a *Uniform Code of Ethics and Procedural Standards for Labor-Management Arbitration* was adopted and published.[6] Since its adoption this code has not only become the accepted one by these national organiza-

---

[6] EDITOR'S NOTE: The text of this Code of Ethics appears in *The Profession of Labor Arbitration* (Washington, BNA Incorporated, 1957).

tions, but it is also in general use by state appointive agencies. The wide circulation of this publication, by both the National Academy of Arbitrators and the American Arbitration Association has done much to improve the practices in labor-management arbitration.

One of the first activities initiated by the National Academy of Arbitrators (designed to take arbitrators out of the "lone wolf" stage) was a series of regional meetings, wherein members could meet, exchange experiences and discuss common problems. Such meetings are held with or without the participation of other interested parties who are not members, depending upon the nature of the subject matter under consideration.

Perhaps the greatest contribution which the National Academy has made toward the strengthening of the arbitration process has been its annual meetings. From the first the members who have been able to attend these events have learned much from the most experienced and most highly skilled practitioners in the field. And it has also been the practice to have on our annual programs some of our most severe critics, those who represent the parties in labor-management disputes. It is through these public meetings that the standards of those who practice professionally in the field of arbitration are elevated and the public learns something of the nature of the profession.

Our Committee on Research and Education edits and, through the cooperation of The Bureau of National Affairs, publishes the proceedings of these annual meetings. This practice was started in 1955 with the publication of *Arbitration Today*. It was continued with a second volume on *Management Rights and the Arbitration Process* in 1956. It is our purpose this year to publish in addition to this volume of proceedings, a companion volume which will include some of the more noteworthy papers delivered at the first seven annual meetings.[7]

This committee also plans to edit and publish a volume on umpireships in major industries, provided those members who have served in this capacity are able to get the cooperation of the parties in a sufficiently representative number of cases.[8]

In addition to the cooperation of The Bureau of National Affairs, the Commerce Clearing House, through its *Labor Law Journal*, has pub-

---

[7] EDITOR'S NOTE: This volume will appear under the title: *The Profession of Labor Arbitration*.

[8] EDITOR'S NOTE: The first such study has just been completed and is incorporated in the present volume as Chapter IX: "The John Deere-UAW Permanent Arbitration System" by Harold W. Davey.

lished a number of papers produced by members of the Academy, some of which have been the direct result of workshops conducted at our annual meetings. Through all of these channels our organization has contributed much to advance the professional status of those active in the field of labor-management arbitration.

While we stated at the outset that it was not our purpose to serve the public as an appointive agency, it is significant that since the beginning of the publication of our membership roster, there has been not only a growing respect for the professional arbitrator, but also a steadily increased demand for those who have been admitted to membership in the N.A.A. Some parties to collective bargaining agreements have begun to specify in their agreements, not a particular arbitrator, nor a panel from which one is to be chosen, but simply that the one who serves them must be a member of the National Academy of Arbitrators. And we are told that the appointive agencies have at times been requested to include only N.A.A. members on the panels which they are asked to submit to the parties.

There is one recent development in the arbitration field which the National Academy did not initiate. We take no credit for the introduction of the proposed Uniform Arbitration Act.[9] While the members of the Academy are divided on the subject, a substantial number believe that the less legislation we have in the field of labor-management arbitration the better it will be for the prompt settlement of grievances. Legislation of this kind invites litigation. And such litigation will tend to stifle the use of voluntary arbitration and to prolong rather than shorten the grievance process.

Today, the generally accepted contract clauses provide for the settlement of grievances by final and binding awards of arbitrators chosen by the parties. Under the proposed Uniform Arbitration Act, an award will be neither final nor binding if one party is unhappy with the result and elects to hire an attorney and appeal to the courts. In this way the pot is kept boiling; the process is prolonged; the expense mounts; and the government lays on a heavy hand. What has been a voluntary, economical and speedy method of resolving grievances may

---

[9] EDITOR'S NOTE: The text of the Act as originally drafted in 1955 appears in Appendix D of *Management Rights and the Arbitration Process* (Washington, BNA Incorporated, 1956). The text of the revised draft (1956) appears in Appendix B of this volume.

well become involuntary, expensive and long drawn-out, if this proposed act is adopted in all of the major industrial states.

While the National Academy had no part in initiating the proposed Uniform Act, it has offered constructive suggestions for the improvement of this proposed legislation.[10] And it will continue, through its Committee on Law and Legislation, to advocate such changes in this and other legislative proposals as will reserve to the parties the greatest possible latitude in resolving their local grievances without becoming involved in needless litigation in the courts.

The work of arbitrators, like that of judges, is in one sense enduring and in another sense ephemeral. That which is erroneous is sure to perish. The good remains, the foundation on which new policies, practices and procedures will be built. That which is bad will be cast off in due time. Little by little, old and outworn doctrines are undermined, both through the process of negotiation by the parties and by the sounder reasoning of those called upon to interpret the language which the parties have hammered out in the heat of economic conflict, and through long hours of patient effort to reach an agreement.

Often we worry overmuch about the enduring consequences of our errors. They may work some confusion for a time. But in the end they will be modified or corrected or their teachings ignored. The future takes care of such things. "In the endless process of testing and retesting, there is a constant rejection of the dross, and a constant retention of whatever is pure and sound and fine."[11]

We take pride in the contributions made by the National Academy of Arbitrators toward the strengthening of the arbitration process. What our critic had to say ten years ago may still apply to some who pose as arbitrators; but we believe that he will agree that the questionable practices referred to by him are not being generally perpetuated by the members of this Academy.

But our contribution thus far is only a beginning. The future belongs to you younger men who accept the challenge of this new and growing profession. Long after many of us have joined the roster of deceased members, and our small part in the arbitration process has been for-

---

[10] EDITOR'S NOTE: See Appendix C of *Management Rights and the Arbitration Process,* and Appendix C of this volume for the reports of the Committee on Law and Legislation.

[11] Benjamin N. Cardozo. *The Nature of the Judicial Process,* New Haven, 1921, p. 179.

gotten, you will be here to carry the torch forward. I know the flame will burn bright while the torch is in your keeping. And in this way the prestige of the profession of labor management arbitration will continue to be enhanced. We cannot afford to permit this process, which has done so much to promote industrial peace, to be undermined by the activities of the cynical, the uninformed, or those incompetent to handle such matters.

John Day Larkin
President, 1956

Chapter I

THE ARBITRATION OF DISCHARGE CASES:
A CASE STUDY

J. Fred Holly

Professor and Head of the Department of Economics
University of Tennessee

Discharge is the supreme penalty imposed upon employees by the employer to maintain discipline in the work force. The serious implications of the penalty are of such magnitude that both contractual and legislative restrictions have been placed upon the employer to assure that discharge is for "just cause." The contractual limitations upon the employer's freedom of action generally leave him free to exercise initiative in the administration of discipline. His actions, however, are subject to the test of "just cause" as determined through the employee's right to question the decision through his access to the grievance machinery. Frequently, the justness of the employer's decision is finally determined by arbitration.

This case study is concerned with an analysis of the awards of arbitrators in cases involving the question of "just cause" for discharge. The study covers the 1055 discharge cases reported in LABOR ARBITRATION REPORTS[1] in the period January 1942 through March 1956. These awards are grouped into two periods for analysis as follows: (1) January 1942-August 1951, and (2) September 1951-March 1956.[2]

The author's concern with this analysis is twofold: (1) have arbitrators generally upheld or modified the discharge penalty? and (2) what considerations or criteria have been important in the arbitrator's

---

[1] The Bureau of National Affairs, Inc., *Labor Arbitration Reports*, (Washington), Volumes I-XXV.

[2] These periods were selected simply because of the availability of an earlier study covering the first period. In 1952, Joseph Charles Honeycutt completed a Masters Thesis at the University of Tennessee dealing with the subject and the first time period. The author is deeply indebted to Mr. Honeycutt for this study.

determination of the propriety of the imposed penalty? The answers to these questions should indicate ways to aid the parties in improving the administration of industrial discipline, collective bargaining, and arbitration. Moreover, the results should make possible the drawing of conclusions on the role of precedent in arbitration awards, and should aid arbitrators by indicating to them those considerations that have been deemed to be important in the various types of discharge cases.

A study of this type has many limitations such as the following: First, there is the problem of the representativeness of the cases analyzed. Specifically, are the cases studied representative of all discharge cases? The Bureau of National Affairs does not publish all discharge cases, and this study includes only those that were published. Hence, this study is representative of all discharge cases only in so far as the BNA reports are representative. Second, it is self-evident that a reader will have difficulty in understanding the whole situation merely from a study of the arbitrator's opinion and award. Finally, do the opinion and award truly reflect the criteria involved, or are the criteria merely rationalizations of the award? In addition, there are other limitations of the study that should be apparent to students of the arbitration process.

The 1055 arbitration awards were classified, for the purposes of this study, into four major categories of reasons for discharge and further subdivided as follows:

1. Violation of Plant Rules (354 cases)
   1.1 Absenteeism (113)
   1.2 Altercation with other employees (74)
   1.3 Dishonesty, Theft, or Disloyalty (81)
   1.4 Gambling (11)
   1.5 Intoxication (33)
   1.6 Other Specific Rules (42)

2. Incompetence and/or inefficiency (265 cases)
   2.1 Damage to or loss of machines and materials (20)
   2.2 Incompetence or Negligence (184)
   2.3 Loafing, Leaving Post, Sleeping on Job (61)

3. Insubordination (200 cases)
   3.1 Acts of insubordination (92)
   3.2 Refusal to accept job assignment or overtime work (108)

4. Union activities and miscellaneous causes (236 cases)
   4.1 Striking, instigating strike or slowdown (167)
   4.2 Other union activities (39)
   4.3 Miscellaneous causes (30)

In this paper, each of these topics is treated separately, both in respect to frequency[3] and important considerations.

1. Violation of Plant Rules

Table 1 shows the distribution of arbitration cases involving discharge for the violation of plant rules. This type of case occurred more frequently than did any of the other major causes of discharge, representing 354 of the 1055 cases. An examination of these data reveals that management's record in this type of case is somewhat improved since 1951. For example, in the period prior to 1951, management was sustained in only 40.5 percent of the cases, whereas this rate improved to 44.5 percent following 1951. While the rate of revocations remained roughly the same in each period, the rate of reduced penalties fell sharply from 30.0 in the first period to 25.3 in the latter period. The areas primarily responsible for this improvement in management's record were absenteeism (45.8 to 50.0) and altercations (48.1 to 54.5).

While this type of study is not designed to reveal the causes for the trends noted above, the author was impressed with several general reasons for such changes. First, all parties to arbitration have a better understanding of the nature of their problems today than they had in the earlier period. Second, experience has given us better criteria for determining infractions, appropriate penalties, etc. Third, more knowledge of this area has led to better administration of discipline in the sense that action is more clear cut, impersonal, and nondiscriminatory. Finally, arbitrators have become more consistent as their experience has led them to give consideration to those elements or factors

---

[3] Caution must be exercised in weighing the frequency factor since there is no way of determining the representativeness of the 1055 cases studied. While this study provides a complete analysis of all discharge cases reported in *Labor Arbitration Reports*, we have no indication of the completeness or the adequacy of the sample of this publication's reporting. As a result, we cannot rely upon statistical measures of realibility, significance, etc.

TABLE 1: DISTRIBUTION OF ARBITRATION CASES INVOLVING DISCHARGE FOR VIOLATION OF PLANT RULES

1942-1956

	Number			Percent		
	1942 1951	1951 1956	1942 1956	1942 1951	1951 1956	1942 1956
1. Violation of Plant Rules:	235	119	354	100.0	100.0	100.0
1.1 Absenteeism:	83	30	113	100.0	100.0	100.0
Management Sustained	38	15	53	45.8	50.0	46.9
Penalty Revoked	24	11	35	28.9	36.7	30.9
Penalty Reduced	21	4	25	25.3	13.3	22.2
1.2 Altercations:	52	22	74	100.0	100.0	100.0
Management Sustained	25	12	37	48.1	54.5	50.0
Penalty Revoked	10	2	12	19.2	9.1	16.2
Penalty Reduced	17	8	25	32.7	36.4	33.8
1.3 Dishonesty, Theft, Disloyalty:	40	41	81	100.0	100.0	100.0
Management Sustained	14	15	29	35.0	36.6	35.8
Penalty Revoked	15	16	31	37.5	39.0	38.2
Penalty Reduced	11	10	21	27.5	24.4	26.0
1.4 Gambling:	8	3	11	100.0	100.0	100.0
Management Sustained	3	1	4	37.5	33.3	36.3
Penalty Revoked	3	1	4	37.5	33.3	36.3
Penalty Reduced	2	1	3	25.0	33.4	27.4
1.5 Intoxication:	21	12	33	100.0	100.0	100.0
Management Sustained	10	6	16	47.6	50.0	48.5
Penalty Revoked	5	3	8	23.8	25.0	24.2
Penalty Reduced	6	3	9	28.6	25.0	27.3
1.6 Other Specific Rules	31	11	42	100.0	100.0	100.0
Management Sustained	4	4	8	12.9	36.3	19.1
Penalty Revoked	13	3	16	41.9	27.4	38.0
Penalty Reduced	14	4	18	45.2	36.3	42.9
Total Sustained	94	53	147	40.5	44.5	41.3
Total Revocations	70	36	106	30.0	30.2	30.0
Total Reductions	71	30	101	30.0	25.3	28.7

Source: The Bureau of National Affairs, Inc., LABOR ARBITRATION REPORTS, Vols. I-XXV.

that have become rather universal in application to each of the various types of cases.

The analysis of the cases involving discharge for the violation of plant rules revealed many considerations or criteria that weigh heavily in the decision of the arbitrator in cases in this category. The general application of these considerations implies that we have gone far in the direction of finding acceptable criteria for the evaluation of discipline in this particular area. The following considerations applicable to plant rules bear this out.

Criteria Established

Arbitrators have consistently held that the employee must know the rule that he has been punished for violating. The usual test here is that the necessary information must be available to the employee in a manner identical with other employees, and must have been disseminated in the usual manner. Moreover, a new policy must not be inaugurated without informing the employees of the change in policy. Also, the rules must be reasonable, and arbitrators frequently look at the reasonableness of the rule as well as the reasonableness of the penalty.

Except in unusual cases, warning must precede discharge. In the absence of specific contractual requirements, the warning may be either written or oral. A "final warning" must be followed by discharge instead of calling each warning the "final warning."

The employer must not be arbitrary, discriminatory, or unreasonable in administering discipline. Consistency of employer action is required and employees must not be "singled-out" for disciplinary purposes. Consistency of action does not always mean uniformity of action. For example, the length of service of the employee is frequently considered relevant, and the seriousness of the alleged offense may vary with the type of work performed or with the nature of the work area.

Arbitrators usually demand substantial proof of the rule violation and the burden is on the employer to prove the violation. Past acts of a similar nature by the employee may diminish the degree of proof required. Thus, the past record of the employee is often important as indicating the probability of the employee having committed the offense. Moreover, the past record is also used in determining the appropriate degree of penalty that is desirable.

In addition to these general considerations involving the violation of plant rules, it was possible to draw conclusions concerning specific factors for the various subdivisions of this category of discharge cases. These are as follows:

1.1 Absenteeism

It has been consistently held that chronic or excessive absenteeism is just cause for discharge. The only real problem here has been to develop suitable criteria for determining when absenteeism is excessive. In this regard there was no finding which indicated that so many absences in a certain time period were excessive. Rather, arbitrators attempt to decide this question by giving considerations to such factors as the following: the length of the time period involved, reasons for the absences, the nature of the job, the attendance record of other employees, and the employer's attempts to correct the problem. Also, absences are generally excused when they are for the purpose of attending funerals of close relatives, or when they are supported by a doctor's excuse.

Frequently, absences occur when an employee refuses to report for work when the employer has denied his request for a leave of absence or given him a less favorable vacation period. In dealing with this type of case, arbitrators have generally agreed that management has the right to schedule work and rule on requests for leaves of absence.

Many contracts require that an absent employee shall notify the employer of his absence. Arbitrators generally hold that a company must have a standard procedure for reporting absences if the employees are required to notify the employer that they will not report for work.

1.2 Altercations With Other Employees

An employee is not usually subject to the employer's discipline for altercations away from the plant outside of working hours. Yet, attacks on customers of the employer, or altercations that may reflect upon the employer's reputation may alter the aforementioned consideration. On the other hand, the "no fighting" rule applies to altercations on company property outside of working hours as well as during working hours.

Discharges are not usually upheld when the employee's actions were those of reasonable self defense. In some cases arbitrators have considered whether weapons were used and whether serious injury was done or threatened. On the other hand, the act of striking one's supervisor is the most unyielding of the bans on altercations.

1.3 Dishonesty, Theft, or Disloyalty

In general, cases in this category have given arbitrators considerable concern because of the serious implications of the charge against the employee. As a result, arbitrators place much emphasis upon full proof of the alleged act. In addition, cases in this category are frequently troublesome because honesty and loyalty are relative matters, and frequently also involve the consideration of intent. Thus, the arbitrator

TABLE 2: DISTRIBUTION OF ARBITRATION CASES INVOLVING DISCHARGE FOR INCOMPETENCE AND/OR INEFFICIENCY

1942-1956

	Number			Percent		
	1942 1951	1951 1956	1942 1956	1942 1951	1951 1956	1942 1956
2. Incompetence and/or Inefficiency	208	57	265	100.0	100.0	100.0
2.1 Damage to or Loss of Machines and Materials:	13	7	20	100.0	100.0	100.0
Management Sustained	5	3	8	38.5	42.8	40.0
Penalty Revoked	5	2	7	38.5	28.6	35.0
Penalty Reduced	3	2	5	23.0	28.6	25.0
2.2 Incompetence or Negligence:	146	38	184	100.0	100.0	100.0
Management Sustained	63	24	87	43.2	63.2	47.3
Penalty Revoked	42	7	49	28.8	18.4	26.6
Penalty Reduced	41	7	48	28.0	18.4	26.1
2.3 Loafing, Leaving Post, Sleeping on Job:	49	12	61	100.0	100.0	100.0
Management Sustained	20	3	23	40.8	25.0	37.7
Penalty Revoked	11	3	14	22.4	25.0	23.0
Penalty Reduced	18	6	24	36.8	50.0	39.3
Total Sustained	88	30	118	42.3	52.6	44.5
Total Revocations	58	12	70	27.9	21.1	26.4
Total Reductions	62	15	77	29.8	26.3	29.1

Source: The Bureau of National Affairs, Inc., Labor Arbitration Reports, Vols. I-XXV.

is in the position of having to establish that the act was actually committed, and that it really constituted dishonesty, theft, or disloyalty. In cases where the employee is caught in an obviously dishonest act, the only problem is the credibility of witnesses. Except in unusual cases, an act committed outside the scope of employment has been considered as a mitigating circumstance.

1.4 Gambling

The arbitration awards in the cases involving gambling were based on the general considerations previously listed at the beginning of this section. No special considerations applying to this type of rule infraction were discovered.

1.5 Intoxication

Cases in this category reveal that discharge is always considered for just cause when there is substantial proof that the employee was intoxicated. Yet, such proof is extremely difficult to obtain. Intoxication must be discovered when the employee is on duty. Evidence based solely on suspicion has not been considered just cause for discharge.

1.6 Other Specific Rules

The majority of the cases involving "other specific rules" included alleged violation of safety rules, no-smoking rules, and bans on political activities on company premises during working hours. The analysis of these cases established that the majority of such rules are concerned with minor infractions which deserve some disciplinary action other than discharge. (The "rule of reason" is applied more generally in this category than in any of the other "plant rule" areas.) Any extenuating circumstances are given considerable weight by arbitrators when hearing cases in this category.

2. Incompetence and/or Inefficiency

As the data in Table 2 indicate, management's record has greatly improved in the arbitration of discharge cases for incompetence and/or inefficiency. In the period 1942-1951, management was sustained in only 42.3 percent of such cases; whereas, following 1951, management has been sustained in 52.6 percent of these cases. In like manner the record on revocations (decline from 27.9 to 21.1) and penalty reduction (29.8 to 26.3) has improved in the latter period. The major reason for this improvement is found in the fact that 24 of the 30 cases involved the charge of incompetence or negligence where, during the first period, management was sustained in 43.2 percent of the cases, and in the latter period in 63.2 percent. A study of the cases leads to the conclusion that the basic reason for this improvement lies in the fact that management simply has better records now to support such charges, and that such allegations are made infrequently when there is no supporting evidence.

The comparatively small number of cases in the latter period in the other two categories renders comparisons almost meaningless.

The analysis of the reported cases on discharge for incompetence and/or inefficiency revealed that arbitrators have been quite specific in applying many considerations to the determination of the propriety of the managerial decision. The following are among the more important of these considerations. The standard of competency must be reasonable, and was frequently based on the average man concept. A standard of competency should not be adhered to strictly where the factors causing incompetence are beyond the control of the individual.

The employee must have been given adequate training to permit him to qualify for the job. The test of adequacy is a comparison with the training received by other workers on the same or similar jobs. Arbitrators have held that an employee may not be discharged justly for inability to perform duties to which he has been promoted beyond his capacities.

The employee is not protected by the "just cause" doctrine during the trial or probationary period. Successful completion of the probationary period does not immunize the employee against later charges of incompetency.

The presence or absence of adequate supervision and suitable equipment has been considered to be crucial by many arbitrators. There has been little question concerning discharges for incompetence where the employee has consistently ignored previous warnings about his job performance. On the other hand, charges of incompetence and/or inefficiency have not been upheld where the questioned practice was sanctioned by the supervisor.

Generally, no distinction is drawn between reasons for incompetence; for example, physical limitations are given no different treatment than any other reason that might render an employee incompetent. However, unusual circumstances outside of the work situation have been given some consideration in discharge cases where the employee has a long record of satisfactory service.

The submission to the arbitrator of production records, work sheets, or samples of workmanship has been considered the most adequate method of establishing a charge of incompetence and/or inefficiency. On the other hand, recently received merit increases go far to nullify charges of incompetence.

Deliberate action, wanton disregard of employer's property, or undue carelessness is just cause for discharge. But if the employee's conduct is more thoughtless and negligent than willful and malicious discharge has been held to be unjust.

One employee cannot get another employee discharged by merely reporting to his supervisor a dischargeable offense. The report must be corroborated to justify discharge. Neither can an employer discriminate against an employee by trying to catch him in some mistake.

In addition to these general considerations involving discharge for incompetence and/or inefficiency the analysis revealed additional specific considerations applicable to each of the subdivisions of this category. These specific considerations follow:

2.1 Damage to or Loss of Machines and Materials

Three additional considerations are found to apply specifically to this category, viz:

> a. When the employer's charge is carelessness, he must show that an undue amount of carelessness existed and that discharge is an established penalty for the type of carelessness involved in the case.
>
> b. An employee's failure to follow an established practice of paying for lost tools or equipment has been considered a just cause for discharge.
>
> c. Probable resultant damage that an employee might have caused has been considered an unjust cause for discharge.

2.2 Incompetence or Negligence

In some types of work, such as creative editorial work, arbitrators have held that the employers do not have to set any standards of competence in order to discharge an employee for incompetence. In jobs with more specific duties, arbitrators have held that the failure of an employee to pass a standardized practical test constitutes just cause for discharge.

In many cases involving incompetence, arbitrators have given major consideration to the effect of the employee's incompetence on the employer's business. In some charges of incompetence, the nature of the product has been considered of major importance in the award. In these cases the primary concern has been with the possible effect of the employee's incompetence on the lives of others.

2.3 Loafing, Leaving Post, Sleeping on Job

Arbitrators require a high degree of proof to substantiate discharge for loafing. Mere suspicion of loafing does not constitute just cause for discharge. Moreover, evidence must show that the time spent loafing was within the scope of control of the employee, and that his loafing affected production. Generally, a warning for loafing must precede discharge for this cause.

Where the employer can prove that an employee repeatedly leaves his post, or is absent therefrom for extended periods, or abuses rest periods, discharge is for just cause. If leaving one's post for a common cause has been a general practice in the firm, arbitrators have held that an employer is not justified in discharging an employee for this offense.

Arbitrators have consistently upheld discharges for sleeping on the job in crucial work. Employees generally, however, have received the benefit of the doubt in a charge of sleeping on the job. Arbitrators have questioned the methods which some employers used in obtaining evidence to support a charge of sleeping on the job.

3. Insubordination

Management has found it difficult to deal with problems of insubordination. It is in this area of discharge cases that management has had the lowest rate of sustained cases, the lowest rate of revoked penalties, and the highest rate of penalty reductions. The poorest record in this category relates to "acts of insubordination" where prior to 1951 management was sustained in only 28.0 percent of the cases and in only 29.2 percent following 1951. (See Table 3). The obvious reason for this poor experience is that management simply has encountered extreme difficulty in deciding where a personality clash or a misunderstanding ends and insubordination begins.

In this category of cases the considerations were found to relate to the specific subcategories. Accordingly, there are no general considerations for insubordination as a whole.

3.1 Acts of Insubordination

Employers must be consistent in disciplining employees for insubordination. Because of the nature of the case and extenuating circumstances, insubordination may be either a just or an unjust cause for discharge.

The use of abusive and threatening language toward the employer and the indulgence in excessive displays of temperament have been regarded as insubordination and just cause for discharge. An employee's personality clash with a superior constitutes unjust cause for discharge. For example, momentary displays of unpleasantness or use of abusive language alone to superiors have been considered an unjust cause for discharge.

TABLE 3: DISTRIBUTION OF ARBITRATION CASES INVOLVING
DISCHARGE FOR INSUBORDINATION
1942-1956

	Number			Percent		
	1942 1951	1951 1956	1942 1956	1942 1951	1951 1956	1942 1956
3. Insubordination:	143	57	200	100.0	100.0	100.0
3.1 Acts of Insubordination:	68	24	92	100.0	100.0	100.0
Management Sustained	19	7	26	28.0	29.2	28.3
Penalty Revoked	15	4	19	22.0	16.6	20.6
Penalty Reduced	34	13	47	50.0	54.2	51.1
3.2 Refusal to Accept Job Assignment or Overtime Work:	75	33	108	100.0	100.0	100.0
Management Sustained	28	11	39	37.3	33.3	36.1
Penalty Revoked	16	4	20	21.3	12.1	18.5
Penalty Reduced	31	18	49	41.4	54.6	45.4
Total Sustained	47	18	65	32.9	31.6	32.5
Total Revocations	31	8	39	21.7	14.0	19.5
Total Reductions	65	31	96	45.4	54.4	48.0

Source: The Bureau of National Affairs, Inc., LABOR ARBITRATION REPORTS, Vols. I-XXV.

3.2 Refusal to Accept Job Assignment or Overtime Work

There has been little question concerning the propriety of discharge for insubordination when there has been a refusal to comply with a valid order. Arbitrators generally agree that proper procedure for an employee in a case involving a questionable job assignment would be to accept the assignment and file a grievance.

Merely protesting that assigned work is not part of a person's job duties has been considered an unjust cause for discharge. Neither is it just to discharge an employee who has merely failed to carry out an order without refusing to do so. Also the employee must know that he is being given an order before he can be discharged for insubordination. Moreover, employees cannot be expected to carry out orders that would be detrimental to their health or in violation of their physician's instructions.

In those situations where the contract made no reference to whether overtime work was mandatory or voluntary, arbitrators generally held that past practice in the firm or industry was controlling.

4. Union Activities and Miscellaneous Causes

As indicated in Table 4, management has made substantial improvements since 1951 in the arbitration of discharge cases in the fourth category. Yet, the number of cases in this category since 1951 is so small that extreme care must be exercised in interpreting the data. All that can be said with assurance is that the available data show that since 1951 the cases in which management has been sustained increased from 40.3 percent to 53.3 percent; meanwhile, revocations dropped from 23.3 percent to 15.0 percent and penalty reductions declined from 36.4 to 31.7 percent.

4.1 Striking, Instigating Strike or Slowdown

Where there is no evidence of anti-union bias or discriminatory discharge, arbitrators generally have sustained the discharge of an employee for violating the "no-strike" clause. The employer must present a high degree of proof to substantiate his charge in this category. The predominance of union members or leaders among those discharged may be significant in pointing out a union's charge of discrimination. Where the leaders of the employees know a strike is illegal and continue the strike despite warnings by both the employer and the union superiors, there has been little question concerning the justness of discharging the leaders.

Production records have been regarded by arbitrators as substantial evidence in supporting discharges for slowdowns. The author could find no general agreement concerning a union official's responsibility for strikes or slowdowns.

4.2 Other Union Activities

If the employer has not been anti-union, arbitrators have generally held that the burden of proof is upon the union to show that a discharge was discriminatory. In the absence of an anti-union bias, and with full proof, arbitrators have upheld management's discharges for illegal union activities. A union representative is immune to discipline when he is

TABLE 4:   DISTRIBUTION OF ARBITRATION CASES INVOLVING
DISCHARGE FOR UNION ACTIVITIES AND
MISCELLANEOUS CAUSES

1942-1956

	Number			Percent		
	1942 1951	1951 1956	1942 1956	1942 1951	1951 1956	1942 1956
4. Union Activities and Miscellaneous Causes:	247	92	329	100.0	100.0	100.0
4.1 Striking, Instigating Strike or Slowdown:	117	50	167	100.0	100.0	100.0
Management Sustained	48	25	73	41.0	50.0	43.7
Penalty Revoked	22	7	29	18.8	14.0	17.4
Penalty Reduced	47	18	65	40.2	36.0	38.9
4.2 Other Union Activities:	32	7	39	100.0	100.0	100.0
Management Sustained	13	5	18	40.6	71.4	46.1
Penalty Revoked	10	1	11	31.3	14.3	28.2
Penalty Reduced	9	1	10	28.1	14.3	25.7
4.3 Miscellaneous Causes:	27	3	30	100.0	100.0	100.0
Management Sustained	10	2	12	37.0	66.7	40.0
Penalty Revoked	9	1	10	33.0	33.3	33.3
Penalty Reduced	8	0	8	30.0	0.0	26.7
Total Sustained	71	32	103	40.3	53.3	43.6
Total Revocations	41	9	50	23.3	15.0	21.2
Total Reductions	64	19	83	36.4	31.7	35.2

Source: The Bureau of National Affairs, Inc., LABOR ARBITRATION REPORTS, Vols. I-XXV.

acting within the scope of his union duties, but is subject to discipline when he steps outside that scope.

Arbitrators have held that it is the union's responsibility to allege and to establish a discriminatory discharge to overcome the prerogative of an employer given by a probationary employment clause.

4.3 Miscellaneous Causes

The few cases involved in this category establish that:

a. Employee conduct, taking place outside the plant premises and during non-working hours, must be related to the employer-employee relationship, if the causes complained of are to be accepted as just cause for discharge.

b. Horseplay seldom constituted just cause for discharge.

c. In most cases discharges have been upheld when they are for true economy reasons.

Summary and Conclusion

As indicated earlier this case study had two major purposes; namely, to determine (1) have arbitrators generally upheld or modified the discharge penalty? and (2) what considerations or criteria have been important in the arbitrator's determination of the appropriateness of the imposed penalty?

Inability to select a sample rendered impossible any statistical measures of significance; however, Table 5 is included as a summary of the findings in so far as the available cases are concerned. These data show that for the entire period under study, management's best record on sustained discharges is in the category of incompetence and/or inefficiency and these amount to only 44.5 percent. On the other hand, the low point of 32.5 percent is reached in the insubordination cases. Thus, in no single category has management's record approached 50 percent; yet, when these data are broken down into two time periods, it is demonstrated that management's record is improving.

As to the second major purpose of the study, many considerations were found in each of the categories that are weighed heavily by arbitrators. Although each case is an entity in itself, and extenuating circumstances are usually involved, many principles were found that govern discharge cases. Briefly stated, the more important of these include the following:

1. Policies must be both known and reasonable.
2. Violation of policies must be proven, and the burden of proof rests on the employer.
3. The application of rules and policies must be consistent:
   a. Employees cannot be singled out for discipline.
   b. Past practice may be a controlling consideration.
4. Where employees are held to a standard, that standard must be reasonable.
5. The training provided employees must be adequate.
6. The job rights of employees must be protected from arbitrary, capricious, or discriminatory action.
7. Actions must be impersonal and based on fact.
8. Where the contract speaks, it speaks with authority.

TABLE 5: DISTRIBUTION OF ARBITRATION CASES INVOLVING DISCHARGE BY MAJOR CLASSIFICATIONS

1942-1956

1942-1951 Cases	Violation of Plant Rules		Incompetence and/or Inefficiency		Insubordination		Union Activity, Misc.		Total	
	No.	Percent	No.	Percent	No.	Percent	No.	Percent	No.	Percent
Management Sustained	94	40.0	88	42.3	47	32.9	71	40.3	300	39.4
Penalty Revoked	70	30.0	58	27.9	31	21.7	41	23.3	200	26.2
Penalty Reduced	71	30.0	62	29.8	65	45.4	64	36.4	262	34.4
	235	100.0	208	100.0	143	100.0	176	100.0	762	100.0
1951-1956 Cases										
Management Sustained	53	44.5	30	52.6	18	31.6	32	53.3	133	45.4
Penalty Revoked	36	30.2	12	21.1	8	14.0	9	15.0	65	22.2
Penalty Reduced	30	25.3	15	26.3	31	54.4	19	31.7	95	32.4
	119	100.0	57	100.0	57	100.0	60	100.0	293	100.0
1942-1956 Cases										
Management Sustained	147	41.3	118	44.5	65	32.5	103	43.6	433	41.0
Penalty Revoked	106	30.0	70	26.4	39	19.5	50	21.2	265	25.2
Penalty Reduced	101	28.7	77	29.1	96	48.0	83	35.2	357	33.8
	354	100.0	265	100.0	200	100.0	236	100.0	1055	100.0

Source: Tables 1-4.

Finally, the study shows that there should be grave doubts concerning the value of precedent awards in arbitration. While earlier cases may have a deceptive relevance to a given arbitration, the awards may be wholly inapplicable for a number of reasons, including the major one of basic differences in the governing agreements. On the other hand, the basic considerations or criteria requisite to a just award are highly similar within each category of discharge cases. Thus, an understanding of these considerations should improve the practice of arbitration.

Discussion—

BENJAMIN AARON

Institute of Industrial Relations
University of California, Los Angeles

Among those of the general public who have no direct contact with labor arbitrations, attitudes toward arbitrators' awards seem to range from profound cynicism to amused tolerance. In my experience not much can be done with persons holding the former view; more likely than not, it reflects a bilious world outlook, a disposition to believe that every decision, from the rulings of the Supreme Court to those of a baseball umpire, is "fixed." The attitude at the other side of this rather narrow intellectual spectrum is perhaps more amenable to change. It is one frequently held by professional people—scientists, lawyers, economists—who regard arbitration awards with a kind of good-natured condescension, seeing them only as interesting, if not always comprehensible, products of an imprecise and hopelessly unpredictable decision-making process.

To illustrate this latter attitude, I quote from a letter I recently received from an eminent law professor, regarding a forthcoming symposium on arbitration: "Two or three of the titles may overlap somewhat," he wrote, "but we are not too concerned about that because we believe that any two arbitrators will differ sufficiently on almost any topic to remove whatever objection there might otherwise be to some slight duplication."

I suppose that the most appropriate retort to my learned friend's implied stricture would be that it applies with equal force to judicial or scholarly opinions in some specialized areas of law, economics, and the physical sciences. Professor Holly's paper suggests, however, that arbitrators may some day be able to advance a more affirmative defense, namely, the fact that the great majority of decisions involving such matters as discipline and discharge are based upon a set of reasonably well-defined principles that have won general acceptance in the field of industrial relations.

I say "some day" because it seems to me that the development of such a set of principles has proceeded quite unevenly, and in some areas it is still relatively immature. With respect to discharge cases, Professor Holly has ventured the guarded conclusion that "the basic considerations requisite to a just award are highly similar within each category." I doubt whether even so cautious a generalization as this would go unchallenged if applied to, say the contracting out of work, or the treatment of employees alleged to be security risks, or a variety of other matters.

I see no reason, however, why arbitrators should be defensive about the fact that precedent counts for so little in their decisions. After all, an arbitrator is concerned with facts, as well as with principles, and the infinite variety of facts permits, indeed requires, a wide range of decision within the scope of a single general principle. It is instructive to recall that as far back as 1898 James Bradley Thayer wrote mockingly of "that lawyer's Paradise where all words have a fixed, precisely ascertained meaning; where men may express their purposes, not only with accuracy, but with fullness; and where, if the writer has been careful, a lawyer having a document referred to him, may sit in his chair, inspect the text, and answer all questions without raising his eyes." Lawyers have not found this Paradise on earth and arbitrators won't either.

If there is any truth in the foregoing observations, then we need not be unduly concerned by the obvious limitations of Professor Holly's statistical analysis of discharge cases—limitations that he has been most careful to point out. Indeed, I find it rather comforting, in this Age of UNIVAC, to know that there are a few areas of human endeavor which yet manage to elude the fell clutch of automatic prediction.

Professor Holly has told us what happened in over 1,000 discharge cases, but he has been commendably cautious in articulating the bases for the decisions. There is a fatal seductiveness about statistical compilations—a cozy invitation to indulge in broad generalizations—that has proven to be the downfall of many an investigator. In this connection I recall the case of the scientist who performed an experiment on 1,000 fleas. He took each flea in turn and held it under his thumb for three seconds. He then released the flea and said in a loud voice, "Jump!" Each flea, without exception, jumped. The scientist next amputated the legs of all the fleas in his sample group and then repeated the experiment; but this time not a single flea jumped at his command. After analyzing his data, our scientist announced his findings: First, fleas learn to respond to commands with great ease and speed. Second, when a flea's legs are amputated, it is rendered completely deaf.

Professor Holly is too careful a scholar to leap at such unwarranted conclusions. Indeed, the tentativeness with which he has put forth his findings suggests that he is a student of James Thurber and has adopted as his creed the following aphorism of that great man: "Get it right or let it alone. The conclusion you jump to may be your own." Few would quarrel with the list of principles he has found to govern discharge cases; some might even wish to expand the list. Moreover, most of us would agree, I think, that the practice of arbitration will improve as some of these principles gain ever wider acceptance.

I wish I could conclude my remarks without some major criticism of Professor's Holly's work, but more in sorrow than in anger, I must call attention to a very, very serious error, just out of intellectual integrity: In discussing the "shall nots" that employers must observe in administering discipline, Mr. Holly has violated not once, but twice, the Rule of Five that was so definitively stated by our esteemed colleague, James Hill, in one of our previous meetings. He says, in the first part of his paper, that the employer must not be arbitrary, discriminatory, or unreasonable, and in the conclusion he strikes "unreasonable" and substitutes "capricious." In short, he has arbitrarily, unreasonably, discriminatorily, and capriciously reduced the Rule of Five to a Rule of Three, and, what is worse, he has not once mentioned the fact that the employer has a duty not to be whimsical. This flaunting of tradition is an affront to the profession, and I know I speak for an overwhelming majority of the Academy when I say that we resist any implication that we will ever use only three adjectives when five are available.

Just one or two concluding remarks. I suppose I should allude to the box score that Professor Holly has kept on the record of management. I just want to beat somebody in the audience to this comment, that I don't know who is being educated and getting a better average —the employer or the arbitrator. I suppose it is arguable which group is improving.

Finally, Professor Holly, who is as modest as he is scholarly, asked me somewhat anxiously whether I thought there was any point in an investigation of this kind, whether the paper was worth while. I told him quite sincerely that I thought it was, that the study perhaps is not too meaningful by itself, but will become increasingly meaningful as we get more studies of this kind, and the kind that Professor Ross has made and will be telling us about. I think we are all greatly in the debt of both gentlemen for the work that they have done.

CHAPTER II

THE ARBITRATION OF DISCHARGE CASES: WHAT HAPPENS AFTER REINSTATEMENT

ARTHUR M. ROSS [1]

Director, Institute of Industrial Relations
University of California, Berkeley

1. Introduction

Law and statistics are notoriously uncongenial. While the original "Brandeis brief" was filed almost fifty years ago, and while some courts are increasingly willing to take notice of economic and sociological data (particularly the Supreme Court in constitutional cases), concepts and principles remain the staple item of diet. So it is in arbitration. Since arbitration is a private system of contract enforcement, and is manned to a growing extent by attorneys, it is not surprising that rules, maxims and precedents are so prominent. The small but developing literature of labor arbitration, insofar as it is not preoccupied with procedural matters, deals chiefly with the emergence and evolution of doctrines and principles to attack the peculiar problems of contractual interpretation which confront the labor arbitrator.

Doubtless this state of affairs will continue in large measure. But logic and legitimacy are not the only tests of a doctrine. The question of how it actually works out is also of interest. In various fields of the law, judges, attorneys and scholars are already concerned with the efficiency of established principles in ordering the affairs of men and solving their controversies. Divorce law, concepts of insanity, the jury system in auto accident cases, anti-trust law and regulation of sexual behavior come to mind readily. If studies of experience under legal doctrines are to be made, contact with statistics cannot be entirely avoided.

In labor arbitration, also, there is much to be gained from studies

---

[1] The author is glad to acknowledge the valuable assistance of Mr. Paul Hartman of the Institute of Industrial Relations.

of experience after the award. For example, we are frequently called upon to decide whether particular employees are qualified for particular jobs on which seniority rights are being asserted. We have developed various tests of capability; we consider certain types of evidence as relevant. We decide that some of the employees are qualified, and order that they be assigned, promoted or recalled to the jobs in question. Are they *really* qualified? It would be instructive, and not very difficult, to learn how many of them actually "make out" on the jobs.

I am reporting today on a study of experience under arbitration awards in which discharged employees have been reinstated. For arbitrators there ought to be an unusual degree of interest in how these reinstatements have worked out. The principal reason is that arbitrators themselves have created the standards of decision for this type of case. This has been a matter of necessity rather than preference; we are a timid lot for the most part. We have had to invent standards because none have been furnished. In no field of arbitration can less guidance be had from general legal doctrines or from the language of contracts and submission agreements than in the field of industrial discipline.

To be sure, an arbitrator is applying the terms of a collective bargaining agreement when he decides a discharge case. Typically the agreement recites that the employer will not discharge without proper cause, and the arbitrator makes a judgment as to whether there *was* proper cause. Technically this is contractual interpretation. But it is contractual interpretation in the same sense as it was statutory interpretation when the O.P.A. decided that $1.00 was a "fair and equitable" ceiling price for a peck of winter potatoes. The Emergency Price Control Act required that ceiling prices be "fair and equitable." It was the task of the O.P.A. to develop standards of fairness and equity, and then apply them to particular commodities. Clearly this task called for a good deal of administrative rule-making as well as adjudication. In the same way the arbitrators collectively have had to contrive standards of proper cause and then apply them individually to particular cases.

It is true that some collective agreements afford more guidance than the familiar rubrics of "just cause," "proper cause," or just plain "cause." The contract may incorporate a list of disciplinary offenses with the corresponding penalties. It may specify that certain derelictions, such as persistent absenteeism or falsification of production records, will be grounds for discharge. The submission agreement may limit the arbitrator to finding whether the grievant was guilty of the offense for which he was terminated. The contract or submission agreement may instruct the arbitrator as to whether he is authorized to mitigate the penalty, as an alternative to upholding it or rescinding it altogether. In these and other ways the parties may "structure" the situation, as the sociologists would say. Ordinarily they do not.

Certainly the antecedent Law of Contracts offers little help. At common law the employer generally had an unrestricted right to discharge, just as the employee had an unlimited right to quit his job. There are, of course, many court decisions in the books involving termination of employment and utilizing familiar contractual concepts such as failure of consideration, mutual mistake, anticipatory repudiation and legal impossibility. These, however, were actions for breach of individual employment contracts for a fixed term. The notion of an individual employment contract is still of help to the courts in rationalizing some of their labor-law decisions; but if such a contract really exists, it is only a contract at will and does not confer any rights of tenure. It is the collective bargaining contract, not the supposed individual employment contract, which is brought into play in the ordinary discharge case. Perhaps the developing standards of "just cause" for discharge under a collective bargaining contract could be translated into more traditional categories such as failure of consideration; but it is not clear that such a translation would accomplish much and, in any case, it has never been attempted.

There were additional reasons for studying the aftermath of the reinstatement award. Although the discharge case is probably not the most important type of grievance brought to arbitration, from some standpoints, it is almost certainly the most numerous type. During a recent year, for example, about 25 percent of all arbitration appointments made by the Federal Mediation and Conciliation Service were in discharge matters.

Many discharge cases are charged with emotion and generate strong feelings among the parties. In fact, the parties may have stronger feelings about the discharge or reinstatement of a single employee than about a wage case involving large numbers of employees and great sums of money. For this reason, it was expected that they would have clear recollections of the cases and definite reactions to the awards. This expectation was generally borne out. I received quite a few interesting letters from company and union officials, amplifying their responses concerning particular cases and commenting on the discharge problem generally.

Finally, some widely divergent theories about the subsequent career of the reinstated employee are current. One theory runs something as follows: He is a marked man, or he never would have been discharged in the first place. His number was up. Management will nail him again soon, and make it stick. Reinstating him merely throws him back into an impossible situation. His best bet will be to pick up his retroactive pay and find himself another job. At the other extreme, it is said that he was probably discharged by an impetuous supervisor in a fit of anger. Everyone is relieved when the arbitrator slaps him on the wrist and puts him back to work. Having been discharged once, he will now get religion and keep his nose clean. In fact he will become a model employee. Neither of these popular theories, nor any of the intermediate positions, has ever been tested statistically.

2. The Arbitrators' Approach to Industrial Discipline

In their search for principles of industrial discipline, the arbitrators have turned not to the Law of Contracts but to modern concepts of enlightened personnel administration, sprinkled with elements of procedural due process in criminal cases. This is not the place to present a full-blown theory of industrial discipline.[2] For the present purpose it will suffice to list a few of the major tenets which are stressed in the literature of personnel administration and in the thinking of arbitrators concerning disciplinary grievances.

---

[2] See A. Howard Myers, "Concepts of Industrial Discipline," and Gabriel N. Alexander, "Comment," in Jean T. McKelvey [ed.], *Management Rights and the Arbitration Process*, Proceedings of the Ninth Annual Meeting of the National Academy of Arbitrators (Washington: BNA Incorporated, 1956), pp. 59-83; Harry H. Platt, "Arbitral Standards in Discipline Cases," in *Lectures on the Law and Labor-Management Relations* (Ann Arbor: University of Michigan, 1951), 233-237; Robert H. Skilton, *Industrial Discipline and the Arbitration Process* (Philadelphia: University of Pennsylvania Press, 1952); American Management Association, *Constructive Discipline in Industry* (New York, 1943); J. M. Porter, Jr., "The Arbitration of Industrial Disputes Arising from Disciplinary Action," in Milton Derber [ed.], *Proceedings of the Second Annual Meeting, Industrial Relations Research Association* (New York, 1950), pp. 262-270; William H. Knowles, *Personnel Management—A Human Relations Approach* (New York: American Book Company, 1955), pp. 277-279, 293; Gordon S. Watkins, *et al.*, *The Management of Personnel and Labor Relations* (New York: McGraw-Hill, 1950), pp. 481-508; and Harry Shulman and N. W. Chamberlain, *Cases on Labor Relations* (Brooklyn: The Foundation Press, 1949), pp. 366-575.

1. The employer is entitled to prescribe reasonable rules of conduct. What rules are necessary will vary from one establishment to another, and the employer enjoys considerable discretion in making this determination.[3]

2. The employee has a right to know what is expected of him. Therefore the employer has an obligation to give adequate notice of the rules, unless they are so self-evident as not to require notice.[4] This requirement gives rise to a number of chronic issues, such as (a) whether a particular rule has been promulgated with sufficient notoriety, and (b) whether violations have been condoned to such an extent as to make the rule invalid.

3. The employer has no jurisdiction over the employee's private life, and no right to impose discipline for behavior off company time and property—this being a task for the civil authorities. The exception occurs when the employee's actions away from the job have the effect of damaging or seriously jeopardizing the employer's legitimate interests. The problem in cases of this type is to decide whether the employer's interests were sufficiently involved as to justify his intervention.

4. The employee must conform with valid rules in good faith and with serious purpose. He must comport himself as a disciplined individual; otherwise goods or services cannot be produced with any degree of efficiency.[5]

---

[3] "An organization requires policy and formal coordination in order to pursue its aims, with adequate authority for internal discipline to effectuate its program." (Myers, *op. cit.* p. 62.) "Any sort of group action, if it is to be efficiently performed, requires coordination, control and personal discipline. Industrial discipline is exactly of that sort. It seeks to eliminate practices that make for group inefficiency and to encourage those that facilitate effective cooperation." (Yoder, *op. cit.*, p. 463.)

[4] "The right to discipline for infractions implies that workers will be informed as to the rules to be followed and that foremen who supervise and administer penalties know what the policies are so as to avoid charges of discriminatory treatment." (Myers, *op. cit.*, p. 63.)

[5] "Management is entitled to have an obedient and cooperative working force and ought not to be subjected to the necessity for retaining in its employ persons who over a period of time demonstrate by their conduct that they cannot accommodate themselves to reasonable shop rules." (Alexander, *op. cit.*, p. 81.) "It is an implied obligation of a worker to be reasonably regular in his attendance, to exert reasonable effort and diligence on his job, to perform adequately, and to render a fair day's work for a day's pay . . . to follow instructions, to accept work assignments, and to obey orders of supervision at all times, except possibly if they would subject him to criminal liability or to safety and health hazards." (Platt, *op. cit.*, p. 234.)

5. The employer must avoid arbitrary, hasty or capricious action when confronted with unsatisfactory conduct. The tendency for supervisors to "over-react" against what they regard as a challenge to their authority is one of the persistent problems of industrial discipline.[6] To guard against this tendency, collective agreements frequently provide that an employee will not be discharged until after a preliminary suspension, or until after consultation with the union.

6. Disciplinary policies should be applied consistently and evenhandedly.[7] This standard is clear enough in disparaging capricious decisions and discriminatory purposes. It does not mean, however, that a mechanical uniformity of treatment must be achieved, regardless of differences in the background or circumstances of particular cases. What is important, as Benjamin Aaron has stressed, is consistent purposes rather than uniform penalties.[8]

7. The punishment should fit the crime. There is a controversy among arbitrators as to whether they have authority to mitigate penalties where the employee is guilty of the offense charged but the penalty is regarded as excessive. In 70 percent of the reinstatement cases covered by the present survey, workers were reinstated with partial back pay or no back pay.

8. Proper industrial discipline is corrective rather than punitive. The purpose is to instill self-discipline in the working force.[9] Both employer and employee lose when the employee is terminated. The em-

---

[6] Porter points out that particularly in cases of alleged insubordination, "there is frequently an over-reaction, by first-line management. . . . The discipline applied need only meet the requirements of management's responsibility for efficient production in the plant, but, in fact, it tends to exceed this need and becomes an action mainly of vindication of status and exercise of authority." (Porter, *op. cit.*, p. 268.)

[7] "Employees want a uniform and consistent application of the rules—the rule of shop policy instead of the whimsical rule of men—and, indeed, adherence to policy is sound personnel practice." (Knowles, *op. cit.*, p. 278.)

[8] See Benjamin Aaron, "The Uses of the Past in Arbitration," in Jean T. McKelvey [ed.], *Arbitration Today*, Proceedings of the Eighth Annual Meeting of the National Academy of Arbitrators (Washington: BNA Incorporated, 1955), p. 12.

[9] "The highest type of control is that which originates within the individual worker. . . . It develops from a man's belief in the personal integrity, in the fairness, and in the understanding of his superiors. Self-discipline in the employee group is the goal of enlightened leadership." (American Management Association, *op. cit.*, p. 5.) "The purpose [of discipline] according to the most modern thinking of industrial relations people, is not to inflict punishment for wrongdoing, but to correct individual faults and behavior and to prevent further infractions." (Platt, *op. cit.*, p. 235.)

ployer must recruit and train a replacement, and must often reckon with ill will on the part of the discharged employee's fellow workers; while the employee loses his seniority and all the valuable rights associated with it. Therefore discharge should normally be invoked only as a last resort, after it has become clear that corrective measures will not succeed.[10]

9. It follows that the evaluation of a given penalty will depend not only on the immediate offense but also on the employee's previous disciplinary record. It also follows that, in the normal case, a series of disciplinary measures—including interviews, formal reprimands, and disciplinary layoffs—should be applied with gradually increasing severity before discharge is considered. "Capital punishment" should not be levied until it has been established that the employee will not respond to lesser penalties.[11] Doubtless many cases of mitigated penalties represent the arbitrator's attempt to apply this principle to a firm which does not make a practice of assigning disciplinary layoffs. Whether the arbitrator should, in effect, impose such a practice on a firm which has never used it is subject to much controversy.

3. Summary of Findings

It was said of the late Dr. Kinsey that no one could study a matter so long and so intensively without developing a certain amount of enthusiasm for his subject. Nevertheless, it is not my purpose to endorse—or disparage, for that matter—the prevalent practices in disciplinary cases. My objective is limited to reporting what they are. In

---

[10] If one views the objective of disciplinary action as the improvement of behavior, then it is clear that insofar as the individual disciplined is concerned, any value in terms of reformed behavior is lost to the company when the man is discharged." (Porter, *op. cit.*, p. 269.) "Corrective discipline imposes upon management a two-fold burden of firmness and patience. . . . [Management must] adopt a reasonably firm attitude against minor violations . . . [and must be] patient. . . . Even though an employee's behavior is aggravating and provocative, the employee must be dealt with objectively and not because of anger or desire to retaliate" (Alexander, *op. cit.*, p. 81.)

[11] "Clearly a duty to issue reprimands or warnings exists as a reasonable first step of discipline, preliminary to disciplinary layoffs and dismissals." (Platt, *op. cit.*, p. 65.) "In the attempt to enforce discipline and secure a fair day's work, the employer should . . . give proper consideration to method. . . . The appropriate first measure may be to warn him [the offender]. Then if he does not improve within a reasonable time after warning, the stiffer penalty may be imposed—disciplinary layoff to discharge." (Shulman, *op. cit.*, p. 409.)

the spirit of Section 206 of the Labor-Management Relations Act, this is a fact-finding report without recommendations.

The reinstatement cases analyzed here were found in the printed volumes of LABOR ARBITRATION REPORTS covering the years 1950-55. I looked for cases in which the grievant was discharged for cause, and subsequently reinstated by an arbitrator or board of arbitration; and providing enough reference information to permit correspondence with the employer and the union. All cases meeting these tests were included, except that I eliminated any case in which I had served as arbitrator. Exactly 207 individual grievants in 145 establishments were found.[12]

Some of the material in this report (including seniority status of the grievants, grounds for discharge, principal reasons for reinstatement, and terms of reinstatement) has been taken from the body of the decisions.

In addition a questionnaire covering each grievant was sent to his employer, along with an explanatory letter. (Appendix A.) A similar but not identical questionnaire was sent to the union representing each of the grievants. (Appendix B.)

The response from employers was unusually good; by the time the replies were tabulated, 60 percent of the employer questionnaires had been returned. A good deal of the information in this report has been derived from the employer questionnaires. The union questionnaires came in more slowly, and only about 20 percent had been returned when the tabulations were made. This was to be expected, because many unions are not in a position to follow the subsequent career of reinstated individuals. In view of the limited response, it has not been practical to make an elaborate analysis of the union questionnaires. Nevertheless, they have yielded some very worthwhile data.

The basic tables are set out in Appendix C below. All statistics cited in the text of the report have been taken or derived from Appendix C. As the appendix tables indicate, some of the respondents did not answer all the questions. For example, some of the questions were not applicable in the case of employees who did not return after reinstatement, or who stayed only for a short time. Where percentages are used in the text, these refer to the employees for whom the par-

---

[12] This is the point to make the conventional disclaimer that cases reported in LABOR ARBITRATION REPORTS are not necessarily representative. At the same time, it has never been shown that they are unrepresentative; and in any event, they are the most convenient source of arbitration awards.

ticular information was supplied. The exact number of employees involved can be ascertained from the appendix tables.

With these explanations out of the way, we can now proceed to the results of the study.

Seniority Status at the Time of Discharge

The discharge problem seems to be concentrated among relatively junior employees. To the extent that seniority information is available, 28 percent of the reinstated workers had two years or less seniority on the date of discharge. (See Appendix Table C-1.) Another 23 percent had from three to five years. Thus, more than half can be classified as junior, if five years or less will serve as a definition of junior status. Only eighteen percent had eleven years or more of seniority at the time of discharge.

While official probationary periods in industry usually run from thirty days to six months, it is well known that a considerably longer period elapses before an employee becomes permanent in the full sense of the word. The first few years of employment are a period of trial and error. Many studies have shown that a large proportion of workers who quit their jobs have low seniority.[13] Layoffs for lack of work are normally concentrated among workers with relatively recent hiring dates. It now appears that the majority of discharged employees are also fairly new.[14] By the time that employees have accumulated substantial seniority, they have likewise accumulated important rights which they are careful to protect. They have become valued members of the work force, and will not be discharged hastily. They have adjusted to their supervisors; the supervisors have adjusted to them. They have arrived, and are likely to remain.

Grounds for Discharge

A majority of the employees were discharged for overt and dramatic types of misbehavior. Twenty-seven percent were discharged for illegal

---

[13] See, for example, P. Eldridge and L. Wolkstein, "Incidence of Employer Change," *Industrial and Labor Relations Review*, Vol. 10, October 1956, pp. 101-107.

[14] It is true, of course, that the present study covers only those discharged employees who were subsequently reinstated. However, there is no reason to believe that discharged employees who are not reinstated have any greater seniority, on the average.

strikes, strike violence, or deliberately restricting production. (Table C-2.) Another twenty-two percent were accused of refusing to perform job assignments, refusing to work overtime, and similar forms of insubordination. Nine percent were terminated on the score of fighting, assaults, horse-play and trouble-making. Thus, almost sixty percent of the cases involved these three types of offenses. All of them represent an open challenge to the authority of management, as viewed by management, or a breach of peace inside the plant.

The quieter, less conspicuous and more gradual forms of dereliction did not account for such a large proportion of all the terminations. Eleven percent were discharged for absenteeism, tardiness or leaving early; eight percent for incompetence, negligence, poor workmanship or violation of safety rules; and five percent for dishonesty, theft or falsification of records. The remaining eighteen percent were scattered among numerous categories, including intoxication, disloyalty, gambling, loafing and miscellaneous rule violations.

If a similar distribution of all discharged employees were made, including those *not* reinstated, the proportions would be somewhat different. Nevertheless, it seems evident that the drastic and shocking episode, such as a fight, an illegal strike or an act of defiance, puts the greatest strain on the employment relationship. Quieter problems like absenteeism and poor workmanship do not produce a crisis in the shop, do not mobilize emotions, and are more likely to be resolved without resort to the sanction of discharge. It may be that the modern theory of corrective discipline, which emphasizes patient educational effort with the delinquent employee, is widely accepted in industry insofar as the less dramatic offenses are concerned; and that fighting, illegal strikes, etc., are regarded by employers as "capital crimes," justifying immediate discharge notwithstanding the employee's previous record. The proper application of corrective discipline to these kinds of offenses has never been fully explored or explained.

Principal Reasons for Reinstatement

In each of the 207 cases, the arbitration opinion has been analyzed to determine the arbitrator's principal ground for reinstating the grievant. It is instructive that the question of literal guilt or innocence has not been decisive in the majority of the cases. The reason most frequently invoked has been the existence of mitigating circumstances. For example, the grievant did assault a fellow worker, but had been sorely provoked. Or the grievant did refuse an overtime assignment, but had worked a great deal of overtime in recent months. Or the grievant's long service and previously unblemished disciplinary record should have been given more weight. In 50 cases, or 24 percent of the total, discharged employees were reinstated because of mitigating circumstances. (Table C-3.)

A closely related ground for reinstatement was that discharge was an excessive penalty for the offense. This ground was assigned in 39 cases, or 19 percent of the total. Here again, the grievants were not held innocent of blame. Rather the arbitrators found they had been dealt with too harshly: that the punishment did not fit the crime.

In 20 cases (ten percent), arbitrators held that the employer had failed to met his own obligations.

In nineteen cases (nine percent), employees were reinstated on the ground of unequal treatment. They were singled out for discharge although other employees, guilty of identical or similar conduct, were not terminated. The employer's actions were held to be capricious or discriminatory.

Among the remaining 79 cases, 43 grievants were reinstated on the ground of insufficient evidence to support the charge against them. Sixteen were reinstated because their actions were found partly or wholly justified. Twenty were reinstated for miscellaneous reasons.

Thus, in over 60 percent of the cases, the crucial issue was not whether the grievant had misbehaved. The issue was whether discharge was a fair and reasonable penalty in view of the nature of the misbehavior, the surrounding circumstances, the employee's previous record and the employer's policy in handling similar cases. Some arbitrators, it is true, accord the employer more leeway than others. Some will uphold a penalty if it is within an area of reasonable discretion. Others will uphold it only if they are personally convinced that it was fair. In either case, apparently the typical discharge hearing is not so much a trial of guilt or innocence as a review of the reasonableness of managerial action.

Terms of Reinstatement

In view of what has been shown, it is not surprising that only a minority of the grievants were reinstated with complete retroactivity. (In practically every case, of course, the unions asked that they be made whole.) Sixty-three, or thirty percent, were reinstated with full back pay; sixty, or 29 percent, with partial back pay; and 84, or 41 percent, with no back pay at all. (Tables C-2 and C-3.)

The extent of back pay varied with the original charge. Most of the grievants who had been accused of insubordination were reinstated without back pay. (Table C-2.) The same was true in cases of fighting, assaults, etc. On the other hand, the larger group of those charged with strike leadership or violence or deliberately restricting production were reinstated with full back pay.

As one would expect, the extent of back pay also varied with the arbitrators' reasons for reinstatement. Where mitigating circumstances were found, the largest group was restored without retroactivity, the second-largest with partial back pay, and only a few were made whole. The same is true of cases in which discharge was deemed an excessive penalty. Where the employer had failed to present sufficient evidence to sustain the charge, the majority of grievants were restored with full back pay.[15] (Table C-3.)

People will have different opinions concerning the frequency of no-back-pay or partial-back-pay decisions. Some will accuse the arbitrator of compromising instead of facing the issue. Some will say that he strained the facts to get the grievant back on the payroll by hook or by crook. In defense, it will be argued that in these cases there was just cause for some punishment, but not for the ultimate sanction of discharge; that the arbitrator should not be required to select between two equally unfair results; and that he should not be stigmatized as a "compromiser" when he finds a reasonable solution. In any event, it is clear that the majority of arbitrators believe they have authority to mitigate penalties when not prevented by the contract, the submission agreement, or perhaps the previous practice of the parties.

---

[15] At first blush, it seems difficult to understand why some of the arbitrators denied back pay after finding insufficient evidence to support the charge. Analysis of such decisions indicates that in the majority of cases, the grievant was accused of several delinquencies. The principal accusation was not supported, but some of the minor charges were admitted or established. Regrettably, however, there were a few cases in which the arbitrators apparently concluded that (a) the grievants were guilty, but (b) the employers had not proved it. This curious concept of "proof," as being something different from persuasion, is widely held by lay juries but has not been characteristic of persons in a judicial role. In one or two cases it is possible that the arbitrators resolved their genuine doubts by splitting the award, an expedient requiring no comment.

How Long Did They Stay?

We come now to the after-history of the reinstatement decision. First, do the reinstated actually return; and if so, how long do they stay? We have this information for 123 employees covered by the employer questionnaires.

Twelve employees never returned to work. (Table C-4.) Six of these had less than two years of seniority. Seniority information concerning the remaining six is lacking, but presumably most of them were short-service men. The probable inference is that the employees who failed to take advantage of reinstatement were too new to have established roots in the plant. Incidentally, eleven of the twelve were ordered reinstated without retroactivity; so that if they pressed their grievances merely to secure back pay, they were sadly disappointed. (Table C-5.)

Of those who returned, thirteen were terminated, for one reason or another, within six months; 22 within a year; and 32 within two years. Among the entire group of 123, 63 are still employed in the same establishment and sixty are no longer there. Thirty-five have quit since the date of reinstatement, including the twelve who never returned. Seventeen have been discharged a second time, including nine within the first year. Eight are dead, have retired, or were laid off in the permanent closing of a plant.

Among those reinstated in 1950, the majority are no longer in the establishment. (Table C-6.) Of those reinstated from 1951 to 1954, about half have left and half have remained. Most of the workers reinstated in 1955 are still employed in the same establishment. Naturally, the more time passes, the more likely it is that a given employee will resign, retire, die or be discharged.

Most of the employees who have been terminated since the date of reinstatement were short-service men (to the extent that we have information concerning seniority status). Conversely, a majority of the short-service men have been terminated. Most of the long-service men (six years or more of seniority) are still employed. *Only one of these has been discharged a second time since being reinstated. Only three have quit.* (Table C-4.)

The implications are obvious. The reinstated long-service employee will probably last. The reinstated short-service employee is not so likely to remain.

With respect to the short-service employees, however, the statistics must be interpreted with great caution. They do not necessarily show that a reinstated short-service employee is more likely to be terminated than any other short-service employee. The quit rate in manufacturing industries tends to run at about two percent per month, or 24 percent per year, and is doubtless considerably higher among junior employees. The discharge rate averages 0.3 percent per month, or 3.6 percent per year.[16] Elaborate calculations would have to be made to establish precise comparisons. My own view, however, is that the reinstated short-service employee is not more likely to quit than others with similar seniority. He is more likely to be discharged, however.

The Reinstated Employee as Seen by His Employer

Employers were requested to state whether the grievant has been a satisfactory worker since reinstatement; whether he has made normal occupational progress in terms of promotions, merit increases, etc.; whether there has been a recurrence of disciplinary problems; whether further disciplinary action has been necessary; how his supervisors have felt toward him; and what has been the grievant's attitude. In some cases it was impossible for the employer to state an opinion on these questions, because the grievant did not return or did not remain long enough to provide any basis for an opinion. The responses were given in the employers' own words, often with supporting details, but have been grouped into convenient categories for presentation here.

Has the grievant been a satisfactory employee since reinstatement? "Yes": 65 percent. "No": 35 percent. Of those employees deemed satisfactory, two-thirds are still employed. Of those regarded as unsatisfactory, about sixty percent have left—primarily by the discharge route. (Table C-7.) Practically all the "unsatisfactory" employees had less than five years' seniority at the time of the original discharge. A majority had less than two years. (Table C-8.) Only three with six years or more were classified "unsatisfactory."

Has the grievant made normal occupational progress? "Yes": 64 percent. "No": 35 percent. (Table C-9.) Of those still employed, however, more than 70 percent have made normal progress, according to the employer. Of course there is more room for advancement in some

---

[16] Turnover statistics are published in *Monthly Labor Review* (Washington: U. S. Department of Labor).

plants than in others. Some of the grievants are in the same jobs which they held at the time of discharge, but are still described as having made "normal progress." But many workers who have never been discharged are assigned to the same jobs for long periods of time. For those employees who failed to make normal progress, another question is whether they failed because of personal deficiencies or because they were working under a cloud. Analysis of the questionnaires does not furnish any clear answer. It is likely, however, that the reinstated employee has a somewhat diminished chance of being promoted.

Has there been a recurrence of disciplinary problems? Have any disciplinary penalties been imposed since reinstatement? The answers to these questions deserve careful scrutiny. As noted above, it is sometimes said that the reinstated employee will be particularly careful to keep out of trouble thereafter; others feel that the difficulty will probably recur, and that supervisors will endeavor to "nail" him a second time.

A total of 123 reinstated employees are covered by the employer questionnaires. No information on subsequent disciplinary history is reported for 27. (Table C-10.) These include the twelve who never returned, twelve who resigned shortly after reinstatement, and three others.

With respect to the remaining 96, employers state that 67, or 70 percent, have presented no subsequent disciplinary problems. Eight have repeated the same offense for which they were originally terminated; four of these have been discharged again. Twenty-one, the employers state, have been guilty of some different offense, and eleven of these have been discharged.

Once more the influence of seniority is striking. Practically all of the "repeaters" were short-service men with five years or less of seniority at the time of their original discharge. (Table C-11.) So far as we have information, only three employees with six years or more have experienced further difficulties, and none with eleven years or more. Apparently the employee with considerable seniority is almost certain to stay out of trouble after being reinstated.

How have the supervisors felt toward the reinstated employee? In 71 percent of the cases, the responses can be classified as favorable or neutral. In the remaining 29 percent, supervisors were reported as holding an unfavorable or resentful attitude. (Table C-12.)

Needless to say, a supervisor will not be overjoyed when a discharged employee is reinstated to his work group. The employee stands as a symbol of two unpleasant facts: that the supervisor's authority is limited, and that the arbitrators disagreed with his judgment. Many employers emphasize, however, that the supervisors have attempted to let bygones be bygones and deal with the grievant as with any other employee. Some employers report that the supervisors have been unhappy over the need to reinstate employees whom they consider unacceptable.

What has been the grievant's attitude since reinstatement? The responses can be classified as follows:

"Attitude good": 54 percent—mostly still employed. In 28 cases, employers state definitely that the disciplinary crisis had a favorable effect on the grievants' behavior.

"Attitude unchanged": fourteen percent—mostly still employed. The significance of this response is not too clear. Presumably what is meant is that the attitude continued unsatisfactory, or else that the original problem was not one of attitude.

"Attitude poor": thirty percent, about half of whom are still employed. Some employers state that the reinstated employees now consider themselves above the law. (Table C-13.)

It would be only human if the employers were somewhat more charitable in describing the attitudes of the supervisors than in characterizing those of the reinstated employees. Nevertheless, it is significant that about three-quarters of the supervisors and a strong majority of the grievants are reported as having satisfactory attitudes. These reports indicate a generally sound adjustment to the difficult human problems attending reinstatement after discharge.

The Arbitration Award as Viewed by the Employer

The final question addressed to the employers reads as follows: "Looking back on the incident, do you believe the arbitrator made the right decision in reinstating this employee? Please give reasons."

This question was not answered in thirteen cases, mostly involving workers who never returned. Of the remaining 110 cases, employers believe the decision was correct in 43 cases (39 percent), and wrong in 67 cases (61 percent). (Table C-14.)

Many of the affirmative responses are explained by the favorable effects of the award. A number of practical benefits were noted. Several employers noted that the grievant became a satisfactory employee after reinstatement. For example:

Since his belligerency and militancy disappeared, we now have a normal, average buffer who turns out a fair day's work.

He has been as good an employee as most of the other employees. Certain facts developed later revealed that this incident was really a clash of personalities. This is borne out in fact that before grievant left, he and supervisor had developed fairly friendly relations.

Other employers believe the decision supported or clarified the company's disciplinary policy.

We retained the services of a trained employee while establishing a three-month disciplinary layoff precedent for offense.

This decision based on interpretation of contract. This arbitration gave us a guidepost for future use.

Although the arbitrator ruled that the employee should be reinstated, he upheld the Company's position that employees do not have the right to refuse a suitable job offer on recall from layoff.

Still others agreed with the decision because they considered it correct on the merits, although some felt the outcome would have been different if the evidence had been fully or properly presented.

Yes—based on facts as presented—although the man should have been discharged. A thorough presentation of all the facts was not made, due to an unwillingness on the part of supervisors to persecute a man of poor capabilities.

While this employee had been troublesome, we were not fortified with enough written evidence of his shortcomings in view of his length of service.

As noted above, employers still disagree with the awards in 67 cases. The reasons assigned mostly relate to the merits of the decisions, as seen by the employers, rather than the practical outcome.

In 33 cases, employers restated their original position on the merits of the discharge. For example,

It was and still is our opinion that circumstances warranted termination of services, otherwise we would not have gone to arbitration.

Naturally had we thought the arbitrator's decision to be correct we would never have taken action to begin with.

Eleven believe that the decision was not based on a sound view of the evidence.

> We feel that the impartial arbitrator based his decision on assumptions and was more interested in discovering where the Company had made errors rather than basing his decision on the facts of the case.

Six accuse the arbitrator of compromising, mediating, departing from the contract, or exhibiting undue sympathy for the grievant.

> Contract called for reinstatement only if the discharge were unjust, and for full back pay upon reinstatement. Arbitrator's decision to the effect that employee had learned his lesson and should be given another chance, but without back pay since he was not blameless, was an attempt at compromise which was satisfactory to neither the Company, the Union, nor the employee.

> Arbitrator was prejudiced in reinstating employee in light of employee's financial difficulties. However, arbitrator admitted employee was a "most misdirected employee."

In a minority of cases the employer criticizes the decision on the ground of its bad effects. In seven cases, the weakening of supervisory authority is stressed.

> Result of having breach of discipline condoned by arbitrator is to make it more difficult to secure cooperation of entire group of employees and maintain supervisor's status as leader of group.

> Such decisions tend to weaken long-established company policy.

> Set mill and community back ten years by failure to uphold disciplinary action.

And in seven other cases, the objection is that the grievant's poor attitude was only reinforced by his being reinstated.

> Being young, was at stage where drastic action was needed to change his thinking concerning authority. If discharge had been sustained and the fact impressed upon him that he must not disregard rights of others, he might have been turned into proper channels of thinking.

> . . . In every respect this employee is marginal and was at the time of the arbitration award. The arbitrator's award encouraged this marginal attitude—which I am fearful is too often the case.

> He has never forgotten the incident and has always felt that management was against him. We have been unsuccessful in erasing this attitude. There should be other means established in awarding the employee . . . other than reinstatement.

On the other hand, several employers who disagree with the decision frankly concede that the employee has turned out well.

> Based solely on the facts presented, the decision was a poor one. However, in the light of [grievant's] fine recovery, I feel we will have gained a loyal and conscientious employee.

As a point of purely scientific interest, it might be noted that the employer's reaction to the decision is not greatly affected by the conditions of reinstatement. Employers believe the decision was correct in 35 percent of the cases providing full back pay, 47 percent providing partial back pay, and 37 percent providing no back pay. (Table C-14.)

Employer Evaluation of the Decision as Compared with Practical Outcome

The employers' reasons for approving or disapproving the decisions have been summarized above. There is considerable correlation, however, between these evaluations, on the one hand, and the practical outcome after reinstatement, on the other. (Table C-15.)

The correlation is particularly striking as to those decisions regarded as correct. There were 43 such decisions. Employers say that grievants have been satisfactory in 80 percent of these cases.[17] They have reportedly made normal occupational progress in 90 percent. Disciplinary problems have recurred in only three cases, less than ten percent. Supervisors have had a favorable, or at least neutral attitude toward the reinstated employees in 88 percent of the cases. The employees' attitude has been considered good in 78 percent.

Favorable experience after reinstatement does not guarantee that the employer will approve the decision, however. In numerous cases the employee has been satisfactory, has made normal progress, has kept out of further trouble, etc.; but the employer continues to disagree with the decision on its merits or because of its supposed long-run effects. About all that can be said is that the employer is more likely to approve a reinstatement that works out well, and is almost certain to disapprove of one that works out poorly.

Outcome of Reinstatement as Seen by Unions

Only 38 union questionnaires had been returned at the time it became necessary to tabulate the results. Because of this rather small response

---

[17] Non-responses are omitted from the percentages throughout this paragraph.

(eighteen percent, as compared with sixty percent of the employer questionnaires), it was not practical to make such an elaborate analysis of the material. However, it has proved helpful for certain purposes.

The first question which arises is whether the union questionnaires are comparable with the larger group of employer questionnaires, or with all the cases originally selected for the survey. In some respects these 38 cases are quite representative. The distribution with respect to grounds for discharge is similar to that of the larger group. The same is true of the distribution of cases according to conditions of reinstatement. The 38 employees are somewhat older, in point of seniority, than the average of all employees involved in the survey. A somewhat larger percentage is still employed than is true of the 123 covered by employer questionnaires (60 percent, as compared with 51 percent.)

The major difference is that most of these 38 cases are ones which turned out well after reinstatement, in view of the employers as well as the unions. That is, in the vast majority of these particular cases, employers reported that the grievants proved satisfactory after reinstatement, made normal occupational progress, encountered no further disciplinary trouble, etc.

The union's view of the outcome of these cases is even rosier. In some instances the unions were not able to reply to all questions, because of lack of detailed familiarity with conditions in the shop. But to the extent that replies were forthcoming, they were almost uniformly favorable.

For example, we asked whether the grievants had been treated fairly after reinstatement. This question was answered affirmatively in 31 cases. *In not a single case did the union complain of unfair treatment.*

Some of the other replies can be classified as follows:

"Do you believe the grievant has been a satisfactory employee, from the employer's standpoint, since reinstatement?" Yes: 29. No: 0. Not reported: 9.

"Has he made normal occupational progress?" Yes: 23. No: 2. Not reported: 9.

"How have the grievant's supervisors felt toward him?" Favorable or neutral: 24. Unfavorable: 0. Not reported: 12.

"What has been the grievant's attitude since reinstatement?" Good: 23. Unchanged or poor: 2. Not reported: 13.

"Does the union believe that the arbitrator made the right decision?" Yes: 33. No: 1. No reply: 4. (Employers disagreed with the decision in a slight majority of these particular cases.)

"From the union's standpoint, was it worthwhile to arbitrate this case?" Yes: 32. No: 3. No reply: 3.

The unions were asked to explain their views on the correctness of the decisions. Most frequently they restated their position on the merits of the case. A substantial number stressed that the grievant was a worthy employee, as shown by his subsequent behavior. Several rested on the arbitrator's reasoning. The single dissenter held that the arbitrator's solution was unworkable and the grievant incorrigible.

Some illustrative passages are as follows:

I feel that the arbitrator did make the right decision in this case. This man although not wholly blameless did not actually violate the agreement between the Co. and the union. His penalty of three months loss of pay was sufficient, discharge would have been too severe.

This man has advanced himself to a more responsible job and is a very responsible and happy worker.

All indications point to the fact that employer made hasty decision to discharge in the light of employee's previous record, and discharge was effected on the basis of supervisory evidence to the employer not substantiated in the arbitration hearing.

To my knowledge he was noted as a chronic troublemaker and was constantly inciting wildcat strikes without reason.

Likewise, the unions were asked to explain their opinions as to whether it was worthwhile to arbitrate these cases. The largest number replied that the grievant had been unjustly accused, so that it was the union's duty as bargaining representative to oppose his discharge; that the grievant was justified in what he did; and that the grievant was worthy, as confirmed by his conduct after reinstatement. Another sizable group explained that the decision enhanced the union's position and vindicated the principle of unionism. One respondent stated that the grievance lacked merit, and one said the decision had a bad effect on union-management relations.

Some quotations:

When there is any doubt, we are obligated to defend a member of the union.

Yes, because the union will go to any extremes for any employee who has gotten unfair treatment from the Co.

It added prestige to the union membership, and the leadership was doing their job in policing the execution of the contract in force.

Management has been very careful and call now when there is a problem. It has also made the union much stronger in the shop.

No, because subsequently the unit chairman and chief steward were discharged after another series of wildcats and resulted in two more cases. The problems should have been handled through the grievance procedure instead of using unauthorized work stoppages as a solution.

4. Summary and Conclusions

It has not been the purpose of this study to evaluate the doctrines which arbitrators have developed to handle discharge grievances. Instead the purpose has been to ascertain how reinstatements have worked out Needless to say, the soundness of a decision cannot be tested primarily by whether the litigants are made happy. If they wish to be assured of a happy solution, they are free to negotiate one themselves and stay out of arbitration. Nevertheless, the prevalent theory of corrective discipline does involve a judgment as to whether the grievant is potentially a useful and acceptable employee. When a reinstatement is based on the theory of corrective discipline, presumably the arbitrator has made an affirmative judgment of this type; or at least, he believes the negative has not been sufficiently established. Therefore it should be of interest to know whether his conclusion is borne out.

The most significant variable revealed in the questionnaires is seniority status. A majority of the grievants had five years or less seniority at the time of discharge. A majority of the short-service men did not take advantage of reinstatement, or were terminated after reinstatement. Those reinstated employees deemed unsatisfactory were practically all relatively junior, and a majority had less than two years at the time of discharge. Almost all the employees who encountered disciplinary troubles after reinstatement were in the junior group.

About sixty percent of the grievants were discharged over dramatic and conspicuous episodes such as illegal strikes, assaults and acts of insubordination. The theory of corrective discipline has never been satisfactorily expounded in relation to this kind of offense, although it is clear enough with respect to continuing problems of a gradual character.

The decision to reinstate was not typically based on a finding of innocence, or a refusal to find guilt. The most common grounds for reinstatement were that mitigating circumstances should be recognized, that discharge was an excessive penalty, and that the employer had failed to pursue a consistent disciplinary policy. Moreover, about seventy percent of the grievants were reinstated with no back pay or only partial retroactivity. Thus it is apparent that the discharge case most frequently becomes a review of the reasonableness of management's action rather than a trial of guilt or innocence.

Ten percent of the employees did not return. Another twenty percent lasted less than a year. Fifty percent are no longer employed. But the normal rate of labor turnover in industry must be taken into account. Probably the reinstated employee is not more likely than other employees to resign, but is more likely to be discharged again.

From an operational standpoint, about two-thirds of the cases have worked out well. Employers say that two-thirds of the reinstated employees have proved satisfactory. About sixty percent have reportedly made normal occupational progress, although there is reason to believe that the reinstated employee is less likely to be promoted. Seventy percent have presented no further disciplinary problems. The attitude of supervisors has been favorable or neutral in about seventy percent of the cases. The reinstated employee's attitude is described as good in about sixty percent of the cases. Since reinstatement creates a delicate human situation in the shop at best, these responses indicate a generally mature and far-sighted adjustment to the difficulties.

A rather small proportion of the union questionnaires was returned.

Nonetheless, it is surely of some significance that the unions did not complain of unfair treatment in a single case. In virtually every case the union reported that supervisors as well as grievants have displayed sound and favorable attitudes.

Employers now believe that the decision to reinstate was correct in thirty-nine percent of the cases. By way of explanation, they stress principally the favorable outcome of the reinstatements. Employers disagree with sixty-one percent of the decisions, chiefly on the merits as they stood at the time of discharge. Thus the employer is more likely to approve of a reinstatement that works out well, and almost certain to disapprove of one that works out poorly.

The unions agreed with the decision, and considered it worthwhile to have arbitrated the grievance, in almost every case. Unions believe they have a primary duty to support a discharged employee unless the merits of the discharge are clear.

Perhaps the foregoing report has somewhat illuminated the processes of discharge and reinstatement under collective bargaining agreements. To avoid a distorted impression, please bear in mind that not every discharged employee is reinstated. Furthermore, general conclusions— no matter how unassailable, and statistical averages—no matter how accurate, can only place a problem in context. They cannot solve the next case. For the next case, and particularly the next discharge case, is certain to be special and unique.

Appendix A on page 45 reproduces the questionnaire to employers. Appendix B on page 47 reproduces the questionnaire to unions.

QUESTIONNAIRE

for Report on "What Happens After Reinstatement?"

Note: *All replies will be strictly confidential. No company or individual will be identified in the Report. Only totals and summaries will be used.*

Name of company ....

Name of employee ....

Classification at time of discharge ....

Date of discharge ....

Date of reinstatement ....

Name of arbitrator ....

Award published at ....

QUESTIONS

(1) Did this employee actually return to work after the arbitration award?
....

    a) If not, why not? ....

....

(2) Is he still employed in your establishment? ....
                          Answer (3) or (4)

(3) If he is *not* still employed:

    a) When did he leave? ....

    b) What were the circumstances of his termination? ....

....

....

....

    c) Was he a satisfactory employee after reinstatement? (Please give comments) ....

....

....

    d) Did he progress normally? ....
       What was his last classification? ....

    e) How did his supervisors feel about him after reinstatement?

....

....

....

(4) If he *is* still employed in your establishment:
    a) What is his present classification? ....

    b) Has he made normal progress in terms of promotion, merit increases, more responsible assignments, etc.? ....(Please give details):

    c) All in all, has he been a satisfactory employee since being reinstated? ....

    d) Has there been any recurrence of the difficulty which led to his discharge? .... (If so, please give details) ....

    e) Has any disciplinary action been necessary since his reinstatement? .... (If so, please give details) ....

    f) How have his supervisors felt toward him since his reinstatement?

    g) What has been his own attitude? ....

    Did the disciplinary crisis have any effect upon his subsequent attitude or behavior? ....

(5) Looking back on the incident, do you believe the arbitrator made the right decision in reinstating this employee? .... (Please give reasons) ....

.... (Name)
.... (Title)
.... (Company)
.... (Address)

Please return to:

Arthur M. Ross, Director
Institute of Industrial Relations
University of California
201 California Hall
Berkeley, California

Appendix B

QUESTIONNAIRE

for Report on "What Happens After Reinstatement?"

Note: *All replies will be strictly confidential. No union, company, or individual will be identified in the Report. Only totals and summaries will be used.*

Name of Union ....
Name of Company ....
Name of Member ....
Classification at time of discharge ....
Date of arbitration award ....
Name of arbitrator..
Award published at ....

QUESTIONS

(1) Did this member actually return to the same employer after the arbitration award? ....

    (a) If not, why not? ....
....

(2) Is he still employed in the same establishment? ....

* * *

Answer (3) or (4)

(3) If he is *not* still employed in the same establishment:

    (a) When did he leave? ....

    (b) What were the circumstances of his termination? ....
....
....
....

    (c) If he left because of a second discharge, did the Union arbitrate that case? .... If not, why not? ....
....
....

    (d) Do you feel he was treated fairly after being reinstated? (Please give details.) ....
....

47

(4) If he *is* still employed in the same establishment:

(a) Has he made normal progress in terms of promotion, more responsible work, merit increases, etc.? ....
....
....

(b) Do you believe he has been treated fairly? (Please give details.)
....
....
....

(c) Do you believe that, from the Company's standpoint he has been a satisfactory employee since being reinstated? (Please give details.)
....
....
....

(d) Has he had any further disciplinary difficulties? (Please give details.) ....
....
....
....

(e) How have his supervisors felt toward him since his reinstatement?
....

(f) What has been his own attitude? ....
....

(5) Looking back on the incident, do you believe the arbitrator made the right decision in reinstating this member? (Please give reasons.) ....
....
....
....

(6) From the Union's standpoint, was it worthwhile to arbitrate his discharge? (Please give reasons.) ....
....
....
....

.... (Name)
.... (Title)
.... (Company)
.... (Address)

Please return to:
Arthur M. Ross, Director
Institute of Industrial Relations
University of California
201 California Hall
Berkeley 4, California

Appendix C

TABLE C-1. Seniority Status of the Grievants at Time of Discharge

Years of Seniority	Number of Grievants	Percentage of Grievants with Known Seniority
0-2	34	27.7
3-5	28	22.8
6-10	39	31.8
11-15	11	8.9
16-20	5	4.0
over 20	6	4.8
Total reported	123	100.0
Seniority unknown	84	
Total grievants	207	

(Appendix C continued on page 50)

TABLE C-2. Grounds for Discharge and Terms of Reinstatement, 207 Cases.

Grounds for Discharge	Terms of Reinstatement							
	Full back pay		Partial back pay		No back pay		Total	
	No.	Percent	No.	Percent	No.	Percent	No.	Percent
Absenteeism, tardiness, leaving early	7	11.1%	7	11.6%	8	9.5%	22	10.6%
Dishonesty, theft, falsification of records	2	3.2	1	1.7	7	8.3	10	4.8
Incompetence, negligence, poor workmanship, violation of safety rules........	4	6.3	4	6.7	9	10.7	17	8.2
Illegal strikes, strike violence, deliberate restriction of production	26	41.2	20	33.3	9	10.7	55	26.7
Wilful destruction or damage to property	3	4.8	—	—	—	—	3	1.4
Loafing, sleeping on job, unnecessary conversation	1	1.6	4	6.7	2	2.4	7	3.4
Intoxication, bringing intoxicants in plant	1	1.6	4	6.7	3	3.6	8	3.9
Physical condition (of grievant)	2	3.2	—	—	1	1.2	3	1.4
Disloyalty to company	2	3.2	2	3.3	1	1.2	5	2.4
Fighting, assault, horseplay, troublemaking	3	4.8	5	8.3	10	11.9	18	8.7
Gambling, soliciting bets	—	—	1	1.7	3	3.6	4	1.9
Arrest, criminal conviction (unrelated to employment)	2	3.2	—	—	1	1.2	3	1.4
Insubordination, refusal of job assignment, refusal to work overtime	9	14.2	9	15.0	27	32.1	45	21.8
Union activity in violation of contract....	—	—	1	1.7	1	1.2	2	1.0
Miscellaneous rule violations (not elsewhere classified)	1	1.6	2	3.3	2	2.4	5	2.4
Total	63	100.0	60	100.0	84	100.0	207	100.0

TABLE C-3. Principal Reasons for Reinstatement and Terms of Reinstatement, 207 Cases

Principal Reason for Reinstatement	Conditions of Reinstatement							
	Full back pay		Partial back pay		No back pay		Total	
	No.	Percent	No.	Percent	No.	Percent	No.	Percent
Mitigating circumstances	5	7.9%	16	26.6%	29	34.5%	50	24.2%
Discharge was an excessive penalty	3	4.8	15	25.0	21	25.0	39	18.8
Charge was unsupported by the evidence	25	39.7	9	15.0	9	10.7	43	20.7
Grievant was justified in his action	7	11.1	4	6.7	5	6.0	16	7.7
Company failed to perform its obligations	5	7.9	7	11.7	8	9.5	20	9.7
Absence of clear company policy, previous lax enforcement, lack of notice	3	4.8	5	8.3	6	7.1	14	6.8
Unequal or discriminatory treatment	12	19.0	3	5.0	4	4.8	19	9.2
No basis for disciplinary action	3	4.8	1	1.7	2	2.4	6	2.9
Total	63	100.0	60	.100.0	84	100.0	207	100.0

TABLE C-4. Seniority at Time of Discharge, and Employment History after Reinstatement, 123 Cases (Employer Questionnaires).

Seniority at time of Discharge	Subsequent Employment History					
	Still Employed	Never Returned	Subsequently Quit	Subsequently Discharged	Other Terminations	Total
0- 2 years	9	6	5	4	—	24
3- 5 years	8	—	6	3	1	18
6-10 years	12	—	2	1	1	16
11-15 years	4	—	—	—	2	6
16-20 years	1	—	1	—	1	3
over 20 years	1	—	—	—	—	1
Seniority unknown	28	6	10	8	3	55
Total	63	12	24	16	8	123

TABLE C-5. Terms of Reinstatement, and Employment History after Reinstatement, 123 Cases

Terms of Reinstatement	Subsequent Employment History					
	Still Employed	Never Returned	Subsequently Quit	Subsequently Discharged	Other Terminations	Total
Full back pay....	18	—	9	6	4	37
Partial back pay	18	1	6	4	2	32
No back pay......	27	11	9	6	1	54
Total	63	12	24	16	8	123

TABLE C-6. Length of Employment after Reinstatement, by Year of Reinstatement, 123 Cases.

Year	Reason for Termination	Length of Employment after Reinstatement							
		Never Returned	Less than 1 Year	1-2 Years	2-4 Years	Over 4 Years	Total Terminations	Still Employed	Grand Total
	Quit	—	1	—	—	1	2		
	Discharged	—	2	—	1	—	3		
	Other	—	—	—	1	2	3		
1950	Total	—	3	—	2	3	8	4	12
	Quit	5	5	1	2	—	13		
	Discharged	—	2	—	3	2	7		
	Other	—	—	1	—	1	2		
1951	Total	5	7	2	5	3	22	21	43
	Quit	2	4	1	—	1	8		
	Discharged	—	2	1	—	—	3		
	Other	—	—	1	—	—	1		
1952	Total	2	6	3	—	1	12	10	22
	Quit	1	—	2	2	—	5		
	Discharged	—	2	—	—	—	2		
	Other	—	1	—	—	—	1		
1953	Total	1	3	2	2	—	8	10	18
	Quit	2	—	3	—	—	5		
	Discharged	—	—	—	—	—	—		
	Other	—	1	—	—	—	1		
1954	Total	2	1	3	—	—	6	6	12
	Quit	1	1	—	—	—	2		
	Discharged	1	1	—	—	—	2		
	Other	—	—	—	—	—	—		
1955	Total	2	2	—	—	—	4	11	15
1956	Total	—	—	—	—	—	—	1	1
Totals:									
	Quit	11	11	7	4	2	35		
	Discharged	1	9	1	4	2	17		
	Other	—	2	2	1	3	8		
Grand Total	....	12	22	10	9	7	60	63	123

TABLE C-7. Employer's Evaluation of Reinstated Employees, and Subsequent Employment History, 123 Cases.

Has grievant been a satisfactory employee?	Subsequent Employment History					
	Still Employed	Never Returned	Subsequently Quit	Subsequently Discharged	Other Terminations	Total
Yes	47	—	14	2	8	71
No	15	—	9	14	—	38
No response	1	12	1	—	—	14
Total	63	12	24	16	8	123

TABLE C-8. Employer's Evaluation of Reinstated Employees, and Seniority at the Time of Discharge, 123 Cases

Has grievant been a satisfactory employee?	Seniority at the Time of Discharge							
	0-2 Years	3-5 Years	6-10 Years	11-15 Years	16-20 Years	Over 20 Years	Seniority Unknown	Total Grievants
Yes	7	13	14	6	3	—	28	71
No	11	5	2	—	—	1	19	38
No response	6	—	—	—	—	—	8	14
Total	24	18	16	6	3	1	55	123

TABLE C-9. Occupational Progress after Reinstatement, and Subsequent Employment History, 123 Cases.

Has grievant made normal progress?	Subsequent Employment History					
	Still Employed	Never Returned	Subsequently Quit	Subsequently Discharged	Other Terminations	Total
Yes	42	—	11	3	7	63
No	16	—	9	9	1	35
No response	5	12	4	4	—	25
Total	63	12	24	16	8	123

TABLE C-10. Recurrence of Disciplinary Problems,
and Subsequent Employment History, 123 Cases.

Recurrence of disciplinary problems?	Subsequent Employment History					
	Still Employed	Never Returned	Subsequently Quit	Subsequently Discharged	Other Terminations	Total
None	48	—	12	—	7	67
Yes, same offense	4	—	—	4	—	8
Yes, different offense	10	—	—	11	—	21
Not reported	1	12	12	1	1	27
Total	63	12	24	16	8	123

TABLE C-11. Recurrence of Disciplinary Problems,
and Seniority at the Time of Discharge, 123 Cases.

Recurrence of disciplinary problems?	Seniority at the Time of Discharge							
	0-2 Years	3-5 Years	6-10 Years	11-15 Years	16-20 Years	Over 20 Years	Seniority Unknown	Total Grievants
None	10	9	12	6	3	1	26	67
Yes, same offense	3	—	2	—	—	—	3	8
Yes, different offense	4	4	1	—	—	—	12	21
Not reported	7	5	1	—	—	—	14	27
Total	24	18	16	6	3	1	55	123

TABLE C-12. Supervisors' Attitudes Toward Reinstated Employees,
and Subsequent Employment History, 123 Cases.

How have Supervisors felt toward grievant?	Subsequent Employment History					
	Still Employed	Never Returned	Subsequently Quit	Subsequently Discharged	Other Terminations	Total
Favorable or neutral	49	—	11	6	6	72
Unfavorable	12	—	10	6	2	30
Not reported	2	12	3	4	—	21
Total	63	12	24	16	8	123

TABLE C-13. Grievant's Attitude Since Reinstatement, as Viewed by
Employer, and Subsequent Employment History, 123 Cases.

What has been grievant's attitude?	Subsequent Employment History					
	Still Employed	Never Returned	Subsequently Quit	Subsequently Discharged	Other Terminations	Total
Good	39	—	1	—	5	45
Unchanged	9	—	—	2	—	11
Poor	13	—	5	5	1	24
Not reported	2	12	18	9	2	43
Total	63	12	24	16	8	123

TABLE C-14. Employer's Evaluation of Arbitration Award,
and Terms of Reinstatement, 123 Cases.

Does employer agree with arbitrator's decision?	Terms of Reinstatement			
	Full Back Pay	Partial Back Pay	No Back Pay	Total Grievants
Yes	12	14	17	43
No	22	16	29	67
Not reported	3	2	8	13
Total	37	32	54	123

TABLE C-15. Employer's Evaluation of Arbitration Award, as Compared with Various Indications of Practical Outcome.

| Various Indications of Practical Outcome | Evaluation of Award | | | |
| | "Correct" | | "Incorrect" | |
	Number	Percent of Responses	Number	Percent of Responses
I. Satisfactory Employee?				
Yes	34	79.1	35	56.4
No	9	20.9	27	43.6
Not reported	—	—	5	—
II. Normal occupational Progress?				
Yes	34	89.5	28	50.0
No	4	10.5	28	50.0
Not reported	5	—	11	—
III. Recurrence of disciplinary problems?				
None	35	92.1	29	52.7
Yes, same offense	1	2.6	7	12.7
Yes, different offense	2	5.3	19	34.6
Not reported	5	—	12	—
IV. Supervisors' attitude?				
Favorable or neutral	36	87.8	35	60.3
Unfavorable	5	12.2	23	39.7
Not reported	2	—	9	—
V. Grievant's attitude?				
Good	26	78.8	18	40.9
Unchanged	4	12.1	6	13.6
Poor	3	9.1	20	45.5
Not reported	10	—	23	—

Discussion—

SIDNEY A. WOLFF
New York City

Arthur Ross' paper is excellent. I read an advance draft earlier this week and found it unassailable. But if he thinks I studied all his tables, he is in for a surprise! There were a few points, however, which I think should evoke discussion and I hope I can provoke discussion.

Ross points out in his paper that a large percentage of reinstated workers did not take advantage of the opportunity of reinstatement. Now this is a matter that we should consider seriously.

The average supervisor is opposed to the return of a discharged worker, and much criticism is levelled at arbitrators who direct reinstatement. If then, following an award requiring re-employment, a worker should refuse to return, the process of arbitration is brought into disrepute.

In a tight labor market where there is keen competition, his return to the job may be of no consequence to the worker. He may have a burning desire merely to clear his record or to recoup his damages. But sometimes his grievance is but a manifestation of a desire to satisfy his ego. He then files a grievance, contesting the discharge.

I am reminded of a recent case I had involving the discharge of a truck driver. While awaiting hearing, he obtained a job elsewhere, but in answer to the usual question put to him by Union counsel, insisted he wanted his job back. On cross examination, he admitted that he did not want his job back, that he wouldn't work for that employer even if it meant starving. When asked why he filed the grievance, he answered—to teach the boss a lesson.

At this point, the Union official withdrew the grievance and directed the employee to appear at the next Union Executive Board meeting. Later I learned he was assessed personally with the entire cost of the arbitration proceedings. Admittedly this is an extreme case.

Wouldn't it be more appropriate, if the worker only wants damages, for him merely to grieve for damages and not ask for reinstatement? If this were done, I am sure that most companies would quickly work out a settlement. The real objection, as I view it, on the part of a company, is to take back what it feels is an unsatisfactory employee. This procedure might cut down the case load, but in the final analysis, it may be better labor relations.

It appears that in many cases, discharged employees were reinstated because, in the arbitrator's opinion, discharge was too severe for the particular offense. This always brings up the question whether the arbitrator goes beyond his jurisdiction in reducing the punishment when the issue submitted is simply whether just cause existed.

As Ross points out, the majority of arbitrators believe they have the authority to mitigate the penalty when not prevented by the contract, and the Court cases tend to support this statement, although the Court decisions are not uniform.

Ross' study, I think, is most revealing and presents a conclusion that should be of interest to all of us. That is that the short service employee, rather than the senior employee, when reinstated, is more apt to repeat his offense and get into trouble so as to be discharged again. Do we find in this the subtle suggestion that we should only show consideration to the senior dischargee?

In my experience, I have found very few instances of a worker's conduct coming up for review after reinstatement by the arbitrator. It seems to me that experience in this field is like that in the world at large. There are a great many more first offenders than repeaters.

Once someone has stepped out of line and has been caught up, he usually takes the experience to heart. Many times the hearing will reveal to the worker inadequacies of which he was not aware. Once they are brought home to him, he makes a determined effort to give no offense.

The return of a man to the job places added responsibilities both on the employee and the company. Management must be careful to avoid the charge that it is picking on him, and the worker must be careful not to give offense.

This recognition of their responsibilities should cause both sides to behave, and in due course, the constraint between them ought to disappear.

When a man is returned by an arbitration award, the personnel people should have a heart-to-heart talk with the man, preferably in the presence of the shop steward. It should be stressed that bygones are bygones, that there will be no retaliation, and that as long as the job is done, there will be no problem.

In turn, the union representative should make it clear to the worker that it is up to him to do his job properly.

In very few contracts have the parties laid down standards to govern us in the field of industrial discipline. We have seen contracts in page after page state how transfers are to be made, and how seniority is to be applied, but when it comes to industrial discipline, all we find is the sentence that the company will discharge only for just cause.

As I interpret this failure, the parties themselves have been unable to set down standards of conduct to govern the worker. Instead, they are ready to leave the question to the good judgment of an arbitrator.

This is clear-headed thinking. What today might be considered just cause may not be so tomorrow. In case of a labor shortage, an employer may not want to discipline a particular employee to the extent of dismissal. With a set of standards in the contract, the employer might find himself forced to take action. Otherwise he would be laying himself open at a later date to a charge of discriminatory treatment.

Also, a set of standards, or as we sometimes find, a list of derelictions and penalties either in the plant rules or in the contract might well place a company in a straightjacket, denying the company and the arbitrator any maneuverability.

I suggest that the arbitrator not be restricted in cases of industrial discipline. Our record in this field establishes that by far and large our judgments have not been too warped.

In his paper, Ross suggests that in the field of the arbitration of discharge cases, we give attention to the employee involved and fit the punishment to the crime. Yet I suggest, if you will, that in many cases by striving to find mitigating circumstances, the arbitrator is seeking to find a punishment to fit the offender.

I am disturbed by his remarks "that the question of literal guilt or innocence has not been decisive in the majority of the cases." As I view his paper, it appears that in passing on the question of reinstatement the arbitrator first determines whether or not the worker is "potentially a useful and acceptable employee."

But is it for us to determine whether a man is potentially a useful and acceptable employee? Isn't that Management's business? Are we opening too wide a road?

In reaching a determination, an arbitrator will latch on to a man's length of service, his prior record, his attitudes towards the job, his supervisors and co-workers and other factors which I need not repeat. But what is this but an effort to have the punishment fit the offender?

Ross also stresses modern enlightened concepts, sprinkled with elements of procedural due process. Today in the enforcement of our criminal law we are using a growing horde of social workers, psychologists, psychiatrists and do-gooders. Are we to do the same in labor arbitration? If so, we must be well rounded persons, experts in the solution of all problems, human as well as industrial. The psychiatrists tell us that we must consider a person's motivations, why he does these things. Will we bring disapproval down on our heads if we start to chart the uncharted sea of human relations?

I have even read that the psychiatrist finds the use of a sexual symbolism by workers when they swear at their foreman using phrases with unprintable suggestions; or that a wildcat strike is occasioned by the workers' desire to defend against an attack on their manhood; or that horseplay in the plant is a symptom of infantile regression.

Are we to delve into these things? Is the day soon to dawn when a medical degree will be requisite for membership in this august body? These are questions which I leave for your consideration.

CHAPTER III

ARBITRATION OF DISPUTES INVOLVING INCENTIVE PROBLEMS: AN INDUSTRY VIEW

OWEN FAIRWEATHER
Member of the Chicago Bar
Partner, Seyfarth, Shaw and Fairweather

It is indeed a pleasure for me to speak to this audience. As an audience of arbitrators, it can properly be called an audience of experts on labor affairs—or even more properly an audience composed of the experts' experts. I am sure that many of you know much more about the "Arbitration of Disputes Involving Incentive Problems" than I, but here goes anyway.

I am sure that you are aware that there is a difference between the attitudes of unions and the attitudes of management concerning incentive standards. Solomon Barkin, a very articulate union spokesman, who is Research Director of the Textile Union, went right to the heart of this difference, when he said:

> The unions and workers seem to *** be in a position to secure additional wage concessions by the negotiation of work standards.
>
> Management tends to be in a better bargaining position if the standards are pre-determined against a fixed wage relationship.*** Unions, therefore, prefer to retain opportunities for negotiation on the individual job.

There you have it. Managements want to establish incentive standards on a factual basis to the maximum extent possible. Managements contend that the time required to perform a job is a fact. When such time is determined by industrial engineering procedures, incentive standards can be established so as to provide a consistent earnings opportunity above the guaranteed base rate on all jobs. For the same amount of effort, managements say, employees should earn the same amount of "extra" pay above the guaranteed base.

Unions want to negotiate standards. They believe this produces more earnings than relying on the so-called scientific measurement procedures of management. Union spokesmen argue that the techniques managements use to measure the time required to perform a job are not accurate enough; hence, the fixing of the incentive standard should be a matter determined by general bargaining.

The reasons for the difference in approach to incentive standards was noted by Robert Roy, Professor of Industrial Engineering at Johns Hopkins University. He described the condition that occurs after the introduction of an incentive system when the low cost, high-wage honeymoon has lost its bloom:

> As time passes, so does the initial sense of satisfaction to the workers. They begin to look upon the incentive increment in their pay as a right rather than a privilege, and to press for a variety of concessions which, taken one by one, seem quite reasonable.
>
> When some of these concessions are granted, wages are enhanced, but low costs are, if not forgotten, certainly hurt.
>
> ***. In any measured work-wage incentive relationship, the pressure of those measured is always in the direction of obtaining more, never less.

This "pressure of those measured for more" causes some of them, in the efforts to obtain more, to charge that, through the administration of the incentive systems, managements continue to squeeze more work from the workers for less money. They call this the "speed-up." To illustrate this, let me quote a comment by Walter Reuther concerning incentive programs:

> The right of the unions to strike over "speed-up" grievances is now established at the time contracts are negotiated. Continuous progress has been made in the fight against "speed-up," but to maintain what has been won, and to continue to fight against it, the steward and the committeemen in the shop must be trained and alert. ***

All thoughtful managements who operate plants with incentive systems recognize these natural motivations and know that they can be stimulated into destructive pressures. Such managements adopt policies which they hope will protect their incentive systems. One position taken by some managements to stave off this pressure for liberalization of incentive standards can be stated somewhat like this:

We, the management, establish the incentive standards to encourage the individual employee to give us the extra effort which he alone can give. Hence, incentive standards are something personal between the management and the individual employee. Since we, the management, are providing these "extra" earnings above the wage rates negotiated with the union, we should retain the final say.

Now, the union representatives, somewhat surprisingly, might reply:

If that is the position you take, that is all right with us. We don't want some inexperienced outside arbitrator settling our incentive problems any more than you do. However, we will be in to negotiate any incentive standard that we think is unfair, and we are warning you now that if you won't agree to correct those we believe to be unfair, we reserve the right to strike.

Management might then say quietly to itself:

Let's agree with the union on this. It is true the union's reasons for not wanting to arbitrate disputed incentive standards are somewhat different than ours, but, after all, the employees won't strike over every dispute over an individual incentive standard and, hence, we will keep the final say and in this way keep control over the establishment of incentive standards.

The difficulty with this approach, which can be labeled, "The Standards Are Not Subject to Arbitration so We Retain Final Control" is that it surrounds the incentive system with a bargaining atmosphere of compromise and contest. The employees believe they face an uncomfortable dilemma—that they have to "take it or strike." Tensions build up and become deep-seated. Then, when collective bargaining time rolls around again, pressures can be ignited to strike level by the use of sloganized attacks such as "speed-up" and "chisel." Then the management, in its turn, faces the uncomfortable dilemma of having to concede to the demands for liberalization of the incentive standards, thus slowly destroying the incentive system, or refusing to do so, and bringing on industrial warfare. Thus, the approach we have labeled, "Standards Are Not Subject to Arbitration so We Retain Final Control," that appeared at first blush to keep management in the driver's seat, turns out to be a very weak shield indeed.

We have as the alternative to this first approach the view that management should submit incentive disputes to arbitration. If a company is willing to do this, it would seem that the emotional pressure which otherwise can build up around an incentive system and which permits suspicions to grow and flourish cannot build up. A claim of unfair treatment can be refuted by simply replying, "Well, let's find out if what you say is true. We will submit the question in dispute to an Impartial Arbitrator."

However, in spite of the persuasiveness of this reasoning, many managements remain frightened. They say:

> The whole idea of removing emotionalism by a willingness to arbitrate seems right, but few of the recognized arbitrators are industrial engineers, and what does one of those regular arbitrators know about incentives? Since our union won't agree to arbitrate such a dispute before a consulting engineer from a management consulting engineering firm, we won't be able to find an industrial engineer to be the arbitrator and hence the arbitration of incentives just won't work.

The belief that since incentive standards are established by industrial engineers they must be arbitrated by industrial engineers, though it may seem reasonable on the surface, reveals a very fundamental weakness. If management believes that it cannot convince an Impartial Arbitrator who is not an industrial engineer of the fairness of a incentive standard, it is admitting that it cannot convince just an ordinary fair-minded person that an incentive standard it has established is fair. If that is true, how can it convince one of its employees, or the union leader, none of whom are trained industrial engineers, that a standard it has established is fair?

The only way management can rectify this sad state of affairs is to do two things:

First, incorporate into the labor agreement, through very careful negotiation, as clear and workable tests as possible to be used by the Arbitrator to determine the fairness of a particular standard.

Second, develop time measurement techniques to obtain the highest level of accuracy and consistency, and also the explanation techniques, so that a fair-minded person, be he an arbitrator or just an employee or a union leader, can be convinced that the incentive standard established by management, when judged against the contractual "test of fairness," satisfies that test.

Tests of Fairness

Since the arbitrator will be asked to compare the incentive standard in dispute against a contractual "test of fairness" contained in the labor agreement, we must identify the different types of "tests of fairness" found in labor agreements before continuing further. This is because the explanation techniques or, if you prefer a more legalistic phrase, the "proof" problems which will arise in connection with the arbitration of a disputed standard will be different under each of the various types.

The type of contractual "test of fairness" we shall classify as Type No. 1 is not a very common type. This test involves the setting forth in the labor agreement of the various procedural steps which are followed by the company's industrial engineers when they measure the time to perform a certain task and the steps they follow thereafter when they compute the incentive standard. The adoption of this type of contractual "test of fairness" results from the assumption that if the industrial engineer is required to follow an agreed-upon procedure step by step, the resulting incentive standard will be correct and fair.

One example can be cited to show that this assumption is fallacious. The contract contained a provision to the effect that a certain minimum number of job cycles must be measured when a time-study of a job is being taken. It was contained in the labor agreement between a union and a nationwide company. The clause was as follows:

A minimum of at least a 30-minute study or at least a study of 20 cycles, shall be made for any time study.

At first blush, this provision sounds reasonable. It is a good industrial engineering practice to observe and measure the time of a sufficient number of cycles. However, this provision in the labor contract permitted a union steward to thumb through piles of work sheets, hunting illegal standards. He found one. It was based on time measurement of only 18 job cycles, rather than 20, and took less than 30 minutes. The steward marked it illegal. The standard was cancelled. Thereafter, the time required for each 20 cycles was measured and a new legal standard was established in the place of the illegal one. When the new legal standard was released, it was considerably tighter than the former one. Hence, the complaining steward got burned and the controversy got hotter.

Now, the point of this story is that contract provisions which specify the methods that are to be followed to measure the time to perform a task do not result in a satisfactory "test of fairness." In fact, they are worse than none at all because they actually multiply the areas of dispute.

Now let us consider contractual "test of fairness" Type No. 2. This type of test consists of standard data, tables, charts or formulas that have been introduced into the contract by an agreement between the parties. There are a great variety of such agreements. I merely want to illustrate them by using one example. I am taking it from an arbitration case in which I participated.

It involved the incentive rates for cutting patterns in a shoe factory. These rates were established by a very simple procedure, which can be called a standard data procedure, and it was part of the labor agreement. It involved a comparison of the pattern to be cut, or the outline of a pattern to be cut, with the outlines in a book, each of which had an incentive rate, finding the most similar outline and selecting the rate for that pattern, and then adjusting it by certain agreed-upon time values to take account of special angles, variations in length and so forth.

Pearce Davis, who follows me on this program, was the arbitrator. I recognized at the time that his task was quite similar to the task of an arbitrator who was being asked to resolve a job evaluation and classification dispute. In such a dispute the arbitrator compares the job content of a particular job as evaluated against certain job content factors with the descriptions of job contents of other jobs in a book of agreed-upon descriptions.

Once the description which is most comparable is located, the rate for the job classification in dispute can be determined quite easily and the dispute is resolved. In other words, the process of resolving the dispute over the incentive rate for cutting the pattern in this shoe industry case, which involved the use of a standard data system, was not difficult.

Let us now examine the third type of contractual "test of fairness." The third type is the most common. Under this type we lump a group of slightly different "tests" which some persons might consider to be different, but which really are the same. These are the "tests" that require the Company to provide with each incentive standard a certain earnings opportunity.

For example, there is an agreement that each incentive standard will provide an earnings opportunity equal to an "expected rate," sometimes called a "target rate," or an earnings opportunity equal to a fixed percentage of earnings above the incentive base rate.

Sometimes these earnings opportunity agreements are expressed in rather general terms—that the incentive standard must provide an earnings opportunity in equitable relationship to the base rate. Such an agreement means that an intentional ambiguity has been left in the agreement. Such an agreement is often given meaning in percentage terms by the arbitrator. Therefore, it is wiser to express the relationship as a percentage above base rate and not leave this question of construction for the arbitrator to clarify.

Sometimes the agreement will provide that the new incentive standard should provide an earnings opportunity equal to the prior average earning of the employees involved. Such contract provisions slowly inflate earnings. They are unsound, but not uncommon. Of course, I classify them as "unsound" from management's point of view.

A final variation of this earnings opportunity "test of fairness" is the provision in the agreement which says:

> The management will provide incentive earnings that will provide at least a minimum earnings opportunity which will be equal to at least (let us say) 15 percent above the base rate for an employee willing to put forth incentive effort.

This test guarantees a minimum earnings opportunity rather than a specific one. Of the various earnings opportunity "tests of fairness" found in contracts, I prefer this last variety. I believe it recognizes the realities of incentive standard establishment and I think it is appropriate to digress briefly at this point and explain why. In so doing, some of the difficulties that confront arbitrators when they are asked to resolve disputes under earning opportunities "tests of fairness" will be pointed up.

Let us assume that a particular management believed that an employee working with full incentive effort would put forth about 25 percent more effort than he would when working on a fixed hourly rate. This management would then conclude that it would be correct to pay such an employee 25 percent more pay during periods when he was engaged in manual activity and was putting forth this full incentive effort.

However, if this management agreed in its labor agreement to a commitment to provide a 25 percent earnings opportunity above the base rate for full incentive effort it would soon be in difficulty. When I say this I am assuming that the incentive standards are established by leveling of manual performance times by judgment and that the management is attempting to provide no more than a 25 percent earnings opportunity.

Leveling of Performance Times

This brings us to the mystery point in the arbitration of incentive standards—that is, the problems involved in the leveling of manual performance times. Professor H. Barrett Rogers of Northwestern University, an outstanding student in this field, says that the possibility of error in the evaluation of manual performance times when they are leveled to a so-called normal time is "plus or minus five percent." This possibility of error is a little more serious than it sounds. The range of error represented by the expression "plus or minus five percent," when plotted, is a bell curve.

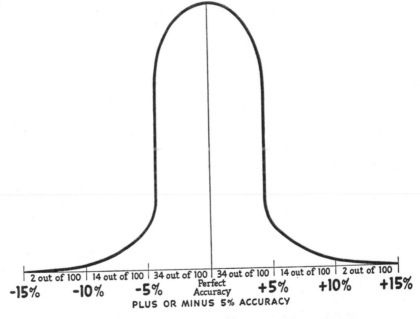

| 2 out of 100 | 14 out of 100 | 34 out of 100 | 34 out of 100 | 14 out of 100 | 2 out of 100 |

| -15% | -10% | -5% | Perfect Accuracy | +5% | +10% | +15% |

PLUS OR MINUS 5% ACCURACY

The Present Maximum Accuracy
that can be obtained when Incentive Standards are established by Traditional Methods

FIGURE 1

Let me illustrate the extremes of error that are contemplated by this curve (Figure 1). Actually 68 out of the 100 standards set by this method would deviate from the correct time only plus or minus five percent. An additional 28 will have an error running up to plus or minus 10 percent (14 between 5% and 10% too "loose" and 14 between

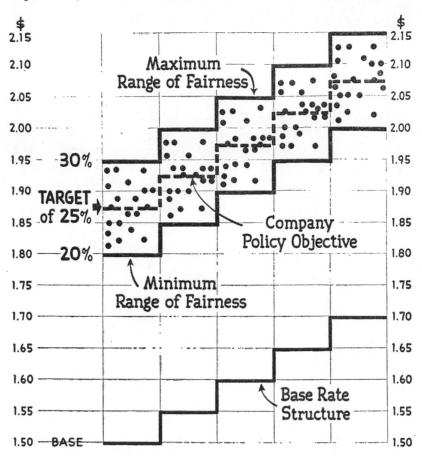

The "RANGE OF FAIRNESS"
of Incentive Earnings Opportunity
Above a Base Rate
FIGURE 2

5% and 10% too "tight"). An additional four percent would have an error up as high as 15 percent too "loose" or too "tight."

We should, of course, remember that the manual performance part of a job is not necessarily the entire job cycle, but this possibility of error

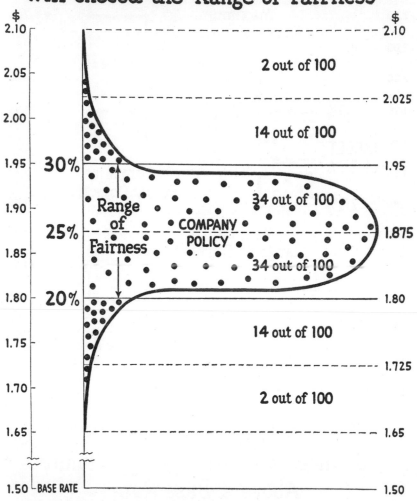

The VARIATIONS in Incentive Earnings will exceed the "Range of Fairness"

FIGURE 3

introduced by judgment leveling is a possibility that undoubtedly is the main reason arbitrators stay awake at night when the dispute involves judgment leveling.

This error is a human error caused by judgments exercised by industrial engineers and they are human beings even though union spokesmen sometimes forget this fact. It means that the actual "earnings opportunities" being provided on a manual job for true incentive effort, if it could be plotted, would actually scatter around the policy target point of 25% above the base rate (Figure 2). Even if a management was making every practical effort to set the standards fairly but was using judgment leveling techniques, we would find that the earnings for precisely the same effort would scatter around the policy target because of the inherent error involved when performance times are leveled by judgment, following observation.

For these reasons, what we should be really interested in determining is whether the earnings opportunities on the various jobs fall within a "band of fairness" rather than upon a specific percentage point above the base rate. If we then identify the minimum of that band and say, "Any standard that produces earnings for an employee putting forth incentive effort below that level is a standard which we will consider unfair," the union can process grievances to obtain the correction of truly unfair standards, but a realistic "margin of safety" has been left between the policy target and the contract commitment so that the industrial engineers can actually be in compliance with the labor agreement as they establish incentive standards on a day-to-day basis.

The practical problem is well illustrated when the bell curve representing the error of "plus or minus 5 percent" is superimposed on top of the chart of the company's policy (Figure 3). You will see that even though the industrial engineers are careful in their initial evaluation of the employees' work pace, they will still make errors, and even though the "minimum of the range of fairness" is set 5% below the policy target, some unfair standards will slip through.

Many people fail to realize the inherent variation from theoretically correct time when manual performance times are leveled by judgment. I think that the industrial engineer is at fault because he does not like to concede to himself, let alone anybody else, that his measurement procedures do not provide precise answers.

Therefore, if a management is going to have an intelligent standard in a contract to work against, it should provide that:

A qualified employee, working with incentive effort, shall have
an earnings opportunity of at least 20 percent over the base rate.

If the policy target of the company is in fact to provide an earnings
opportunity of 25 percent, a 5 percent margin of safety for error has
been provided between the policy target and the contractual commitment.

This explanation has been somewhat oversimplified. There are many
more facets of the problem of incentive standard establishment to be
considered before a complete policy can be spelled out. We are considering here only the problems that arise when judgment leveling is
used, because the differences in opinion concerning the work pace of the
employee is a main source of grievance complaint over incentive standards.

When judgment leveling disputes get to arbitration they are difficult
to handle. The arbitrator is being asked to look through the eyes of the
timestudy observer at an employee whom he never saw perform a job
that can never be performed again even by the same employee at exactly
the same pace, and to determine whether the judgment estimate by that
observer of the work pace of that employee was correct.

The arbitrator's dilemma is further increased when he finds that no
one can clearly explain to him what mental "normal pace" the observer
had in his mind when he compared the work pace he was observing and
evaluated it as a certain percentage above or below his mental picture
of "normal pace."

Walter Reuther explains the dilemma that confronts the arbitrator
when the issue finally sifts down to a dispute over the judgment conclusion upon which the manual performance times were leveled to
normal time. He said:

> The ordinary stop-watch time study involves use of a leveling or
> rating factor. This is the time study man's guess. He puts down a
> percentage figure which is supposed to indicate the degree to which
> the worker studied was performing faster or slower than some
> hazy idea of normal.

If a union representative also observed the employee performing the
job and reported his conclusions to the arbitrator, the dispute does not
become easier to resolve. It then involves a variation between the
level in judgments of two observers. Which is correct? And beware of
the "split-the-difference compromises" between the two, because such
a principle spells slow death to equities and to the incentive system.

In his attempt to work his way out of the fog which surrounds disputes over leveling, the arbitrator should also refrain from being influ-

enced by earnings information. The employees are claiming that they are working with incentive effort and do not have the earnings opportunity provided in the agreement. Of course, they will not prove that they have it by earning in excess of the level provided in the contract.

There was a time when many arbitrators were, to say the least, rather naive when it came to handling questions of this kind. They would support the union's claim that the standard was incorrect upon a showing that the employees were unable to make the expected earnings level. For example, one arbitrator, ruling that a standard should be increased, said the following.

> It is extremely unlikely that employees having an average of 24 years of experience would accept a serious loss of earnings over many months merely to establish that the rate was improper. Some allowance should be made for the obvious difficulty of such employees in adjusting to the new method.

When the arbitrator holds the standard incorrect on such a basis, the future earnings information when the employees raise their production level will prove only one thing—his naiveté. Employees have no compunctions about making a "chump" out of the arbitrator and arbitrators should always remember that the subsequently produced earnings information will prove they have been a "chump" if they are taken in by the self-serving earnings evidence that employees working on a job manufacture.

In recent years the more astute arbitrators have recognized these facts of life. They reject evidence of low earnings as unreliable evidence. In this connection, I should like to read a quotation from an award by Ralph Seward (20 LA 38):

> Such earnings, it is true [measured against an expected earnings level] have not been realized in actual practice. The umpire has given the union every opportunity to analyze the time studies and line speed studies on which the rates were based, and to point out errors or defects in those studies which would account for the failure to reach the target earnings.
>
> The union has failed to make such an analysis or to demonstrate any inadequacy in the studies or any errors in the assumptions which the company based upon those studies.
>
> *   *   *
>
> *It has offered the umpire no grounds for holding that the reasons for the failure to reach target earnings lay with the rates, rather than with the employees themselves.*

Under the circumstances, the umpire has no alternative but to hold that the union has failed to establish that the incentive rates . . . are not in equitable relationship to the old rates and to deny the grievance on that basis. (Italics added)

Thus, the union has the burden of proving that the standards were unsound. Low earnings evidence by itself is not sufficient to overcome the presumption that the rate is established correctly.

Similarly, Harry Platt pointed out the same thing. He said (15 LA 195):

*** I cannot help but conclude that the union has failed to meet the burden of proof requisite to establish the present price . . . as an unfair and improper rate. According to the evidence, the company made five time studies of the job in question (one of which was made jointly by a union and company representative) and they all show rather conclusively that the present gusset cutters could, by exerting normal effort, bring their earnings in line with their former earnings, if not exceed them.

Thus, another experienced arbitrator has rejected low earnings as evidence and has concentrated his attention on evidence concerning the measurement of the time required to perform the incentive task.

If an arbitrator should not rely on earnings evidence in hunting his way out of the fog that usually settles over a judgment leveling dispute, what evidence can he rely upon to increase his confidence that the award he must render will be a just award?

There are various ways to demonstrate the relative accuracy of a leveling judgment in an arbitration proceeding. Each of the various methods of proof of the accuracy of the normal time to perform the manual portion of the job has its uses. A detailed exposition of all of them would require more time than is available but we should not pass the question of proof of the correctness of manual time without discussing pre-determined manual performance time systems which I believe are bringing some real sunlight to the arbitrator when he faces this type of dispute. There are two well known pre-determined time systems in use in many, many plants in this country.

The first system is known as the Methods Time Measurement system, called MTM, and the second is the Work Factor system. Both of these systems use a table of fundamental motions and matching time values. The normal time for the manual portions of a particular job can be developed by analyzing the motions that are employed on the job including the measuring of distances, determining weights, pressures, etc.

Then, the normal time for each motion is found by totaling the values that have come off the chart and converting them into time. No stop-watch need be used and hence the pace of the employee performing the job is of no consequence as no judgment leveling of observed and measured manual performance times is necessary.

The MTM Association conducts a continuous research program and is working in conjunction with the University of Michigan. Many incentive scholars are working on projects for this Association. There is a great deal of academic support for this program, from some who have been critical of MTM and pre-determined time systems in general. One of them, incidentially, is Professor Nadler, who teaches at Washington University, where Bill Gomberg is now teaching. He claims that pre-determined time systems do not produce theoretically perfect time findings. It is not claimed by the advocates of these systems, nor am I stating here, that these pre-determined time procedures produce theoretically perfect answers. However, I am saying here that they become a working tool for handling incentive problems which are immeasurably better than the traditional tools, because they do not involve the subjective judgment involved in judgment leveling. In other words, the use of these systems frees the establishment of the incentive standard from the thing which causes most of the trouble—the judgment leveling of manual performance times.

Let us examine how pre-determined time information can be used in arbitration. The job involved can be set up in front of the arbitrator or can be photographed on motion picture films. In this way, the various motions involved can be identified and listed—the distances, the weights, the pressures used are determined. If any dispute arises over any of these facts, the issue can be resolved by the arbitrator.

Then the arbitrator will receive an explanation of how the time values are selected for each motion from the table. The union representative is in a position to challenge the judgment exercised by the company's industrial engineer in his selection of one or another of the available time values from the table, but the difference here is that all the cards are face up. No determination is done in the secret way that is involved when actual performance times are leveled by judgment.

The arbitrator may be presented with two alternative applications of the time values in the table—one urged by the union and one by the company representatives. He might ask each side to again explain the reasons for its proposed application. From that point on the process he will follow is very similar to the process an arbitrator follows when the issue in dispute involves the determining of evaluation points for a particular job under a particular job classification manual, or, for that matter, the process would resemble quite closely the process that Pearce Davis went through when he had to compare the outline of the shoe pattern in dispute with the outlines of shoe patterns in the book to determine by arbitration the proper rate for cutting the particular pattern in dispute.

Even if the incentive standard were first established by judgment leveling, the relative accuracy of this leveling can often be determined by using pre-determined time information. Where pre-determined times are not used generally within the plant so as to become validated by actual use, they are, of course, a more difficult tool to use.

New Standards for Changed Jobs

Let us leave the dispute over leveling which is likely the most difficult problem in arbitration of incentive disputes. The second major problem is whether or not there has been a method of change sufficient to permit the issuance of a new standard.

Labor agreements usually provide that management may not establish a new incentive standard for the performance of a particular incentive task unless there has been a change in the method of performing that task. This provision results from the desire on the part of the management to assure employees that the standards will not be "tightened" merely to reduce high earnings so that the employees will have more confidence and will put forth high effort.

If we remember that the standard is merely a measurement of the normal time to perform a certain task by a particular method, a change in method justifying a new standard must be a change that will affect the time to perform the job. It should be equally obvious that when a change in method has occurred which changes the normal time, a new standard *must* be established if a fair and equitable system is to be maintained.

Where you have a change in the feeds and speeds of a machine, such a change will affect the time cycle required to perform the job. When this occurs, the revision of the standard is not difficult and is generally accepted by the employee. The employee can see the machine go faster when the feeds and speeds of the machine are increased. The effect of such change can easily be calculated. In spite of this, the claim that a speed or feed change is not a methods change has often gone to arbitration and has unfortunately confused some arbitrators.

The methods change problem becomes much more difficult to handle in arbitration when the methods change that has affected the manual time consists simply of a change in the employee's motion pattern. Let me illustrate this latter problem by taking an example from an actual arbitration case.

The employee took a washer from a box and held it with his thumb around a hole drilled in a piece of angle iron. He put it into a spot-welding machine and tripped the spot welder, welding the washer to the angle iron. Then he took the piece of angle iron out of the spot welder, *turned it around in his hands,* put it back in the spot welder, tripped the spot welder again welding the other side of the washer to the angle iron. Then he removed the piece from the spot welder and put it in the tote box. That was what he did when he was timed.

As soon as the incentive standard was released, the employee picked up the washer, held it over the hole in the angle iron with his thumbs, put it in the spot welder and made two welds with a spot-move-spot motion and then dropped the part in the box.

This job was a short-cycle job. The normal time of Method One, involving a "taking out and turning around" procedure was about twice the normal time of Method Two, involving a spot-move-spot procedure. Unless the standard was changed, the employee could about double his percentage earnings above base without putting any additional effort into the performance of the job. The operator had changed his method or motion pattern. The company established a new standard. The dispute went to arbitration.

The arbitrator held that the company had a right to establish a new time standard because of the change in the motion pattern which he considered a new method. Incidentally, if the arbitrator had found that the normal time determined by the clumsy method was to apply to the job performed by the improved method, he would have made a determination that would have been contrary to the basic concepts upon which the pre-determined time systems are based. That is, that the normal time to perform a job can be determined from an analysis of the motions involved in performing it.

Fundamentally, incentives are to compensate for the expenditure of energy and when you simplify the motions involved in performing the job, the job becomes easier. Why should you pay a man for a difficult operation of taking a piece out of the machine and turning it around when you are only asking him to perform a simpler task which involves only a spot-move-spot operation while the part is still in the machine?

Now, some unions and some arbitrators incorrectly believe that a change such as the one described above is an employee-invented method for change, and as such, does not justify a change in the method. Such a concept puts a premium on the presentation of false motions to the industrial engineer when the task is being analyzed in an attempt to gain an unfair advantage. In the spot-welding case it was pointed out to one of the employees who had appeared as a witness that the "taking the part out and turning it around in his hands for the second spot" procedure that he had been using when the job was being timestudied, was a very clumsy and inefficient method. The witness replied, "We always do spot-welding jobs that way when we are being timestudied." Is the subsequent change in method a manifestation of some form of invention? I think not.

Now, the arbitrator who decided the spot-welding dispute understood that incentive standards are time measurements that should be used only with the task for which they were designed. Since the standard as first released covered an element of work involving the "taking out and turning around" it should not be used when the work element is "spot-move-spot." If a system is to be truly equitable, only standards designed to cover tasks as they are in fact being operated should be used.

An analysis of arbitration decisions unfortunately reveals that some arbitrators lack an understanding of this simple truth. For example, some arbitrators are quick to hold that if there is a methods change, the mere passage of time will make the normal time required to perform a task by an employee by a prior method applicable and correct for the performance of that job by an entirely different method. For example, an arbitrator whose awards seem to me generally sound, stated that the right to change an incentive standard, if there is a change in a method, should have incrusted upon it by implication a limitation to the effect that that right must be exercised within a reasonable time.

I think the fallacy of such a holding can be easily demonstrated:

1. If you are going to have sound incentive systems, the standards should be accurate. Therefore, the normal condition should be that the incentive standard which is being applied should be the incentive standard designed to cover that particular job performed by that particular method, and anything else is an erroneous application, and

there should be no vested rights in errors created by the mere passage of time.

2. If management has the right to direct the manner in which the work is to be performed, and we find there was a methods change which had, in fact, taken place, but that no new applicable standard had been issued, the management could ask the employees to perform it by the prior method. An interesting case was decided by Benjamin Selekman in 13 LA 585 on that very point.

Since the management had asked the employee to go back to a prior method, using a standard based on the normal time to perform the task by that prior method, the standard should be considered correct.

Now, after the passage of some additional time, the management could instruct the employee to perform the task by the new method and would then release a standard concurrently with this officially-instructed change. Would the same arbitrator then hold that because once in the past, the company failed to establish an appropriate standard promptly after a methods change had occurred, it could not now establish an appropriate standard for the methods change that had just occurred? I think if this were the set of facts, he might realize that his reasoning in the prior case was rather thin.

Management must maintain its incentive systems as accurately as it possibly can if its system is to produce fair and equitable incentive payments to all employees. The natural pressures for looseness and liberality can become very intense. The arbitration process can remove much of the tension that sometimes surrounds incentive rate establishment, but it can only do this if it does not itself engender further compromise and inaccuracy. If arbitration does bring compromise and inaccuracy in any case, such action cannot be justified on the theory that a little adjustment by way of a compromise will "keep peace in the family." It is the small compromise that may start the process of disintegration and inequity—a disease that can spread very rapidly once it gets started.

I appreciate that many of the limitations imposed upon the maintenance of a sound incentive system by arbitration awards are nothing but very fair construction of the clumsy contract language that management has often agreed to, for reasons known only to them, but I hope that the tendency of some arbitrators to *imply* restrictions into language when the restrictions are not truly there, or to compromise an incentive dispute in the belief that such action is "good labor relations" will continue to diminish so that the arbitration of disputes over incentive standards can be espoused by managements with enthusiasm.

Discussion—

PEARCE DAVIS

*Professor and Chairman of the Department of Business
Economics and Industrial Engineering
Illinois Institute of Technology*

Owen Fairweather's interesting and provocative paper deals, as you have seen, with broad concepts and also with numerous matters of detail.

I pass over most of his discussion of detail—because of time limits— to comment on some of the larger issues either raised by his presentation or suggested by it.

Union-Management Attitudes Toward Incentive Arbitration

I agree that it is proper and appropriate to arbitrate incentive griev- ances. To do so is both theoretically sound and conducive to better labor- management relationships. Therefore, to me it appears salutary that a constantly widening circle of management representatives is accepting this view. I am sure this trend will continue until arbitration of incentive disputes becomes as routine as discipline and discharge cases are today.

Unions, it seems to me, have never really been broadly opposed to this phase of arbitration, though there are notable present-day exceptions, as has already been noted. The hard core of resistance has clearly been on the Company side.

The upshot of the trend now developing will certainly be a sub- stantially increased workload of incentive disputes in the arbitration portfolio. Such statistics as I have seen support this forecast.

As Mr. Fairweather has emphasized, some unions and some man- agements still prefer to reserve the right to strike and lock out rather than arbitrate grievances that involve the incentive system. Concerning these I would venture the prediction that they will seriously modify or wholly abandon this position in the not-too-distant future. Retention of these weapons carries the constant threat of the use of force to settle differences at the very time that industry—by agreement—is operating under an established regime of constitutional government. Resort to "self-help" for resolution of such disputes is a stark contradiction where union-management contracts are in force. Those who cling to methods of coercion are running against the tide of modern labor-management relations. In time, the measures they now advocate may be expected to wither away.

Justification of Incentive Arbitration

Mr. Fairweather justifies arbitration of incentive grievances primarily on practical, good human relations grounds. Not to do so, he says, establishes an atmosphere of conflict, creates a sense of frustration among workers. With all this, I agree. But I would go further. I would say arbitration of incentive disputes is fully justified on pure theoretical grounds.

In terms of the basic philosophy of the firm, there is no more reason why management should transfer to an impartial outsider authority to make final decisions in matters involving *discipline* and *discharge* than in disputes concerning *incentives*. Management responsibility for discipline in the plant and composition of the work force is surely no less fundamental than management's authority for operation of an incentive wage plan. One is not more "sacred" than the other. Neither represents a more crucial management "right" than the other.

Further, I seriously doubt that potential criteria for determination of incentive disputes by arbitration are less precise, or more vague than those utilized for discipline or discharge cases.

Arbitration of disciplinary issues functions, of course, within the benchmarks set by the "just or proper cause" concept. Certainly, these limits cannot be called narrow!

Indeed, I would say they probably are *broader* than criteria potentially applicable in incentive arbitration. Today, many incentive contract provisions and stipulations of the parties set up reasonably discernible boundaries within which the arbitrator is to function. If not, they certainly can be designed to accomplish this end.

It is appropriate to arbitrate incentive grievances for still another reason. I am quite certain that everyone professionally conversant with the subject will acknowledge that the setting of incentive rates—in fact the installation of the entire system—is a "scientific art" rather than an exact science. All who are informed would agree that there is an appreciable margin of human judgment implicit in the process.

Because it is generally recognized that substantial areas of subjective evaluation do exist, there is no longer any basis for the old claim that an arbitrator may upset a purely scientific determination that has been made with unique and unassailable precision.

The Incentive Arbitrator's Qualifications and Independent Judgment

The theme of Owen Fairweather's presentation is, first, that management should arbitrate incentive disputes and, second, that management should prepare its cases so that the "lay" arbitrator can understand the issues involved and, incidentally, be convinced of the rightness of the Company's position.

As already stated, I am in wholehearted accord with proposition one. With regard to the second I have *no disagreement*. I applaud any effort by the parties which is calculated to simplify the thoughts and the lives of those of us who arbitrate incentive disputes.

But I would not stop at this point. Speaking as an arbitrator to arbitrators, I would urge with as much vigor as I can command, that incentive arbitrators must be equipped and prepared to pass *independent judgment*—I repeat, *independent judgment*—on the merits of the Company and Union positions and arguments.

I do not wish to appear pontifical. But I do sincerely say that if we are truly to discharge our mandate of impartiality we cannot possibly be "innocents abroad." Incentive arbitrators themselves must possess sufficient technical knowledge and experience to evaluate, from the neutral corner, arguments persuasively urged upon us.

Offered at least two doors through which we may pass, we must, in fairness to ourselves, be ready to make a confident choice. I would add and emphasize that the more accomplished and adroit the presentations of the parties, the greater is the need for the capacity of independent judgment.

There is to be more incentive arbitration. More arbitrators will, therefore, decide incentive cases. I would think that the practitioners of our art who are not suitably equipped—especially those in the stage of younger maturity—would want to reassure themselves by adding to the tools at their disposal.

It is scarcely necessary for me to say that the remarks immediately preceding are obviously not directed to my "live" audience. I am sure all you before me have long since become aware of the point I make.

Your own practice demonstrates that you have. These immediate thoughts are directed, rather, to arbitrators now moving up the line and arbitrators yet to come.

I am not suggesting that anyone go back to school or that it is necessary for young arbitrators to become professionals in the field of industrial engineering. Such a course is unnecessary. Means are available for equipping one's self without undue effort and time.

The Not-So-Mysterious Scientific Art of Industrial Engineering

I would be happy if my next remarks were considered against the background fact that I know industrial engineers rather well, have worked with them for a considerable period of years and have a high opinion of their general ability and competence. Certainly I am not anti-Industrial Engineers. If anything, I am in the "pro" category.

Nevertheless, I believe Owen Fairweather is entirely correct when he states that unions commonly refuse to accept industrial engineers, from management consulting firms especially, as arbitrators.

Speaking with frankness, I think the unions are right—from their perspective — to take this attitude. Industrial Engineers as a group, indeed engineers generally, tend to be management-oriented. This circumstance arises (1) because of the climate of their professional training, first interests, and professional societies and (2) because by far the greatest number of their economic opportunities lie with the management team. Their bread is buttered on the management side and in their own interest they must lean heavily in that direction.

Because of the foregoing facts, I suggest that management not include in their arbitration clauses the frequently encountered provision requiring that the arbitrator of incentive grievances be a "qualified industrial engineer." Avoid the resultant search that leads round and round to nowhere.

Instead provide that the incentive arbitrator be one familiar with incentive systems and incentive methods—or words to that effect. The consequences will be more expeditious and fruitful. Such persons can now be found and will, I hope, be available in increasing numbers in the future.

In conclusion, I think you might be interested to know that even in the most "liberal" industrial engineering college curricula only a small fraction of total training time is concerned with training which bears directly on incentive systems and problems.

The relevant area typically is composed of one course in motion and time study, one in job evaluation and wage incentives and, possibly, though not regularly, a course in advanced motion and time study.

A "liberal" industrial engineering program would also require work in factory planning, quality control and production planning amounting, in very approximate terms, to 6 percent. The remainder would be distributed as follows:

1. Mathematics 15%

2. Natural Science 15%

3. Engineering proper 30%

4. General education 20%

5. Business subjects 10%

From the foregoing it is easy to see that arbitrators who are not industrial engineers should not develop too deep a sense of anxiety in the presence of professional industrial engineers. Those who are not already equipped have only a moderate amount of preparation to do. Do it, and when an industrial engineer passes by, hold your head high!

Chapter IV

ARBITRATION OF DISPUTES INVOLVING INCENTIVE PROBLEMS: A LABOR VIEW

William Gomberg
Professor of Industrial Engineering
Washington University
St. Louis, Missouri

The principal problems faced by arbitrators arise generally in disputes over the setting of the production standards underpinning the wage incentive payment structure. These problems are closely related in their treatment to disputes over work load problems in day work factories.

This relationship was graphically brought out in the recent dispute between the Westinghouse Corporation and the International Union of Electrical Workers. The company was attempting to set production standards for maintenance workers on time work. The Union stated its position as follows:

> The IUE has maintained that no work standards should be imposed by Westinghouse on its employees unless the job is put on incentive. The union maintains that to impose work standards without incentives is to create third class citizenship among Westinghouse workers. Dayworkers on standards would have all the disadvantages of dayworkers (in that they would get no incentive pay) and all the disadvantages of incentive workers (in that they would have to work against a standard).
>
> The company would have a one-way street on this. It claims it can discipline or discharge those who do not meet the standard, but would provide no extra pay for those who exceed it.
>
> We maintain that this is not only an unfair and unworkable program, but in fact, it is contrary to the generally accepted best practices in American industry.[1]

---

[1] *Position Paper, IUE,* November 25, 1955.

This was an interesting reversal of usual positions where it was the union instead of the management that was demanding the extension of the wage incentive payment plan. To be sure the issues were much more complicated than stated here. They were confused by the feelings of threatened status of maintenance workers who were now to be subjected to time studies like ordinary production workers but this basic reversal did emerge.

In reviewing the problem that the arbitrator faces, it is therefore my intention to confine myself to the problem of the establishment of production standards.

When labor first raised the problem of the setting of production standards within an incentive payment plan of reference, it found itself confronted by two concepts with which it had to deal. The first was the concept of *extra* pay for *extra* work. The second was the concept that production standards were based upon scientifically discoverable facts and therefore non-arbitrable. The generally accepted definition of wage incentive payment plans follows:

> An incentive wage payment plan is a method of wage payment by which workers receive extra pay for extra production. In establishing wage incentive plans, consideration must be given to (1) the base rate for the job; (2) the amount of work required to earn the base rate; and (3) the relationship between extra work above the base and extra pay for the extra performance.[2]

Most plans at their inception called for worker lost time, caused by machine or production breakdowns over which the workers exercised no control, to be compensated for at the base rate of pay. The movement has been away from this practice. Workers generally are compensated now at the average hourly rate which they demonstrated they could maintain in some defined past period.

The accepted concept was that the employer was responsible to the worker for his base rate as long as he was in the factory; that the premium payment for extra production was more in the nature of a reward rather than an obligation. That is now changed.

Wage incentive payment plans might more properly be renamed "production wage plans" to describe the new relationship. An implicit contract obligates management to furnish an opportunity to the work

---

[2] *Incentive Wage Provisions; Time Studies and Standards of Production*, U. S. Department of Labor, Bureau of Labor Statistics, Bull. 908-3, p. 1, 1948.

force to earn a specified hourly wage at a specified pace. The worker in turn obligates himself to met the production standard which is agreed upon.

If either party fails to met his obligation, he suffers the consequences. The management, in the event of a breakdown in the production organization, must pay to the worker the average wage. The worker, unless he meets the standard, receives less than that wage.

This approach is to be recommended for more than rhetorical purposes. It resolves the question of normalcy by making it an equitable concept rather than a rigid artificial scientific concept.

The consequences of the rigid view of the production standard as a quasi-scientific measurement rather than the result of an equitable agreement are found in the Stolper Steel case. Briefly, the facts of the case are as follows:

> On the fifth day of August, 1948, the Stolper Manufacturing Company and the Union executed an agreement. Section 12 of this agreement set up a wage incentive payment plan. The agreement provided that this section go into effect April 15, 1948, and continue until October 14, 1948. It was to renew itself automatically for periods of six months unless notice was given by either party in writing at least sixty days prior to any six months' expiration date.
>
> Under this agreement, production climbed to anywhere from 120 per cent to 131 per cent of standard. It seems to have been higher in the early days of the agreement (around 131.3 per cent) and fell off to around 121.7 per cent on February 6, 1949.
>
> As a result of dissatisfaction with the operation of the plan, the Union gave proper notice and terminated the agreement as of October 14, 1948. The company unilaterally announced that it was continuing the wage incentive payment plan. Production, beginning February 13, 1949, fell to 100.3 per cent and then varied between that per cent and 104.0 per cent. The men said in effect that they would give a fair day's work for a fair day's pay; they were not interested in the incentive increment; they wished neither to exert extra effort nor to receive extra pay.
>
> The Wisconsin State Labor Relations Board has denounced this action as interference with production and as a slow down, and has ordered the Union to restore the "incentive level" of production. In other words, because the men had demonstrated that on a

voluntary basis it was possible to reach 125 per cent of a fair day's work, the Board has in effect ruled that this now becomes an obligation on the part of the men. Naturally, the labor member of the Board dissented and pointed out that even if the company were to discontinue paying the premium for extra effort, the union would still be obligated to produce at 125 per cent of a fair day's work.[3]

The application of this doctrine would lead workers' organizations in the state of Wisconsin to boycott all wage payment plans keyed to productivity if it had been maintained. Fortunately it has been abandoned.

The union approach to the problem of work standards puts it in the same realm of discourse as hourly wages. There is no more a scientific work standard separate and apart from a concept of equity than there is a scientifically set hourly wage. This approach puts the technician in his proper place. He is an expert advisor to the principals. This point of view frees both parties from what John Commons used to call the tyranny of the expert. This tyranny perhaps best expressed itself in the Louden doctrine of the non-arbitrability of production standards. Louden advised management "... A standard must be based only upon facts and changed only by facts; therefore standards must not be subject to negotiation or arbitration in their establishment or in their change."[4]

Even in those cases where management was strong enough to impose the Louden doctrine of non-arbitrability, the logic of events imposed a change. For example, the agreement between the Ford Motor Company and the UAW had specifically made the setting of production standards a management function. Eventually there was a strike over an alleged speedup. Harry Shulman, impartial chairman of the three-man arbitration panel in the course of the majority decision defined and distinguished the nature of the right to set a production standard from other rights. He wrote:

> ... The "right of the company" (to establish, determine, maintain, and enforce standards of production) which is "fully recognized" is not a right to make a final and binding determination. It is not like other "rights" specified in Article IV, as for example,

---

[3] "Trade Unions and Industrial Engineering," *Industrial Enginering Handbook,* Edited by Grant and Grant, William Gomberg, Prentice-Hall, 1955.

[4] J. Keith Louden, *Wage Incentives* (John Wiley and Sons, New York, 1946), pp. 161, 162.

the right to "decide the number and location of plants" or the "products to be manufactured" or the "schedules of production" or the "starting and quitting time." As to these matters, the company may make *final* determinations which the union must accept for the term of the contract and which may not be made the basis of strike action during that term. Such is not the case with respect to production standards. There the right "to establish and determine and to maintain and enforce" is more in the nature of *a right to* initiate. . . .[5]

What is particularly amusing about this concept of the non-arbitrability of production standards was the eventual use to which it was put by the United Auto Workers. The original agreement between International Harvester and the Automobile Workers permitted the latter no voice in the setting of production standards but allowed the union to strike over the issue. This clause was originally inserted, probably, because it was assumed that the union would never develop the power to exercise this right effectively. In 1955 the union found this right to strike so attractive that it endured a long drawn out strike in order to preserve it.

This time it was the company that was demanding that incentive disputes be resolved by arbitration. Finally clause twelve of the new agreement between the parties compromised the issue by leaving open either route at the discretion of the parties.

At this time we can take it for granted that the pace setters of American industry by and large have accepted the concept of the arbitrability of production standards.

Let us now review this problem of setting standards of production. Industrial jobs may be classified into the following categories.

1. Completely man-paced jobs
2. Jobs that are made up of a fixed machine cycle and a man-paced component
3. Completely process-paced jobs
4. Jobs where man pace and production are unrelated

A set of typical man-paced jobs would be bricklaying or sewing machine operating.

---

[5] *Ford Motor Co.*, 12 LA 949 (July 1949).

Jobs that have a fixed machine cycle and a man-paced component are found in the metal cutting industries where the setup time and clean away time are generally small components of the overall time dominated by the fixed machine cutting cycle.

Completely process-paced jobs are those found on the automobile assembly line and the textile industry.

Jobs where man pace and production are unrelated are found in highly automated factories where the worker is a watchman or maintenance worker on automatic equipment.

Obviously the most critical type of job to treat is the 100 per cent man-paced job. The solution to this problem would at once make the task of treating the other three types of jobs that much more simple. How can an arbitrator go about setting an equitable rate when the parties come to him with a dispute?

This is one area where the usual bromide offered to the arbitrators, that "it is your job to interpret the contract not to write the contract," is not particularly enlightening. All too often the parties find themselves on a hook because problems arise that are completely unforeseen or could not be spelled out operationally. The false assumptions about the dynamics of worker motivation that both parties made when they wrote out the contract come back to haunt them when the operating reality of the plan shows altogether different results than they assumed when they agreed to a plan.

For example: I have seen three inconsistent clauses in a contract: The first will declare that the piece rates shall be set to yield an average earning opportunity of 130 per cent of base. The second that the piece rates shall be consistent in their yield. The third that no rate cut shall take place as long as the material and equipment remain unchanged.

Now the plan is permitted to operate. What happens? The rates are set on a specific line of operations. The men really apply themselves and the rates in the plant average 150 per cent of the base. Have the initial rates been set too loosely or are the men giving an extra increment of effort beyond what should be expected of them?

The arbitrator has to answer this question when new lines of merchandise or new operations come up for review and a dispute breaks out between the men and the management whether or not they are entitled to be rated at 150 per cent of base or set back at the same effort level to 130 per cent of the base. The agreement more often than not will provide little guide to the arbitrator. It will piously state that incentive payment plans are extra pay for extra effort. There, no doubt, will also be the usual statement that a fair day's work is expected of the men. It is defining this level that is the most troublesome aspect of the arbitrator's task.

The nature of the task faced by the arbitrator was spelled out some years ago by one of Frederick W. Taylor's associates. His name was Carl Barth. He was no friend of collective bargaining. In fact, when he was questioned about his attitude towards treating with unions, he exclaimed he would have nothing to do with them for the same reason that he does not treat with the devil. Yet his deep knowledge of time study led him to observe as early as 1922 that

> . . . It is hardly conceivable that two time study men, however well equipped by training and experience and with physical means, would arrive at exactly the same time allowance for any job each might in turn be independently assigned to study. And still, the time allowance of either would be undoubtedly fully satisfactory for use in establishing a fair contract between the worker and the management, though the two would not be identical.[6]

Now this description of the standards setting process is much more modest than the advice of Louden.

The approach of Barth indicates a range of measurements within which disagreement may take place and call for the services of an arbitrator.

It very often happens that the percentage disagreement between labor and management is less than the reliability range of the measurements of the time study technician and the time study technician can contribute little to the solution of the problem.

The Industrial Engineer has brought a plethora of time study techniques and methods to the rate setting process. The use of all of these techniques however remains controversial and unless the agreement specifically directs that one of these techniques is to be used to resolve differences between the parties, it would be foolhardy for the arbitrator to impose any one of them on the parties.

One of the reasons that labor usually prefers a non-engineer in the position of arbitrator in rate setting disputes is that the nationally

---

[6] *Symposium on Stop Watch Time Study*, p. 108, 1922.

known engineer generally is pledged to some particular technique which he has publicly espoused. It is in the nature of his occupation.

For example, if your engineer has publicly advocated the use of the rating films of the Society for the Advancement of Management for the resolution of standards disputes, he cannot abandon this commitment and retain his professional integrity. If he is a serious advocate of one of the microscopic predetermined motion time systems like Methods Time Measurement, or the Work Factor System or the Basic Motion Time Study system, then he would feel obligated to impose this criterion in the absence of any other.

This is hardly the place or the time to go into an exhaustive review of the controversies that rage among engineers over the proper rate setting techniques or the most scientific time study system.

The important thing for the arbitrator to remember is that when the SAM rating films appeared and represented themselves to be an official consensus of the pooled judgment of the country's engineers on what is a fair day's work, they drew a condemnatory editorial signed by William Green in the *American Federationist*. Walter Reuther circulated a letter among his officers warning them against the use of the films for arbitration purposes. The labor movement resented this attempt to impose upon it a unilateral concept of a fair day's work. A technical examination of the films' deficiencies can be found in my own *Trade Union Analysis of Time Study*.

Similarly, students of industrial engineering have proved that if one of the microscopic motion time study systems is true, then all the others must be false. They give mutually contradictory results.

Therefore, unless any one of these specific techniques is included in the agreement, it would be unwise to make any one of them the final measuring rod against which to measure the standard.

The Steelworkers did include in their agreements with United States Steel Corporation a provision that workers were expected to maintain a working rhythm equivalent to a walking pace of three miles per hour. This never came to mean very much. It was predicated upon a school of time study thinking in which pace is kept separate and distinct from method. Actually production speed is an interdependent complex of these two dependent variables. The variables are impossible to separate to any significant extent. What is more important, the transferability of a walking pace to the various working paces is virtually impossible to effect. The clause therefore could not be very meaningful.

On the other hand, where there is a macroscopic system of standard data in use, the job of the arbitrator is made that much easier. Although the elements may not be exactly additive in any combination, nevertheless their very existence acts as a stabilizer on the working environment and provides an emotional climate that encourages settlement of disputes.

Likewise, film records of typical operations in the factory, which both labor and the management have agreed are to serve as keys to rating, can likewise be very helpful where they are available.

The principal difficulty of the arbitrator in these rate disputes is how to extrapolate to the new operations the same equitable sense of effort that was expected on the old operations. His decision of necessity may be an unskilled approximation that in the future will encourage the parties to come to a rational settlement of their own. Inasmuch as it is the arbitrator's purpose to make his function obsolete, even this too will serve a useful purpose.

Most rate setting procedures are predicated upon the assumption that a worker should be judged in terms of a theoretical effort expended uniformly throughout the day. His actual working procedure, of course, will vary with his temperament and his disposition. Some like to accumulate a large bank of work early in the day and then coast the rest of the time. The number of patterns of work varies widely. Walker and Guest[7] have described them in detail. It is the battle of the assembly line. However he is to be left free to determine this pattern for himself, provided there is no interference with the working of the assembly line.

The myth of uniformity protects the worker and cannot be used by management for its purpose. This was brought out in the Ford case. The company had distributed jobs along the assembly line. Technical limitations dictated that all of the jobs were not uniform in their demands upon the worker. Some stations would carry a 50 per cent task, others a 90 per cent task. Still others a 95 per cent task. Obviously the speed of the line was dictated by the bottleneck operation. The company attempted to speed up the line. This meant that certain jobs would be in excess of the firm's determined 100 per cent. The company argued that it had the right to do this because the rate of work was the amount of total work achieved in a full day; that random delays to which the line was subjected compensated the man over 100 per cent for his extra

---

[7] "The Worker on the Assembly Line," Charles Walker and Robert Guest, *Harpers*, 1955.

effort. The arbitration commission again ruled that if the company wanted to run the line in excess of any member's 100 per cent rate, then it had to bargain out some compensating deal to which the worker would consent. The rate, therefore, was determined to be a rhythm from minute to minute rather than a sum of work over a day.[8]

We may summarize as follows:

The central problem in the determination of most wage disputes under wage incentive payment plans is the dispute over the production standard. The determination of this standard for 100 per cent man-paced jobs is critical. Once it is solved at this level, the solution for less than 100 per cent man-paced jobs becomes that much easier.

The concept of the uniformity of rate is critical in machine-paced operations. The setting of the production standard is a problem in equity. The function of the expert and the engineer is to aid the layman to extropolate this concept of equity from old jobs to new jobs.

The determination of what production level achieves a sense of equity is not the monopoly of the expert but the task of the principals to the bargain, aided if need be by the arbitrator.

Engineers are primarily useful to set up a rational range within which the principals can bargain. It is the function of the arbitrator to help the parties overcome the barrier when the collective bargaining process grinds to a halt.

Discussion—

RONALD W. HAUGHTON
Director, Institute of Industrial Relations
Wayne University
Detroit, Michigan

In the course of discussing Mr. Gomberg's paper I will mention some of the techniques which I have found helpful in the arbitration of incentive wage disputes. Here, I will limit my remarks to a consideration of the two industries where I have had the most experience in this type of work. These are automobile and rubber. This, of course, does not mean that these are the only ones which should be considered if one were to undertake a complete survey.

---

[8] Ford Motor Company, 12 LA 949 (July 1949).

The extent to which third parties are included in the decision-making process for the establishment of standards varies by industry. In the rubber industry, the matter of incentives is handled by the arbitrator in substantially the same manner as are disputes on non-wage questions. There is some arbitration of standards provided for in automobile supplier agreements. On the other hand, in the automobile industry itself, arbitrators are precluded by contract from deciding production standards. Sometimes, even there, the matter is brought in by the back door of the discipline procedure. That is, the question of just cause for discipline for failure to meet a standard might be raised.

A new method of determining incentive disputes recently has been included in a Cleveland automobile supplier contract. There, the parties have agreed to appoint a qualified time-study engineer as an impartial fact finder, without authority to decide matters of contract. They then have provided that a regular arbitrator will be called in to decide any dispute which is still outstanding after the determined facts have been considered.

With specific reference to Mr. Gomberg's paper, I agree with him that the central problem of most wage disputes under incentive wage plans is over the production standard. However, I would include also a reference to matters of interpretation of what little contract language is available to guide the parties and the arbitrator in setting standards. Unfortunately, while the objective evidence often is clear, the proper method of handling it is covered under such broad language as: "Standards shall be set in accordance with the time study practices of the Company."

Frequently the contract provisions are so vague and ambiguous that the conscientious arbitrator must make extensive investigations in the plant in order to try to understand practices with respect to which there is sharp disagreement. Each party can be expected to give a clear but diametrically opposed statement of how the standard should have been set. Both claims are based upon straightforward testimony and both are persuasive. A typical example of how this can happen can be found when one considers the able presentations of Mr. Gomberg and of Mr. Fairweather. One would like to agree with each of them, but that is not possible.

I am not sure that my company and union technician friends would take issue with some of the implications contained in Mr. Gomberg's statement that: "There is no more scientific work standard separate and apart from the concept of equity than there is a scientifically set hourly wage."

This seems to assume a certain lack of objective criteria available for the setting of an hourly wage. It is true that in most cases relationships within a wage structure have evolved from the collective bargaining process. However, once those relationships have been set, the arbitrator has available rather precise objective guides to aid him in deciding specific disputes over individual jobs or classifications which may come to him.

Just as a particular hourly rate can be set rather precisely, so can a standard when the company and union technicians present evidence which has been obtained in accordance with a commonly understood method. I believe that Mr. Gomberg has this necessary ingredient of mutuality in mind when he warns against applying any one specific time study technique unless it is included in the agreement. I agree with him wholeheartedly.

I have already noted that the details of time study methods are seldom spelled out in any helpful detail in the contract. This means that the arbitrator must turn to past practice as an aid to resolving incentive disputes. Here, he can use skills which he had developed in handling non-time-study cases. He will need them because many times he will encounter what appears to be almost unbelievable disagreement even as to the basic criteria to be used and as to the methods which have been followed.

When there is such disagreement, the parties can be asked to make a further investigation, or the arbitrator might ask them to accompany him while he tries to dig out the facts himself. When he undertakes the latter course, he may find a skeleton in a little used closet which will surprise all concerned.

Even though an investigation can be time consuming, I believe that it is absolutely essential that the arbitrator make no final decision until he is satisfied that he knows how a particular time study system works and how it has been applied. In addition to conducting careful fact-finding when possible, the arbitrator should insist that joint time studies be available so that he can make comparisons of particular values. Often he can then find that what are seemingly sharp differences simply occurred because two time-study men used different break points in making their studies. Such differences can be resolved by a lumping of several values together for purpose of comparison.

Of course, when all possible facts have been obtained, the arbitrator still must make up his mind regarding the remaining disputed matters. Even at this point, joint discussions with competent company and union technicians can be most helpful. If they act as board members, they will serve the important function of making sure that the arbitrator does not make a devastating error because of lack of knowledge. I believe Mr. Gomberg would consider the technician's roles as arbitration board members as an important complement to what he refers to as their function as expert advisers to the principals.

The technicians sometimes can be jolted into renewed efforts at narrowing areas of disagreement if the arbitrator uses a scare technique. In one rather far-reaching case where two good time study men were some sixteen per cent apart on their speed ratings, I almost frightened them to death by threatening to go out in the plant and make my own ratings. Just yesterday I asked one of the principals involved if he recalled the occasion when I made the threat. He answered, "Yes—I hear that both the technicians fainted!"

The fact is that most time study cases are resolved before the arbitration stage. Furthermore, of the incentive cases which are decided by arbitration, only a small percentage relate to differences in such matters as elapsed time, and speed and effort rating. Speed rating disputes are without a doubt the most vexing. Questions relating to effort rating should not be difficult to resolve. Presumably peg points are available in regard to jobs of like or similar difficulty. Differences in elapsed time findings can usually be resolved by a further check.

In the main, I have found that given competent technical assistance the arbitration of incentive disputes lends itself to the same procedures and techniques as does the arbitration of the other contract issues more frequently submitted to a third party for decision. This means that the setting of a production standard is not necessarily wholly a problem in equity as might be implied from one statement in Mr. Gomberg's paper.

In closing, I have one final word. Perhaps the advance of automation and the oft-resulting machine-paced jobs will minimize subjective decisions, and make setting standards an easy task based upon objective evidence.

CHAPTER V

HALTING THE TREND TOWARD
TECHNICALITIES IN ARBITRATIONS

JOHN F. SEMBOWER
Chicago, Illinois

Much of arbitration's effectiveness may be credited to its simplicity and informality. Not having to administer an elaborate code of procedure, arbitrators with the advantage of a clear understanding of the industrial scene, are able to render decisions with a dispatch that is all but incredible to those who are familiar only with ordinary courtroom litigation.

To the extent that a dross of technical procedures and formalistic approaches may form on the surface of the arbitration cauldron, boiling and bubbling as it is with an ever-increasing number of cases, this simplicity and informality which is such an attribute of arbitration may become submerged.

It is a common experience of arbitrators that those who present arbitrations for the parties tend to become more technical and legalistic in their approach. Human nature is all too prone to be led off into the woods of complications. An arbitrator often finds that unless he keeps a firm checkrein on a hearing, he is drawn into technical complications which should not have arisen.

"Simplicity is the character of the spring of life, costliness becomes its autumn," wrote Longfellow. Arbitration actually antedates our court systems, but its renascence in our time has been a springtime now maturing into summer. Will its autumn find that those forces which seem to complicate the affairs of men have eliminated many of the advantages it once held over more cumbersome and costly procedures of ordinary litigation? It seems a worthwhile goal for arbitrators and parties alike to try to maintain this strength and suppleness of arbitration's vigorous youth.

John Ruskin said that, "It is far more difficult to be simple than to be complicated; far more difficult to sacrifice skill and cease exer-

98

tion in the proper place, than to expend both indiscriminately." Justice Harlan F. Stone, when he was attorney general of the United States, lectured in the Hewitt series at Columbia University on "Law and Its Administration," about the period English law had to go through when the tendency toward legal formalism reached its height in the system of procedure at common law.[1] It is a cycle arbitration ought to avoid if it can.

It was found that at least 60 per cent of the decisions of the courts related exclusively to points of practice, and there was a far greater chance of a matter being disposed of on a point of practice than on its merits. This led to the development of the Chancery courts to help remedy the situation. In a sense, arbitration has fulfilled such a role today.

But it is the disconcerting aspect of almost all human endeavors that they start out simply enough in order to meet a felt necessity, and then begin to proliferate complications until the new is almost as bad, if not worse, than the old. With arbitration as it still is today, however, its practitioners should be able, with reasonable effort, to halt any trends toward over-complication before it goes too far.

It is reminiscent of the story of an old mountaineer in one of our hilly sections, who had learned that a letter had arrived for him at the crossroads post office. He pulled himself together and started down the mountain, breaking into a slight jog. "What's the matter, Uncle Jed?" called out a youngster. "Ye in a hurry?" "Nope," was the answer. "Jest too *tired* to hold back!"

Those who have seen what arbitration can do with simplicity and informality, must have the energy to hold back against breaking into a trot that will land it in the same thorny thicket of unwanted complexities that plague other litigation devices evolved in the never-ending search for a more perfect administration of justice.

In a sense, these opportunities for technicalities and complications lurk along the whole path of an arbitration from its very inception to the granting of the award. Every juncture bears watching to see that it does not begin accumulating an encrustation of technical barnacles, but there are several points where the attack already seems to

---

[1] Harlan F. Stone, *Law and Its Administration* (New York: Columbia University Press, 1924), p. 11.

have begun. These involve the submission, time limitations, efforts at discovery procedures, the "rules of evidence," citations of past precedents, and the use of the record.

The Submission

As the point where the switch is thrown to shunt a matter down the track toward arbitration, the submission always has involved technicalities, and necessarily so. In commercial arbitration, it is here that the contractual requirements of legal competency of the parties, legality of object, and even requirements of memoranda under the Statute of Frauds, come into play; because, of course, the authority of an arbitrator cannot rise higher than its source. Fortunately for labor arbitration, these matters tend to take care of themselves.[2]

Labor arbitration, however, does encounter technical menaces at this point. Just as the small town lawyer once explained that he started every case the same way, "by moving to quash the indictment!" many respondent parties now make it virtually a routine to raise the issue of arbitrability at the outset, with the result that the proceeding is launched upon a legalistic footing.

Just a year ago, Jules Justin gave a valuable summary of how arbitrators are coping with that issue.[3] This is as good a place as any to point out that halting a drift which can be deleterious to all of arbitration is not solely the responsibility nor even entirely within the power of arbitrators; the parties themselves have a big stake in it. Suffice it to say here, that to raise the issue of arbitrability should be regarded as strong medicine to be used only where it is truly significant. To abuse it as a trumped up plea in abatement or a harassing tactic is to encumber arbitration with the very sort of technicality that should be eschewed by all those interested in its continued effectiveness.

Stipulations

The greatest potential danger at this stage is, however, the matter of stipulations. Many parties with much arbitration experience take

---

[2] 3 *American Jurisprudence* 865, "Submission Agreements."

[3] Jules J. Justin, "Arbitrability and the Arbitrator's Jurisdiction," in *Management Rnghts and the Arbitration Process* (Washington: BNA Incorporated, 1956), pp. 1-40.

to stipulations like ducks to water. With the permission of the arbitrator, those in charge of the respective presentations proceed immediately to eliminate from controversy and the need of proof all the undisputed facts and contentions. If they strike a snag and are unable to stipulate on a point, it is saved for proof and argument until later. The issues are narrowed and the hearing is effectively expedited.

There is a growing school of arbitration technique, however, which holds that the arbitrator should at this point insist upon the parties agreeing upon exactly what is in issue between them. Some arbitrations have been delayed a day or even two or more while the parties try to agree upon what to disagree about, and how. Also, in the same general category, are the increasing number of quibbles which are arising over the *form* of grievance statements. It is true that many of these are hurriedly and not too expertly written under shop conditions, and they are vulnerable to criticism as to form.

These latter two situations afford an entering wedge into labor arbitration of the age-old abomination of courtroom litigation, the requirement of "stating a good cause of action," or the case will be summarily dismissed. In embryo form, arbitration offers a clinical example of the beginnings of the classic old common law actions.[4] If arbitrators do not press the parties unduly to arrive at an exact statement of their submission, and are liberal in their construction of grievance statements and replies, matters purely of form will not crowd out those of substance and merit. The law courts have remedied this situation in our time with a liberal policy of permitting amendments even on the face of the pleadings, and arbitrators might take refuge in this also. However, it is better to avoid altogether if possible the time-consuming distractions of what amounts to the development of a concept of a "cause of action" in arbitration.

Time Limitations

In this same general category, parties appear increasingly inclined to plead "statutes of limitations." If the parties have observed quite faithfully the time schedule set up in their agreement for grievance filings and arbitration demands, the arbitrator usually applies the rule as a matter of course. However, where both parties have been

---

[4] Harlan F. Stone, *ibid*, 105f. Oliver Wendell Holmes, Jr., *The Common Law* (Boston: Little, Brown and Company, 1946).

quite casual toward the time schedule, there is good authority to support an arbitrator's proceeding to hear the grievance on the merits.[5]

Discovery

There is a mounting pressure upon arbitration to provide a machinery for discovery of documents and to ascertain the gist of adverse
testimony before the hearing. This is a natural concomitant of the
emphasis on this pre-trial procedure in the newer rules for state courts
and the Federal rules of civil procedure. In the absence of statute to
that effect, arbitrators lack the power to compel witnesses to attend a
hearing or to subpoena documents.[6] If this power is added, it will
broaden inevitably the complexity of arbitration.

Discovery proceedings have much to recommend them, because of
the full and frank disclosures which often result and the elimination
of surprise. However, there also is the strong point that the parties
in an arbitration—particularly in a labor arbitration—occupy quite a
different relationship from most litigants in the courts. They live and
work together from day to day; are in possession of most if not all
of the common papers between them in the pending matters, and in
prior negotiations and the steps of the grievance procedure have as a
practical matter had an opportunity in most instances to make "dis-
coveries."

Again, the parties in this connection have an important stake in keeping arbitration as simple and informal as possible. Expenses are sure
to mount if arbitrators have to supervise what amounts to a deposition
procedure as well as to conduct ordinary hearings. Parties wishing to
keep their arbitrations essentially as they are today may well plan to
base their proof on their own witnesses and papers, carefully and
effectively organized, and upon cross examination of such opposing
witnesses as are presented.

Rules of Evidence

The "rules of evidence" always haunt arbitration as a threat of complexity to be avoided. It is all very well to give lip service to the truism
that the "rules" do not govern arbitration, but underlying them are
so many widely accepted attitudes toward proof and believability that

---

[5] Frank Elkouri, *How Arbitration Works* (Washington: BNA Incorporated,
1952), pp. 81-88.

[6] 3 *American Jurisprudence* 109.

the rules of evidence always seem close at hand, bidding to be recognized.

For instance, almost everyone has a negative reaction to someone testifying about what someone else told somebody else, and so on— the "hearsay rule." When a witness talks about a particular piece of paper or document, it is natural to think that the paper itself should be produced as the best possible indication of what it really stands for —the "best evidence rule." We are not receptive to people trying to change the terms of a written instrument which seems to be full and complete on its face, by relating that it did not *really* represent the agreement—the "parol evidence rule."

If those who present arbitrations would recognize these general principles and organize their testimony along those lines—not technically but generally as a common-sense proposition—the rules of evidence would not be constantly knocking on the door. In demonstration arbitrations, labor-management conferences, and in other forums where arbitration is discussed, the opportunity could be seized for rudimentary training in the presentation of arbitrations, having in mind these things.

As for the arbitrator in the actual conduct of a case, however, he opens the door to complication if he tries to apply them, even by another name. Much argument is heard currently about "burdens of proof" and "weight of the evidence" in arbitrations. An American Arbitration Association tribunal clerk related some time ago that he grew gray hairs while in a particular hearing an arbitrator ruled out one item of evidence after another, "because it was not part of 'the *res gestae'* "! During an intermission, the man presenting the case took the clerk aside and asked, "Hey! Who is this Res Gestae?" Res gestae, of course, has its dark corners for lawyers with long trial experience. It is a technical hobgoblin to be avoided in an arbitration.

Precedent

The accumulation of reports of past decisions constituting the Anglo-American common law has been described as a great coral reef of precedent, with each case dropping its shell to help form the great barrier reef. Such coral reefs now are building up in arbitration, although of course, the doctrine of *stare decisis,* which commits the Courts, all things being equal, to adhere to past precedents, does not apply with the same force to arbitrations.

Nevertheless, there is a great prospect of arbitration shouldering a huge pack of custom and precedent on its back, enough to all but break it down in time. This was ably discussed at these meetings two years ago by Benjamin Aaron.[7]

The regular reporting of decisions is a great service, and, so long as the parties do not object, is wholly desirable. Taking cognizance of past practices within the particular plant where an arbitration is being held is particularly pertinent. But we can be aware of the precedents, and even use them, without erecting them as a great panoply of authorities without which no arbitration can be held, brief written, or award prepared.

Contrary to the widely held belief in this country and England that the Continental countries of Europe, and other peoples following so-called Code legal systems, do not respect precedent, that is not entirely so. In France there is a public official who appeals a case on the Government's initiative if he believes it is contrary to precedent, even if the parties do not wish to do so. The review does not alter the decision as to the parties in such a case, but the precedent is kept straight. That in a system said not to be concerned with precedent! The point is that in a code system each case stands on its own feet as to the facts and law, without borrowing from past reports. So it is with arbitration.

John F. Sullivan, the former American Arbitration Association regional manager in Chicago who taught me much about the practical aspects of arbitration, passed on to me the praise of *both* parties which had received one of my first awards and opinions, "because it was so short and to the point." I doubt that I have written as short an Opinion since, or incidentally, received a more favorable reaction. I guess that I have been adding complications—succumbing, as I am sure virtually all of us must at one time or another, to over-complicating this process we all regard so seriously and respectfully.

The Record

Finally, the "record" of the hearing is a fruitful source of impending complication to arbitration. Just as a spirited clash over the form of the submission sets the stage for later objections to evidence and argument on the ground that they do not come within the issues delineated there, more and more objections are being heard to oral argument which

---

[7] Benjamin Aaron, "The Uses of the Past in Arbitration," in *Arbitration Today* (Washington: BNA Incorporated, 1955), pp.1-23.

the opposite party contends relates to matters not brought out in the hearing. Supplemental briefs are being filed with increasing frequency to contend that matters referred to in opposing briefs go beyond the record of the hearing.

Not nearly all arbitrations are stenographically reported, but this does not deter such objections, which often lead to long and inclusive recapitulations of everyone's memory as to just what *was* said! An unpleasant experience of this kind can well lead to the parties resolving in the future always to have a record taken. But then the plot is likely to thicken, because now there is a transcript against which to compare what comes afterward. The complications of appellate procedure in the regular courts arise as a grim spectre for arbitration when the stenographic record assumes such importance.

Conclusion

If I have made out a prima facie case that it is inherent in human nature to complicate those things which start out refreshingly simple and informal, and that arbitration, unless we watch out, may fall victim to this natural gravitation toward technicalities and complexity, then there remains the question what to do about it.

By preserving an informal and nontechnical tone in their hearings, and indicating to the parties that while they will duly note technical objections to forms of submission, arbitrability, time limitations, and the like, their concern chiefly is to cut through to the merits of the matter, arbitrators can do much to preserve the present character of arbitration.

There is no requirement that arbitrators observe technical rules and formalities, so long as the proceedings are honestly and fairly conducted, and this is fully supported by legal authority.[8] Even where arbitrations have wound up in the courts, it has been held that no inference is raised that the arbitrators have gone beyond the submission from the mere fact that they have admitted so-called "incompetent evidence."[9]

Formal rules as to admissibility and the weight and sufficiency of evidence do not bind arbitrators. Arbitrators are the judges both of the "law" and the "facts," and the parties may well be reminded of this. Arbitrators can take full cognizance of all these things, and the precedents too, but they need not be bound by them.

---

[8] 3 *American Jurisprudence* 101.
[9] 3 *American Jurisprudence* 106.

The stake in keeping arbitration a non-technical means of adjudication of disputes is as great, if not more so, for the parties as for the arbitrators. Hence, it is appropriate for the parties in their presentations to see that arbitration cleaves to the merits, rather than becoming preoccupied with technicalities.

Finally, we as arbitrators would do well to make sure that we do not become so beguiled by the possible technicalities which may be applied, or so infatuated with the complications of our calling and our accretion of knowledge concerning it, that we do not effectively resist whatever inclinations arbitration has to take on a bewildering array of complexities.

To this end, it would be well to make a survey of the reported awards and opinions to determine how many of them are grounded upon the merits or upon the procedural aspects, and to regard any rise in the latter as a "fever chart" indicative of a condition not conducive to maintenance of our present concepts of arbitration as a simple and essentially informal procedure for deciding issues promptly and economically.

Discussion—

G. ALLAN DASH, JR.

Philadelphia, Pennsylvania

I extend to Mr. Sembower my thanks for expounding in this paper, in the terse manner in which he wrote one of his first decisions and opinions, on a subject which has been of growing concern to me on many of those occasions in the past half dozen years that I have stepped briefly out of the relatively luke warm "pot" of Impartial Chairmanship and Umpireship arbitrations into the "boiling and bubbling . . . cauldron" of ad hoc arbitration. As I have been called to participate in more and more "one case" arbitrations, I have many times stood aghast at what, today, is considered proper arbitration procedure in many areas and relationships, when I recall my first arbitration cases just twenty years ago.

On occasions I have felt I have failed to change with the times, have neglected to improve my approaches in fulfilling the function expected of me by those who have, themselves, grown "modern" in their arbitration procedures; in short, have become an "old fuddy-duddy." On still other occasions, I am certain that my attempts to steer the parties into my old and simple methods of procedure have caused counsel for both union and management to doubt my competency. It is indeed a reassuring thing to me that the Academy has recognized the growing trend toward technicalities and complexities in arbitration and has chosen Mr. Sembower to present this paper on that subject.

First, let me dispel some of the reactions that might otherwise be engendered by my remarks by noting that I am not against technicalities in arbitration in all situations. In some areas of the country, arbitration has undoubtedly been a World War II (War Labor Board) phenomenon, almost imposed on labor and management through government edict. In many such areas, the arbitration process started off on a technical footing with counsel present for one or both sides almost from the beginning. It was quite natural in such instances that use would be made of the technical procedural details of the submission stipulation, "statutes of limitations," arbitrability arguments, swearing of witnesses, informal use of "rules of evidence," stenographic record of the proceedings, post-hearing briefs, etc. Where the parties initially adopted an arbitration process inclusive of such technicalities I, for one, find no room for argument.

Second, may I further try to dissipate the concern of my good friends in arbitration as to my fuddy-duddiness by observing that we old-timers in arbitration can gain much in bowing to some of the technicalities relatively new to arbitration. While it may be a trite cliché to observe that experience is a good teacher, I am certain that those of us who have been in this work for many years will find in some of these technicalities real help in resolving more readily and equitably many of the issues that are submitted to us.

In this connection, I have particular reference to the assistance which attorneys or skilled advocates can render in arbitration hearings in developing the facts of the case more clearly and expeditiously than is possible by those advocates not skilled in separating fact from opinion, fact from argument. Additionally, I agree that there are many advantages in the submission of post-hearing briefs, particularly in those ad hoc cases in which no record is made of the proceedings.

I would also agree that in many cases an arbitration stipulation is of significant meaning in the completion of the arbitration process, though it is ofttimes true that a particular case is submitted to arbitration because the parties cannot agree as to the exact nature of the issue between them. In such cases, if the parties were able to agree upon the issue, there would be no need for arbitration.

Third, and last, I am well aware that some of the use of technicalities in arbitration is dictated by the need to observe the requirements of arbitration statutes in particular states. Failure to adhere to certain procedural technicalities can result in the setting aside of arbitration decisions in particular states. Our colleagues from New York seem most aware of these legal pitfalls in the arbitration process and seem to us in the "hinterland" to be overly occupied with such matters. Perhaps the "buzzing around" of some of the hinterland "flitter" arbitrators that sometimes finds them "raiding" the territory of their New York colleagues for the "honey" cases so prevalent there, in retribution for the "raids" much more numerous in the opposite direction, causes some of these technicalities to stick to the "fur" of the "flitters" to be transported back to their home hives.

With the areas of technicalities in arbitration that I have just expressed, I am in reasonable accord. But it is against the trend toward the greater use of technicalities and complexities in arbitration that I join Mr. Sembower today.

We in arbitration should not lose sight of the fact that arbitration is simply an adjunct to the collective bargaining procedure and not a substitute for it. When the parties to a labor agreement adopt a grievance procedure with arbitration as the final step thereof, they ordinarily do so as a means of settling their day-to-day disputes without recourse to the economic weapons of strike and lockout. Arbitration is a kind of safety valve that permits the whole grievance procedure to function in resolving disputes without the blow-up that might otherwise occur if the union had to resort to strikes or the company to lockouts to enforce their respective positions on particular issues. When the parties adopt arbitration as that safety valve, they choose a particular type of arbitration which best suits their mutual interests. From time to time they change or modify that type of arbitration as their relationship matures, but it is always to their own mutually satisfactory pattern that they seek to change it.

The argument which I have with the growing trend toward technicalities in arbitration is that a large part of it comes from persons external to the parties to labor agreements who have originally fashioned their arbitration procedures to suit themselves. Persons with growing skill in advocacy—lawyers, "shop lawyers," consultants, and plain laymen, alike—are increasingly injecting into arbitration the techniques and procedures well suited to court litigation but glaringly out of place in the simple arbitration procedures which many unions and managements have initially adopted. And, as Mr. Sembower suggests, much of the trend toward technicalities is encouraged if they are not outright introduced by arbitrators "infatuated with the complications of our calling."

If the parties to a labor agreement start out with a simple arbitration procedure, or one with a minimum number of technicalities, and are satisfied with the results thereof, the injection of technicalities by outsiders can serve no useful purpose. When the local union representative and company personnel manager, who initially handled arbitrations directly with the arbitrator, find themselves shunted down the arbitration table several seats, with skilled counsel, advocates and consultants sitting between them and the arbitrator, it can be understood if doubts crop into their minds about the process they have thus far found so acceptable. When the simple, inexpensive and expeditious procedures they previously followed in securing their arbitration decisions have substituted for them the complex, expensive and time-consuming procedures of pre-hearing briefs, arbitration stipulations, arbitrability arguments, stenographic records, post-hearing briefs, rebuttal briefs, etc., their growing consternation can be readily appreciated. When, in addition, the actual arbitration hearing is conducted in a pseudo-court atmosphere, with swearing of witnesses, examination, cross-examination, re-examination and re-cross examination of witnesses, objections to witnesses' competency, objections to witnesses' expressions of opinions instead of facts, objections to the witnesses' lack of responsiveness to questions, objections to the leading of witnesses, objections for the record, exceptions noted in the record because of the arbitrator's ruling or refusal to rule on objections—when these occur, the growing lack of confidence in the arbitration process by the union and the company personnel may well reach the breaking point.

Frustration of the arbitration process through technical procedures, pseudo-court-like in intent or implementation, may eventually destroy that process and force labor and management to resort to some other process in culminating their collective bargaining on unresolved grievances. No-strike, no-lockout provisions of labor agreements can be expected to exist only as long as the orderly steps of a grievance procedure continue to serve the function of resolving day-to-day disputes in an expeditious and equitable manner. Extreme legal technicalities, mannerisms or hocus-pocus injected into the final step of the grievance procedure—arbitration—may well lead to the destruction of arbitration as an effective support of the grievance procedure. Persons who introduce overly technical approaches and complexities into the arbitration process should weigh carefully the alternative process they are thus encouraging, resort to the right to strike and lockout.

Most day-to-day grievances that arise under a collective bargaining agreement concern a company and a union interlocked in an intimate working relationship. These day-to-day problems require solutions that are formulated on a recognition of the fact that the relationship between the principals in most cases is a continuing one. Solutions that are based on the cleverness or astuteness of representatives or counsel of one or the other party in raising technical barriers to the development of a fully factual presentation by the opposite party are not solutions that will sustain a sound day-to-day relationship between a company and a union. Such solutions may be evidence of the skill of the representative or counsel or one of the parties to the arbitration, but they seldom enhance the status of the relationship between the company and union who somehow must continue to live together.

Some disputes are presented in arbitration by representatives or counsel for the two parties as though these two individuals are "champions" selected by the parties to serve them in a joust. It seems almost as though they charge at each other on their trusty steeds (of pseudo-court procedures) with their spears (of legal technicalities) thrust out before them to unseat the opposing "champion." If they succeed in unseating their "worthy opponent" (and "win" the case), the result takes on the aura of a worthy joust "won" by him who is still seated on his charger, the true "champion."

The parties to a labor agreement ordinarily want a grievance settled on its merits in a manner that will be fair and equitable, and which will encourage the right development of their day-to-day relationships. Usually they are not interested in a solution based on procedural maneuverings, as Mr. Sembower so ably suggests. A "champion" who "wins" a case in arbitration through resort to technical or procedural maneuverings encourages nothing but ill will on the side of the opposition which will be well aware of the unfairness of the "win."

Technical procedures in arbitration that evidence the skill of the individual protagonists likewise fail to recognize the continuing nature of the relationship between a company and a union. Of course, if that relationship is based on a shotgun wedding which one party is anxious to dissolve as soon as possible, overly technical procedures in arbitration are peculiarly suited to encouraging such a dissolution. But where parties evidence any real intent to live together in a sound working relationship, individuals who encourage technical procedures in arbitration are usually more concerned with furthering their own self-interests than they are in encouraging the expressed intent of the parties.

Litigants before a court usually leave the court proceedings with a permanent rift between them. Parties who seek solution of their problems through the arbitration process are not litigants before a court expecting to have their relationship permanently dissolved. Technical procedures such as are followed in court litigation can do no harm in further deteriorating a relationship destined to be dissolved, but can have a grave impact on the relationships between the parties to a labor agreement who must continue to live together after the arbitration process has resolved their dispute of the moment. Individuals who conduct themselves in the arbitration process as though they are serving litigants in a court procedure may "win" their cases, but will not thus serve the best interests of the parties who have selected them.

The doom of the arbitration process which I suggest as a potential result of an unarrested trend toward technicalities in arbitration is obviously more pessimistic than that which is anticipated by Mr. Sembower in his excellent paper. But it explains why I join him, most emphatically, in urging all who play a part in the arbitration process, the parties, their representatives and counsel, the arbitrators, and the appointing agencies to halt the clogging of the arbitration "safety valve" with the obstructions of excessive technicalities. If the "safety valve" is ever thus clogged, the "boiling and bubbling . . . arbitration cauldron" may well explode to the detriment of the industrial self-government of which we, in this country, are so justly proud.

CHAPTER VI

THE PROPOSED UNIFORM ARBITRATION ACT:
A PANEL DISCUSSION

A. Introduction

CHAIRMAN RUSSELL SMITH: The subject scheduled for discussion today is the Proposed Uniform Arbitration Act. We have, as members of our Panel this morning: Professor Maynard E. Pirsig, Dean of the University of Minnesota Law School; Professor Robert L. Howard, one of our brethren, of the University of Missouri; and former Professor Whitley P. McCoy. I want to dignify him by the title of Professor before referring to the fact that he is now a full-time arbitrator.

We are very happy to have with us Dean Pirsig, who is not a professional arbitrator, but who will find, I am sure, that arbitrators treat visitors courteously, even though they disagree with them sometimes.

Dean Pirsig is one of our national authorities on Procedure. As a matter of fact, he was formerly a member of the United States Supreme Court Advisory Committee on Civil Procedure. He is the author of a two-volume work on Universal Pleading; a case book on Judicial Administration, and a book just recently off the press, which bears the very austere title, "Cases and Materials on Standards of the Legal Profession," which, I understand, means, in short, Legal Ethics.

He has been a Commissioner on Uniform State Laws since 1947, and was Chairman of the Committee or Subcommittee of the Commissioners on the Uniform Arbitration Act. He, therefore, knows intimately the progress and development of the Uniform Act, which we have for consideration today.

We are very happy to have you with us, Dean Pirsig.

In addition, we have one of our brothers, Professor Howard, who has been at the University of Missouri Law School since 1925. His particular academic fields of interest are Constitutional Law, Administrative Law and Labor Law. He has authored numerous law review articles in the legal journals, and is one of the co-authors of this "socialist" case book on labor law. When I said "socialist," that meant "collectivist," of course, which means that some 30 authors got together and pre-empted the field by editing this volume which has all the basic material in it and people have to use it. May I add, it is a very good book.

Professor Howard wrote an article recently which appears in the January, 1956 *Missouri Law Review,* entitled: "There Ought to Be a Law; or, Ought There?" This has reference to the Uniform Act.

He has a rather interesting background with which I think some of you are familiar. He has been a Commissioner on Uniform State Laws since 1946. He is an alumnus of the War Labor Board, as are a good many members of the Academy, having been a panel member and a public member of the 7th Regional Board, and then, more recently, Chairman of the Regional War Stabilization Board, functioning in Kansas City.

The third member of our panel needs no introduction to this audience. He is Whitley McCoy, one-time Professor of Law at the University of Alabama for nigh on to 30 years; Director of the Federal Mediation and Conciliation Service, 1953 to 1955; co-author of a book with another of our brothers, Clarence Updegraff, on *Arbitration of Labor Disputes;* and, as we all know, a leading authority on industrial discipline in the telephone industry.

Our procedure will be as follows:

We are going to have statements of points of view, by Dean Pirsig, and Mr. McCoy, and Mr. Howard, in that order. I presume there will be some disagreement among them, some areas of discussion which will remain open as a result of what they say, or which may remain open in your minds, anyway, and it would be hoped that in due course we will have some discussion of questions in relation to the Uniform Act, in which you may be interested.

I should say, this is not a meeting to review further the Academy's position on the subject of the Uniform Act. You will all recall that the Academy did take a position last year, in opposition to the promulgation and adoption of the Uniform Act. Since then there have been certain amendments of the Act which may or may not result in a modification of the Academy's position, but, in any case, as of the moment, at least, the Academy officially is opposed to the adoption of the Uniform Act, my authority for that being resolutions adopted at the last annual meeting of the Academy, which stand at the moment unmodified.

What our position will be after we have the enlightened discussion this morning and the further discussion of the matter by the membership, I do not profess to try to say.

B.

MAYNARD E. PIRSIG

Dean of the Law School
University of Minnesota

I do not know whether you know or not that the Conference of Commissioners on Uniform Laws considered very seriously and carefully the report that was made by the Committee[1] headed by Professor Smith —incidentally, we thought it an excellent report—and in light of that report, the Conference, on the recommendation of the Committee of which I was Chairman, changed the Act with respect to what we thought was the major objection that this group had to the Act; namely, certain provisions in Section 12, dealing with the setting aside of an award on the ground that it was contrary to public policy, and that it was so grossly erroneous as to imply bad faith.[2]

Let me suggest that, notwithstanding the fact that your Academy disapproved the Act, in the light of the subsequent removal of the major objections to the Act, I would assume that your minds are not closed to a discussion of its merits.

Now, let me give very briefly a description of the National Conference of Commissioners on Uniform Laws. The Uniform Act is, of course, only one of numerous uniform acts, extending over the whole range of law in any area where uniformity of legislation is deemed desirable.

The organization is over 65 years old. It is made up of 150 members, two to seven commissioners from each State, appointed usually by the

---

[1] EDITOR'S NOTE: See Report of Committee on Law and Legislation and Resolution on Proposed Uniform Arbitration Act in Appendix C, *Management Rights and the Arbitration Process* (Washington, BNA Incorporated, 1956).

[2] EDITOR'S NOTE: For text of the Act as originally proposed see Appendix D of *Management Rights and the Arbitration Process.* The revised draft is included in this volume as Appendix B.

Governor, the Attorney General, the Chief Justice or some combination of Judges, or even by the legislature.

The Commissioners meet once a year, the week preceding the meeting of the American Bar Association. The Commissioners, almost exclusively are lawyers, judges, some legislators, some Law Deans and professors. The Conference is organized into sections which, in turn, have various committees to whom the drafting of the various proposed acts is assigned. The spade work is done by these committees between the annual conferences. Then at the annual conferences there are separate meetings of sections, where these drafts are examined, reorganized, revised, then considered by the Conference as a whole, and each section is read, gone over section by section, carefully analyzed, criticized, and usually revised.

That process is gone over twice, and no Act is adopted, with certain exceptions that have to be acted upon by the Conference, without two years of consideration, and, I may say, the Uniform Arbitration Act had more than that. It had four or five years of consideration before it was finally adopted.

These committees, in considering these acts, invite and consult with different organizations interested in the Act and with individuals who are specialists in the field. With respect to the Uniform Arbitration Act, drafts were sent to this organization, to the American Arbitration Association, to the Committees of the American Bar Association, and to numerous individuals who were known nationally for their interest in this subject.

The result is, I think, with respect to this particular Act, that it is as good an Act as you are likely to get on a national scale upon which people can generally agree.

Any particular individual may find this or that item with which to disagree, and I am sure that he could to his own satisfaction do a better job. But, in terms of a uniform generally acceptable Act, it is my opinion that it is as good an Act as you are likely to get, with the objective in mind of promoting arbitration as a means of settling disputes.

Let me give you very briefly some of the highlights of this Act, in order to enable us to get some background of what we are discussing.

Briefly, the Uniform Arbitration Act is an improved version of those statutes which were originally adopted in New York, New Jersey and by the United States Government in the early '20's, and followed with infinite variety by some 15 states. Taking that as the pattern, here are some of the major things accomplished by the Act:

First: It validates written agreements to arbitrate, relating to existing or future disputes. That is one of the important features of the Act. I might tell you that back in the early '20's, this Conference of Commissioners on Uniform Laws undertook to write a uniform arbitration act and they bogged down in that conference over the question whether it should apply to future disputes. The general attitude of judges and lawyers at that time was against arbitration. They regarded it as an interference with the judicial process, as in competition with the courts, as in competition with the practice of lawyers, and they were "agin" it, with the result that future disputes did not appear in the original Uniform Act. It was later withdrawn by the Conference and the subject was dead, until revived by the procedure I just described, resulting in the present Uniform Act.

Under this Act, the written agreement need not be signed, verified, recorded or acknowledged. The simple written agreement is all that is required. It is not confined to disputes arising out of the agreement, if the parties so wish, which is a provision common to most of the modern arbitration acts.

With respect to labor and management agreements to arbitrate, the draft permits the State to choose whether to allow the parties to provide that the Act shall not apply.

Second: The Uniform Act provides a simple method for court enforcement of the agreement to arbitrate and for enforcement of the Award. All applications to the Court are by way of the motion procedure of the State. Actions in the normal sense are not contemplated. Thus, all such applications are to be heard within five to ten days after they are made. Two such types of motions are contemplated.

Motions to Compel or to Stay Arbitration

The first type is motions to compel or to stay arbitration. The motion to compel may be either by an original application or in a pending action involving an arbitrable issue accompanied by stay of the action. The motion to stay arbitration is in substance a substitute for a declaratory judgment procedure, which will be found in most of the States of the United States. It substitutes the motion for the usual action for obtaining the declaration.

Now, the principal issue in these various motions to comply with the agreement or stay the arbitration will be whether the issue in dispute comes within the agreement to arbitrate. While not specifically stated under the Act, this is a question for decision by the Courts, unless the parties have agreed to leave it to the arbitrator.

The Committee section and the Conference as a whole were aware of the arguments, under existing arbitration acts, that the Courts have assumed the arbitrator's function, under the guise of determining arbitrability. These critics point to some of the New York cases as exemplifying that tendency and to the New York doctrine that there must first be a bona fide or substantial dispute. These critics also hold that arbitrators are better qualified than judges to construe the arbitration clause, and that therefore this is the question that should be left to the arbitrators.

Under the Act, there is nothing to prevent the parties from agreeing that the subject of arbitrability shall be left to the Arbitrator, and they may do so in most modern Acts following the New York pattern.

The fact that they have not done so, despite the urgings of prominent writers and of lecturers and speakers before labor discussion groups, seemed to us to be an indication that the parties are not inclined to give the arbitrator that authority. Therefore, to write that provision into the contracts by legislation seemed to the Commissioners unwise.

The problem, then, is essentially one of educating the Courts to their proper role in this area and that means essentially the Appellate Courts. A recent article in the *Arbitration Journal*, indicating a recession by the New York Courts from their earlier position on the issue that I have just mentioned, would indicate that courts are not immune to the processes of education.[3]

After all, when those decisions were written there was very little in legal literature, and certainly nothing in the decisions to which the courts could turn for some guidance on this question, and it may be fairly assumed that with the rather widespread discussion that has occurred you will find a different attitude on the part of the courts in dealing specifically with that question.

The Uniform Arbitration Act provides that it shall not be a ground for setting aside or refusing to enforce the arbitration agreement, "that the claim or issue lacks merit or bona fides, or because any fault or grounds sought to be arbitrated have not been shown." It may be of

---

[3] EDITOR'S NOTE: See article by Ralph E. Kharas and Robert F. Koretz in *Arbitration Journal*, Vol. 11, n.s., No 3 (1956), pp. 135 et. seq.

interest to you that in the middle of this month I am attending a meeting where I shall have to defend that particular modification.

Motions to Reduce the Award to Judgment

The second type of motion contemplated by the Act is the motion for the reduction of the award to judgment, in the course of which the validity of the award is passed upon.

Sections 11, 12 and 13, dealing with confirmation, vacation or modification of the award do no more than recognize the traditional grounds for correcting or setting aside an award. They are grounds that exist under modern arbitration statutes and are grounds that existed in common law, and it was in those sections where the objectionable grounds appeared which have now been removed, as I said, in very substantial part, because of the action taken by your group. Those that remain, then, are essentially:

1. Fraud or corruption in securing the award.
2. Partiality or misconduct on the part of the arbitrator.
3. Acting beyond the powers of the arbitrators.
4. Improper conduct of the hearing; and,
5. The non-existence of an agreement to arbitrate, if that question has not been previously settled at an earlier stage.

That, then, is essentially a broad summary of the motion procedure.

Third: Another important feature of the Act appears in Section 9, which provides, more extensively than any legislation existing on the books of any State or Federal Government today, a modification of the old Common Law doctrine that the Arbitrator's powers cease with the signing of the award. This section provides that after an Award is made, on application of a party, or, if a motion has been made affecting the award, on order of the court, the arbitrator may then modify or correct the award or clarify it.

Heretofore, the Court itself has had to construe an ambiguous or uncertain award and if it was too uncertain and too ambiguous to be enforced, it was thrown out altogether. Now, on application of the parties, that question may be sent back to the arbitrator to fill in and clarify what he has undertaken to award.

Fourth: The Act contemplates the traditional informal arbitration hearing and procedure, unencumbered by any technical requirements. There is no requirement that a record be kept of the hearing; there is no requirement that rules of evidence prevail; there is no requirement that the award be in any particular form, except that it be in writing and signed.

Representations were made to us that there ought to be something requiring an opinion along with the Award. That seemed to us simply to introduce another technical requirement which is undesirable.

There are a few provisions that are designed to effectuate the proceedings, such as that a decision by the majority of the arbitrators is sufficient; waiver in case of failure to appear; appointment of arbitrators where the method provided has failed; and the authorization of subpoenas and depositions, under the complete control of the arbitrator.

There are also some safeguards which the parties may not have provided for, such as notice of the hearing; right to present evidence; and right to counsel. Most of these specific provisions can be modified by the parties if they desire, by their own agreement.

This is, of course, just a very rapid, sketchy summary of what the provisions of the Act are. Maybe I have omitted some of those that you deem important, but I think it should be sufficient to illustrate the simplicity and the limited area of court control that is contemplated by the Act.

The whole design of the Act is to make arbitration effective and to insure an effective, simple, non-technical arbitration procedure. Its use of the judicial procedure is solely to insure that purpose and to keep the judge out of the arbitrator's business. It repudiates the notion that arbitration is like a judicial proceeding and therefore should be subject to judicial review.

I am confident, after examining many of the Acts of this country and various States, that the adoption of this legislation would give arbitration a prestige, a strength and effectiveness that would advance arbitration in this country beyond anything achieved on the subject in the last one hundred years.

Friends of arbitration, in my opinion, should therefore get behind the Act and support it as a uniform measure throughout the country.

Now, two attacks have been made upon it, neither of which to us seemed to be persuasive.

Is Any Legislation Needed?

First it is said that, with respect to labor arbitration, it is undesirable to have any legislation. Management and unions have learned to live together in harmony with arbitration voluntarily set up to settle any disputes that might arise. Litigation over the subject matter of arbitration in those states which do not have the more recent arbitration statutes is practically unheard of. Introduce this legislation and it is an open invitation to the parties to resort to litigation with all the expense and delay that goes with it. We are happy now, so leave us alone. I believe this was the tenor of an article attacking the Act, written by the late Herbert Syme.

It seemed to us there are several reasons why we could not accept that point of view.

First: No one questions that in the great majority of cases the parties live up to their agreement to arbitrate, but still there are cases in which bona fide disputes arise over the interpretation of the scope and applicability of the arbitration agreement and over the conduct of the parties or arbitrators in obtaining the award. To those parties involved in that dispute, and without means of resolving it, it is of no comfort to know that in other cases in which they are not concerned, no disputes arise and no remedy is needed. They are entitled to have their problems settled expeditiously, economically and in accordance with the principles and rules of law.

Second: The assumption that those who now maintain amicable relations would abandon them under this Act and go to Court, seem to us an unrealistic appraisal of the good faith and motives of these people. Under existing law now an astute lawyer can find more effective legal procedures for frustrating the arbitration process than would exist under this Act. The parties do not resort to them because they abide by the agreement they have made in good faith. They would also do so under this Act.

Third: The universal harmony assumed by this objection to the Act is probably not a true description of the situation. It was not verified to us by any representative of the committee appointed by Mr. Arthur Goldberg of the CIO, or by the American Arbitration Association and its committee, or by the general consensus within the National Conference of Commissioners on Uniform Laws, all of whom have their contacts and ties within their own particular States.

As Mr. William Isaacson has pointed out in the June, 1956, issue of the *Labor Law Journal,* the frantic efforts, particularly by union lawyers, to seek enforcement of arbitration agreements by resort to Sec. 301 of the National Labor Relations Act indicate that there is a very real need and demand for some legal procedure and some legislation to permit the settlement of these disputes by a simple and effective judicial procedure.

Fourth: The number of New York cases appearing in the reports pointed to as proof of the objection we are now considering do not substantiate that objection. They reflect, rather: (1) the large extent to which arbitration is used in New York, a large industrial center; (2) New York is peculiar, in that lower court cases, including those of trial courts, county courts and even municipal courts, are reported and therefore distort the picture of the number of legal procedures or cases there are involving arbitration; (3) New York has a heterodox, patchwork type of statute, which is likely to invite rather than prevent resort to courts.

Obviously, a State providing no remedy will have no court cases. Contrasting such a State with New York, in terms of reported cases, warrants no conclusion invidious to the Arbitration Act. Every reported case compelling arbitration represents an arbitration saved, as well as a warning to others to heed their arbitration agreement. In States having no means of compelling arbitration, no one knows how many arbitration agreements are disregarded. They never see the light of day, either before an arbitrator or a court.

Should Labor and Commercial Arbitration Be Combined?

The second attack that has been made on the Uniform Act is that it combines both labor and commercial arbitration. The argument is that arbitration in each case serves essentially different purposes. In labor arbitration it is the end product of a grievance procedure within the plant, and is a procedure agreed upon by the parties as a substitute for the strike and the lockout. In commercial arbitration, it is said, arbitration is a substitute for litigation. In the one the parties must continue to live together. In the other, it is concerned but with one customer of many. Hence, the approach is different and the statutes should not be alike. Otherwise, the courts will carry concepts appropriate to one over to the other to which they are not applicable.

Again, for several reasons, the Commissioners could not see their way clear to accepting this contention. Let me summarize those reasons very briefly. All I can do is to state them, without developing them:

(1) For the most part, discussions in this tenor remain theoretical, and concrete demonstration is lacking. Pointing to the objectionable

New York cases involving the no-dispute doctrine is no answer, because they are as objectionable in commercial arbitration as they are in labor arbitration, and, as I have said, the Act specifically negatives that doctrine.

(2) The trend in recent legislation—a recent example is Ohio—is to the contrary. Both are being included in a single Act.

(3) Procedures, as distinguished from content, for both commercial and labor arbitration are essentially the same. The subject matter and content are, of course, different. There are objections to having two separate arbitration procedures in a single State, one dealing with labor and the other with commercial arbitration, and, I suppose, a third dealing with neither. We got away from the separate procedures when we joined law and equity, which, of course, differ as widely in content, approach and disposition as do labor, commercial and other types of arbitration. The same simplicity should apply to arbitration, whether labor or commercial.

(4) One would suppose that labor leaders should be the first to object to being included in the same act as commercial arbitrations. Yet the national labor leaders with whom we consulted and from whom we have heard did not disapprove of this combination.

(5) If anyone should object to this particular act, I would suppose it would be the commercial people, because this Act is drawn essentially with an eye to labor arbitration, as distinguished from commercial.

(6) A point that never seems to be discussed or dealt with in criticisms of the Act is that under the Act the parties are perfectly free to contract that the Act shall not apply.

Finally, there is, I think, a very real point and let me say that this argument was suggested to me by labor leaders on the national level, that separate labor arbitration statutes are likely to have less objective treatment when it comes to enactment than an Act which deals with all arbitration, commercial, labor and other types; that if labor arbitration is separated from the other types of arbitration, you open it and expose it to attack from hostile interests, and those with the greatest political power are going to determine the content of the Act.

For these reasons, then, the Conference felt that the two ought to be combined.

Coming back, then, to what I said to begin with, it seems to me that this Act might well serve as a milestone in the history of arbitration in this country; there are only some 15 or 18 States that have anything like a modern arbitration act, based on the New York Act. All of the rest either have no arbitration act or they have some ancient or ineffective statutes with which they are completely dissatisfied.

One reason the Commissioners got into this is because there is a movement throughout the country in different States for legislation covering labor arbitration. The Commissioners thought they would be doing some service if they could provide an Act which would have some degree of objectivity, which would incorporate what was thought to be the best on the subject, and which had some prospect of general acceptance.

Without such example, without such a model, you are likely to get a heterogeneous and inadequate system of State legislation on the subject. I hope, therefore, that you gentlemen will give serious consideration to the re-examination of the Act, particularly since, as I understand it, your previous objection was based upon provisions which have now been removed.[4]

C.

WHITLEY P. McCoy
Washington, D. C.

So much has been said and written on the subject of the Uniform Arbitration Act, that in the little time allowed me here I cannot be expected to cover the subject. I can only suggest briefly the reasons, in general, that have led me to the conclusion I have reached.

The obvious purpose of the proposed Uniform Arbitration Act is to make arbitration more attractive to parties to disputes, and thus to stimulate its use, while diminishing litigation in commercial disputes and strikes in industrial disputes. No one can reasonably quarrel with that purpose. It is only on the means to attain that end that there is honest, and I hope entirely friendly, disagreement.

I am strongly in favor of the Uniform Arbitration Act, with an amendment providing that it shall have no application to Labor-Man-

---

[4] EDITOR'S NOTE: At the conclusion of the tenth annual meeting the Board of Governors decided to review the position taken by the Academy during the 1956 meeting on the subject of the Uniform Arbitration Act and to present at the 1958 meeting its recommendations as to whether the Academy position should be changed as a result of the amendments to the Uniform Act approved in August 1956 by the American Bar Association.

agement disputes. The reasons for my favoring the proposed law will indicate why I also favor the restricting amendment. The very reasons for a uniform Act covering commercial arbitrations are reasons against applying such a law to Labor-Management arbitration.

1. Arbitration of commercial disputes will be stimulated by enactment of the Uniform Act because of the factor of expedition. Our court dockets are crowded, the judges are overworked. Arbitration of cases that would otherwise take their slow, weary, and tortuous way through the courts would relieve those heavy dockets and result not only in speedy disposition of the cases arbitrated, but also speedier disposition of cases remaining in litigation. The fact that recourse could still be had to the courts, by motions to compel or stay arbitration, or to enforce, set aside, or modify awards, would not offset this advantage too much, for arbitrators would still have done a great deal of the court's work.

Now it is quite clear, without the necessity of elaboration, that this reason does not operate in favor of a uniform law to cover Labor-Management disputes. Quite the opposite. Such disputes are not in the courts but are already in common law arbitration. The effect of a uniform Act covering them would be to throw many of them into the courts, further crowding already overcrowded dockets, slowing up not only the arbitration process but also cases in litigation.

2. The Uniform Act will stimulate commercial arbitration because of the factor of economy. As contrasted with litigation in court, arbitration is a relatively simple and economical means of deciding the ordinary commercial case; for example, how much, if anything, does the X Corporation owe the Y Corporation? The slow wasteful procedures of pleading, of empanelling a jury, the wearisome technical arguments of corporation lawyers, the high court costs, the motions, the continuances, the appeals, the writs of certiorari, the new trials, the further appeals— the total cost can be frightful. I should like to hear from an authoritative source a rough estimate of what the average cost of a commercial arbitration is. I am sure it is not one-tenth of the cost of litigating the average case in court.

Now this reason, economy, is likewise a reason against including Labor-Management disputes in the Act. To do so would add to the present cost of arbitration, court costs and attorneys' fees in those cases where resort is had to the courts. An arbitration that might otherwise cost the Union and the Company $150 apiece, would be more apt to cost $1500 or $3000 apiece after the motions and the appeals. How could a small Company, up against one of the larger and wealthier international unions, stand it for long? How could a small local union, up against a multi-million dollar Company, stand it for long? Pass this Act as it is now written, and arbitration of Labor-Management disputes might soon suffer a severe decline, at least in some industries and some sections of the country, with a consequent rise in strikes and other forms of self-help.

3. The Uniform Act will stimulate commercial arbitration because of the factor of truth and justice. Parties to commercial disputes, if they can be persuaded to arbitrate under a fair uniform Act which gives them adequate protection, are much more apt to get the correct result, for they can pick an arbitrator expert in the particular field of business, economics, or law involved. They may pick an insurance man for an insurance case, an accountant for an accounting case, a patent lawyer for a patent case, etc. They can pick the man for the case, instead of having to take whatever judge is assigned. And the arbitrator, not being entangled in the red tape of the law, can expeditiously find the facts and base a just award on it.

Does this apply to Labor-Management disputes? Quite the contrary. Ninety per cent of the 100,000 or more collective bargaining contracts now provide for arbitration; a body of competent arbitrators exists, knowing the field and trusted alike by companies and unions. Their awards are respected and lived up to with very rare exceptions. To apply the uniform Act in this field would subject the awards of recognized specialists to the review of men without the essential knowledge of industrial relations and plant problems. Truth and justice would be diminished, not enhanced.

I have given three reasons for the Act and for the restricting amendment. If I had time I could give others, and in each case the reason for the Act would be also a reason for the amendment, except with respect to specific enforcement of agreements to arbitrate and enforcement of awards. It would be well if we had some law to cover those aspects of Labor-Management arbitration, but if the cost of getting such a law is the acceptance of all the other provisions of the proposed Uniform Act, the price is far too high. I am afraid that if we can get such a law only at that price, there would soon cease to be so many labor arbitration agreements to seek specific performance of, or so many awards to seek enforcement of.

The proponents of the proposed Act in its present form, have, in my opinion, simply overlooked the fundamental differences between commercial arbitration and labor-management arbitration—differences that have been pointed out by Professor Howard, in the *Missouri Law Review,* and by Herbert Syme in the *Labor Law Journal.* The proponents think that the Uniform Act will increase labor arbitration. In the opinion of the opponents, passage of this Act will have the opposite effect.

It has been said that everybody is for the Act except the professors and the arbitrators. Of course this was never quite true, and becomes less true every day as the issue is studied and publicized. But even if true, the professors at least have studied the problem, and I know of none better qualified than arbitrators to speak on the subject of arbitration. And I suggest this thought to legislators: Where does the self-interest of the arbitrators lie? Are they in favor of more arbitration or less arbitration? If arbitrators thought that passage of the uniform act would increase arbitration, you may be very sure that they would be unanimously in favor of it. Instead, the great majority of arbitrators are convinced that passage of the Act would greatly curtail if not end labor-management arbitration, and would consequently lead to cancellation of no-strike clauses and a return to industrial warfare.

Now obviously this is not the expression of a hope. We hope our fears are unfounded. But it is a real fear, based upon our intimate, day to day contacts with the people involved in labor arbitrations, our knowledge of the problems involved in making arbitration work satisfactorily, and our familiarity with the psychology, the emotions, the thought processes of the people concerned.

Labor leaders have already been alerted to, and recognize, the danger to arbitration, but many of them are not too concerned because they have never really lost their first love—self-help, strike, slowdown. Some are openly opposed to arbitration, and would welcome an excuse to abolish it with consequent abolition of no-strike pledges. Management leaders, though of course in favor of the safeguards which the Act would give them, have begun to see the threat to arbitration and no-strike clauses involved in passage of the Act. I think that they too see the cost of the safeguards of the Act as too high, especially since the need for them is largely imaginary and theoretical. I am informed that the Labor Relations Committee of the National Chamber of Commerce has just in the last two or three weeks expressed concern over this Act, pronounced it inappropriate legislation, and has so notified the State Chambers.

Arbitration of labor-management disputes on a purely voluntary basis, conducted under the common-law without benefit of statute, has had in just 16 years time such a tremendous growth and almost universal acceptance as to be amazing. It is accepted as a part of the grievance procedure, part of the everyday running of the plant. As long as it is working, let's let it alone. The risks in tinkering with it are too great.

I have said that I favor an amendment to Section 1 excluding labor-management disputes from the coverage of the Act. I think, perhaps, I might go along with a compromise. At least I have a compromise in mind that I think should be considered and discussed. I therefore propose for your consideration an amendment to the Act reading as follows:

> Strike out the last sentence of Section 1 and substitute in lieu thereof the following:

> "This Act shall have no application to the arbitration of so-called labor-management disputes, that is, disputes between employers and employees or their duly constituted representatives or agents, but the arbitration of such disputes shall continue as now to be conducted under the principles of the common law and of equity, except where the parties to such disputes, after the effective date of this Act, shall have expressly agreed in writing, in their collective bargaining agreement or otherwise, to arbitrate under the terms and provisions of this Act, in which case the terms and provisions of this Act shall apply."

I will not suggest arguments for or against this amendment, at least until we get some reactions from other members of the Panel or from the floor.

D.

ROBERT L. HOWARD
Law School, University of Missouri

It is a reasonable assumption that all persons present at this meeting have a friendly interest in labor-management arbitration, and would like to see it improved, perfected and encouraged as an instrument for the promotion of industrial peace.

I take it we are concerned today with two questions: First, whether we do or do not need legislation applicable to labor-management arbitration, and second, if we accept an affirmative answer to that question, whether the present Uniform Arbitration Act is an appropriate instrument to meet that need.

In order that my position may be clear initially, I may say that I am convinced that in most areas of the United States we do not need such legislation; and that where legislation may be regarded as desirable, the present Uniform Act does not satisfactorily supply the need, for the reasons, among others, that it goes too far; that it contains many provisions that may possibly be appropriate enough when applied to commercial arbitration, but which have no proper place in a measure applicable to labor-management arbitration; that it injects the court into the picture where it was never the intention of the parties to an arbitration provision in a collective bargaining agreement to have it enter, and allows it to encroach upon the function of the arbitrator; that it has in it the very great danger of weakening, if not destroying, that expeditiously final and binding character of the arbitration determination which is the chief merit of this process of industrial dispute settlement; and that it may well weaken or destroy the completely voluntary character of labor-management arbitration as it exists today.

In any consideration of this problem, the first alleged justification for even talking in terms of a need for legislation is uniformly asserted to be the common law rule by which a party to an agreement to arbitrate may repudiate that agreement any time he may see fit to do so, and that he may withdraw from an arbitration *proceeding* any time before an award is made, and repudiate his agreement to arbitrate.

If that statement accurately reflects the common law situation now existing in most jurisdictions, and if labor and management, as the parties to an arbitration provision in a collective bargaining agreement, commonly, or with any substantial frequency, assert their right to repudiate their obligation to arbitrate, then a strong case is made for some sort of legislation.

It is submitted, however, that where such a situation exists, and where some legislation as a remedy therefore is deemed desirable, the first sentence of the first Section of the Uniform Act largely supplies the need, without all of the complex provisions that follow. When a statute provides that "A written agreement to submit any existing controversy to arbitration, or a provision in a written contract to submit to arbitration any controversy thereafter arising between the parties, is valid, enforceable and irrevocable, save upon such grounds as exist at law or in equity for the revocation of any contract," the foundation has been provided upon the basis of which a court, in the exercise of its common law authority, and without further statutory elaboration, can provide all the remedy that may be required.

But that is not the only answer to the alleged problem created by the asserted common law rule.

In the area of the country from which I come, the representatives of management and of labor habitually, traditionally and uniformly consider their agreements to arbitrate as binding obligations, and they conduct themselves accordingly. They do not repudiate those obligations.

In the middle west where I am most intimately conversant with the arbitration process we do not need this legislation, not even the first sentence, because the problem does not arise. Furthermore, we do not want such legislation, and when I say we, I include both labor and management.

There is also another angle to this first aspect of our problem that must not be overlooked in any long range consideration. And that goes back to the soundness of the common law doctrine in its application to labor-management arbitration.

We are all aware of the fact that that doctrine is commonly said to have had its origin primarily in the jealousy of the courts over the feeling that parties to a contract, who agreed to by-pass the court and submit any dispute arising therefrom to final and binding arbitration, were improperly interfering with the jurisdiction of the court. Absent the agreement to arbitrate, the dispute would have gone to the court for disposition. To say that the court was being deprived of jurisdiction seemed like a reasonably clear assertion, and the doctrine that one may repudiate his agreement at any time has persisted in many, and perhaps most, jurisdictions.

But however applicable this common law rule may be to commercial arbitration in which it had its origin, if there is any strength in the commonly asserted adage that when the reasons for the rule do not exist, the rule should not apply, then no reason could ever possibly have existed for the application of this rule to labor-management arbitration. By no stretch of the imagination could it ever be said that labor-management arbitration encroached upon, restricted, or took from what would otherwise be within the jurisdiction of the court. Labor-management arbitration is not a substitute for litigation, as is commercial arbitration, but rather a substitute for resort to economic force. And it is almost invariably joined with a no-strike, no-lockout agreement which the parties and the courts do regard as binding and enforceable. Thus, whether we may prefer to rely on the dictum of Lord Coke that an agreement to arbitrate is in its nature revocable, or that of Lord Campbell that it is against public policy because it ousts courts of jurisdiction and for that reason revocable, it stands on no stronger ground with reference to labor-management arbitration.

This whole problem has been pointed up by a recent decision in the Chancery Court of Monroe County, Mississippi, in a case with which you are all probably familiar, and which is now pending before the Supreme Court of that State. The arbitration provisions of the agreement in that case were coupled with a no-strike provision. The Chancery Court called attention to the fact that the Supreme Court of the State had held that "a written agreement for submission to arbitration is revocable by either party before an award is made" in cases involving commercial arbitration, but pointed out that the "Court had never ruled on the question of whether an arbitration clause in a collective bargaining contract is enforceable," an observation that would be equally applicable to the courts of most other jurisdictions.

The opinion then goes on to point out that since a decision in 1931, the State Supreme Court had put its stamp of approval on contracts made by unions with employers; that with the Mississippi Theatres Case in 1936 the State Supreme Court had held that a court of equity could properly enforce obedience to collective bargaining agreements by injunctive relief, on the ground that such agreements advance the general public welfare by avoiding boycotts, strikes, lockouts and other evils.

Then, after commenting on the recognized merits of arbitration as the most satisfactory method of settling disputes between labor and management, and emphasizing the no-strike provision of the arbitration clause as adding to its value to the company, to the union, and to the public generally, the Chancery Court concluded that the arbitration clause in a collective bargaining contract is likewise in the interest of the general public welfare and should be enforced in the same manner as any other lawful provision of the contract is enforced," and accordingly issued its mandatory injunction.[5]

I submit, gentlemen, that the approach of the Chancery Court to the problem in this case, and its reasoning and decision, are eminently sound; that they should commend themselves strongly to the Supreme Court of Mississippi in its review of this case, and in like fashion to other courts wherever the question may arise.

Incidentally, I assume that this case, and others like it, serve to give vital content to the suggestion of our good friend Alex Frey when, in his testimony before the Pennsylvania Governor's Commission in 1953, he called for the correction of some judicial errors in this field that would eliminate the need for legislation.

Obviously, if the Supreme Court of Mississippi can be persuaded to accept this challenge to correct a "judicial error" which it, incidentally, has not been guilty of with respect to labor-management arbitration, and if other courts will follow suit, the most commonly asserted reason for legislation of the nature here under consideration will have ceased to exist.

If I may now be permitted to pass on to the assumption being widely made that legislation is desirable, at least in some areas, and to comment more directly on the Proposed Uniform Arbitration Act, I would suggest that the combination of commercial arbitration and labor-management arbitration under application of the same legislative measure is one of the major defects of the Uniform Act. I have yet to encounter any one, personally, or by way of the printed word, who has been willing to admit that the combination is otherwise than desirable.

I have no purpose to controvert the contention that many, and possibly most or even all, of the provisions of the Uniform Act may be desirable for commercial arbitration, just as they were so considered desirable by those who drafted the same or similar provisions included in earlier statutes, all of which were directed in their application solely to commercial arbitration.

But just because both processes are called "arbitration," does not necessarily mean that the same statutory provisions are equally desirable in both cases.

---

[5] Machine Products Co. v. Prairie Local Lodge No. 1538, Miss. Chanc. Ct. 27 LA 285. ED. NOTE: Subsequently reversed by Miss. Sup. Ct., 28 LA 339.

The long time relationships between the parties to a collective bargaining agreement containing a provision for arbitration coupled with a no-strike, no-lockout provision bear almost no similarity to the relationships between the parties to an ordinary commercial contract. The two types of arbitration are designed for very different purposes. The one, as has been stated, is a substitute for litigation, the other a substitute for resort to economic force. Commercial arbitration concerns itself with business relationships for the breach of which a dollars and cents award ordinarily provides an adequate remedy.

Labor-management arbitration, in contrast, deals not with dollars and cents issues, but, for example, with the technical details of a wage incentive plan as applied to the various skills in a modern steel mill, with the application of a technical plan of job evaluation to the varying duties of employees engaged in the numerous aspects of any of our many complicated industrial establishments, or even with the matter of promotions, lay-offs and rehires in the application of combinations of plant-wide and departmental seniority in any large scale production enterprise. All are likely to be matters with which the average trial court is wholly unfamiliar; to the disposition of which the court process is ill adapted; which neither party to a collective bargaining agreement had any purpose to entrust to the disposition of a court; and which must be disposed of finally and without delay if the parties to a collective bargaining agreement are to go on living together and working together with any degree of harmony. The delay incident to court intervention in the arbitration process may produce small injury to the relationship of the parties to commercial arbitration, but such is not the case with labor-management arbitration. And one of the major objections to the many provisions of the Uniform Act that invite court intervention is the consequent inevitable delay.

While it is true that some concessions have been made by way of accepting amendments that delete the most objectionable features of Section 12 of the Uniform Act, the basic offense of trying to apply a commercial act to the labor-management relationship still exists.

The very nature and purposes of the labor-management arbitration process makes highly inappropriate the application of most of the detailed provisions of the Uniform Act.

The process is one based solely on the voluntary agreement of the parties, and the element of complete *voluntarism,* together with that of *finality,* constitute the two most significant and essential aspects of the whole process. And the provisions of this statute do violence to both.

The essence of labor-management arbitration as provided for in most modern collective bargaining agreements lies in the fact that it is coupled with, as its necessary counterpart, a no-strike, no-lockout agreement. The parties have voluntarily agreed to give up these remedies of self-help, but only for a price, and only on terms which they, themselves, have determined to substitute therefor. They have not agreed to subject their relationship to the application of some statute or to the intervention of a court. What they have agreed to do is to forego their right to resort to the strike or the lockout, in exchange for an arbitration process under which the determination of the arbitrator or the arbitration board selected by the parties is to be final and binding, and they do mean final and binding.

When a statute provides for court appointment of an arbitrator, even under the restricted language of the Uniform Act, something is taken away from the essential characteristic of voluntarism, to say nothing of the fact that the average trial judge is not well equipped to make an effective appointment.

When we further provide for a species of judicial review by the various provisions set forth in Sections 12 and 13 for vacating or correcting an award, and when we add the multiplicity of opportunities for appeal provided by Section 19, those basic and essential elements of voluntarism and finality are left bearing small resemblance to the original intention of the parties.

The provisions of the Uniform Act with its many open invitations to a party to call upon a court to intervene in the arbitration process is, in my judgment, fundamentally inconsistent with the basic major features of voluntary labor-management arbitration, intended to be the terminal point in every dispute, and not the signal for the beginning of court intervention, review, and a process of appeals.

I have elsewhere entered the plea that we should exercise some degree of patience with a system that is yet in its experimental and developmental stage, and that we may find it much wiser to let the processes involved in labor-management arbitration have a chance to mature unrestricted, instead of attempting to put them into a legislative straight jacket, or authorizing the court to barge in upon that very sensitive development. This is peculiarly a field in which legislation should not enter unless the necessity therefor to save the usefulness of the institution has been demonstrated beyond all rational doubt. No such urgent necessity has been been discerned in the part of the country with whose arbitration practices and needs I am most intimately familiar.

E. General Discussion

I. ROBERT FEINBERG: Some of the speakers have made the point that one of the reasons they are opposed to the Uniform Arbitration Act is that the courts are not familiar with labor relations, or would get into such questions as seniority, discharges and other matters with which the courts necessarily would not be familiar, and that, consequently, the arbitrator who has been selected by the parties, as an expert, should ultimately decide the case.

Now, isn't it true that under the Uniform Act, just as under the New York and other statutes, the courts are prohibited from getting into the merits of the dispute and can only set aside an award on collateral grounds, so that, consequently, those issues, in any event, would not be submitted to a judge?

PROFESSOR HOWARD: That is a question I definitely wanted answered by someone who is not particularly for or against the statute. It has seemed to me that Section 2, for instance, of the Act, especially in (c) and (d), which deal with "an issue referring to arbitration", and "an issue subject to arbitration", implies that the court is going to have to determine the question of arbitrability. My theory is, that when they deal with that question of arbitrability, they are going to get into the very problem of interpretation of the provisions of the contract that were intended to be left to the arbitrator.

There are certain other provisions that, it seems to me, lend themselves to the same possibility.

CHAIRMAN SMITH: Do you consider this an answer to your question, Mr. Feinberg?

MR. FEINBERG: Only in a limited sense.

ARCHIBALD COX: I would like to elaborate a little a sentence in Dean Pirsig's remarks, which I think we sometimes have not thought enough about, and perhaps some of the other speakers would comment upon it, so I would ask Dean Pirsig if I may turn it into a question.

Dean Pirsig suggested, and I think rightly, that a lawyer today could do more to tie up a labor arbitration and to haul people through the courts and to make it expensive to challenge the award, without any statute, than could possibly be done under this statute.

There are decisions that support the view that you can go in and get a stay of arbitration, where the arbitrator is going to decide something not arbitrable. There are grounds in common law for attacking awards that are broader than the grounds set forth in the statute. It is true, people have not done that on a very wide scale, but there are indications that it is being done more broadly.

We have had two cases in the Supreme Judicial Court in Massachusetts where this was done, and the proceeding was tied up below—part of it permanently. I have an award of my own in court now that has been there for a year, where the employer was challenging it, because I ordered reinstatement instead of simply finding that a person had been discharged without cause.

These things can be done, and I think they are going to be done increasingly. I think the real point here is that in the past, arbitrations and industrial relations have been carried on separate from the law, and it is likely to be true that the union lawyers are trying to take advantage of the courts as much as employer lawyers, and I venture the suggestion, that Dean Pirsig is not only right, but 15 years from now, without arbitration statutes, you will find a host of situations in which the courts are exercising their existing powers.

My other thought follows along in line with the first. I sat here wondering when Professor Howard spoke about a court decision enforcing agreements to arbitrate, and Whitley McCoy said he liked the first section of the Uniform Act, but nothing else, just what powers he thought the courts would exercise under such a common law decision or under such a general declaration. They will surely make up some rules for deciding when they will send you to arbitration and when they won't send you to arbitration. They will surely make up some rules for deciding what awards they will set aside and which ones they will enforce. The real question there is whether you have more confidence in a statute that is drawn at the present time somewhat in advance, before people have too much vested in a line of court decisions; or whether you have confidence in the courts to work out a better set of rules than could be worked out in a statute.

I do not detect that confidence, and I wonder whether someone could answer this?

MR. McCOY: I think Professor Cox is pessimistic in thinking that the trend is going to be toward more appeal to the courts in the absence of statute.

It seems to me that the trend is entirely the other way, that labor and management, which were at each other's throats 20 or 30 years ago, are learning more and more to live together and there is less danger of going to courts today than there ever was, and there will be less in the future, unless you adopt a statute which invites the parties to go to court, and that is what the statute would do. It would be an open invitation.

Today when you get a situation of a company or a union losing a case, and they say to the lawyer, "What can I do?", the lawyer doesn't start to tell them all their common law remedies. He says, "You can't do anything; it is final and binding." But what would the lawyer say under this Act? He would say, "Oh, under Section So-and-So, we will take this to court," so I think the trend is the other way.

PROFESSOR HOWARD: I would like to say just one word to what Professor Cox had to say on the earlier question.

My chief plea is that we not adopt this as a Uniform Act and try to get it enacted in the states where people feel that they do not need it. My people, I am strongly convinced, feel that they do not need it.

In comformity with what Mr. McCoy just said, not long ago I had a conversation with one of the leading lawyers representing industry in St. Louis, who spends his whole time in the field of labor-management relations, and he gave voice to exactly the same situation. He says, "Today, when one of my companies is disgruntled with an arbitration award and asks me what I can do, I say, 'You agreed that this arbitration should be final and binding, didn't you?', and they say, 'Yes.' " And, he says, "I say, 'Forget about it', but, if they had the statute and with these provisions, where you can ask the court to modify or vacate the award, I would be forced to tell them, 'There is a statute allowing you to do it,' and we would be getting into court every day, and that is the primary reason I am opposed to the Act."

A lot of industry and labor lawyers in that area are of the same view.

CHAIRMAN SMITH: I am sure the lawyer would feel he had to tell his clients about remedies available at common law.

ABRAM H. STOCKMAN: Did the Commissioners consider the suggested change in the last sentence of the first section, as suggested by Professors Howard and McCoy?

DEAN PIRSIG: Yes, they did, and it was felt, as a matter of fact, the disposition was even not to put in the qualifying clause now. The qualification was put in essentially at the insistence of labor representatives with whom we consulted, and they were completely satisfied with the provision as it now stands.

In effect, the purpose of this reversal of the language is to exclude the provision and make it a subject of bargaining between labor and management. It seemed to us, if this is a good Act, and we think it is, then the weight ought to be on the other side; that if it does not apply in this particular case, then, let the parties discuss that. I think there is a good deal of risk that a contract might not provide for it, on the assumption that it is already covered by the Act, so that in many cases it would defeat the intention of the parties.

I might just add one word to Professor Cox's observation. It seems to me that that Mississippi case will invite the very kind of obstructive legal tactics that he is anticipating, because, if a court may go in as an equity court to tie up the enforcement of the award, or for specific performance of an agreement to arbitrate, you can tie up an arbitration for years by an action, and this Act was specifically designed to substitute a quick and economical procedure to replace it.

CHAIRMAN SMITH: I suppose it would be interesting to find out statistically the extent to which one side or the other might introduce at the bargaining table in contract negotiations in any state adopting the Uniform Act, the question of whether the parties should agree to exclude its application in a particular case.

Are there any other questions?

REV. LEO C. BROWN: Like Professor Howard, I am from Missouri. My remarks are based upon the assumption that this Act, laying the basis for appeals, will facilitate appeals. If that is true, it seems to me that the Act will very definitely discourage arbitration.

I think most of us have seen very few cases in which people have refused to arbitrate or refused to abide by an award, but I think many of us have seen cases where one party had somewhat unwillingly submitted to arbitration, or cases where one party has insisted that you will arbitrate only one case at a time, the reason being quite obvious, that they wanted to increase the costs and discourage the other party from arbitrating.

Even in instances where the arbitrator was entitled to a very substantial fee, even in cases where parties wanted to discourage arbitration by increasing the costs, I think, with an Act that invites litigation, they have this opportunity, and while I am not saying there are a large number of cases where this is likely to be true, I think there are many more such cases than there are instances of people refusing at the present time to arbitrate or to abide by an award.

NATHAN P. FEINSINGER: It seems to me that one thing that is lacking in this Act is a statement or declaration of policy at the outset.

As it stands now, courts, unfamiliar with the process of arbitration, have no guide by which to determine what is to be accomplished, and I am wondering, Dean, whether it wouldn't be worthwhile to insert a policy statement at the outset which would still some of the fears that have been expressed here, as to what would be the ultimate outcome of the adoption of the proposed Act.

I was thinking of something along these lines, a policy statement which would read somewhat as follows:

1. The object of the Act is to encourage resort to arbitration as a voluntary and peaceful and expeditious procedure for the settlement of commercial and labor disputes (assuming both remained connected in the same Act).
2. To make agreements to arbitrate enforceable.
3. To clarify and limit the grounds on which awards intended to be final and binding may be attacked through judicial proceedings and in the same vein, to discourage frivolous attacks on arbitration awards intended to be final and binding.

Have you given any thought to such a statement?

DEAN PIRSIG: Let me give you a little background on that. I think it is a very good statement. I have no objection to it.

The policy of the Conference of Commissioners on Uniform Laws, after having had experience with prefatory introductory policy statements, and having found that it gets itself into all kinds of difficulties with them, not with just this Act, but all acts, has been not to include policy statements.

A good deal of what you have mentioned in that prefatory statement of policy is now included in the prefatory note, which accompanies the

Act itself and is before all the legislatures through their commissions, so, what you have in mind is, in substance, accomplished by this prefatory note.

This does not, of course, get on to the statutes, but I think it would be rather ample annotation that accompanies the Act, so we can anticipate that it will be before the courts.

MR. FEINSINGER: Is that note available?

DEAN PIRSIG: Yes.

ALBERT J. HOBAN: On the point raised by Mr. Feinsinger, we actually had that come up in Rhode Island, where one of the lower courts, assuming the Act had been drafted from the New York Act, has ruled that, of course, we adopted the New York decisions, which was not the intention of the legislature at all, and if you do not have either a policy statement or something very strong in the notes, I am afraid you will run into that in the adoption of the statute.

WILLIAM SIMKIN: I don't know whether this is a comment or a question, but it seems to me that we all would agree that for perhaps the bulk of relationships, there is no problem with or without an Act. Where relationships are good, there will be no problem. But where there is a reasonable degree of reluctance, either to arbitrate or to comply with the award, then I would suggest, and I think it is implicit in what has already been said, that the existing sanction and the reason so few cases get into court, is the fact that the union has given up the right to strike, and that when there is undue reluctance either to arbitrate or to comply with an award, that sanction comes up.

My question is this: Would the enactment of an Act like this weaken the sanctions which exist, which are primarily the union's likelihood to strike where reluctance exists?

DEAN PIRSIG: I am not sure about the kind of case you are assuming. If you are assuming a case where the reluctance is based upon a bona fide claim that the arbitration agreement does not apply, then, essentially, it comes down to an argument that a man ought to forego his right to be heard on that, lest he run into a strike.

Now, if the claim is not bona fide, then I suppose that the order will result in an order to arbitrate and you will have arbitration in a very short time.

I am not sure that I get your point.

MR. SIMKIN: Realistically, I don't think it makes much difference whether it is a good case or a bad case. If it is a bad case, in the present situation, we, as arbitrators, have a question of arbitrability at the hearing, but the hidden force of the strike is what forces it into the hearing, and we decide that question, rather than the courts. I don't know whether that is answering your point or not.

DEAN PIRSIG: Well, I do not quite see how this Act could substantially affect the motivation of those people. Maybe I am wrong, but I mention that as a factor. I suppose, if a man still wants to maintain his good relations with management or labor on the other side, that that will continue to be a factor which will avoid resort to courts.

MR. SIMKIN: The reason for my comment is, my observation is only as to cases that go into the courts, where one side or the other has no economic strength. Those are the only cases, by and large, that ever get into the courts.

PROFESSOR MCCOY: I wanted to add this thought along the lines that Mr. Simkin has been suggesting, at least. I don't suppose there is an arbitrator here who has not been amazed at times, at the theories of companies as to what is a proper raising of the issue of arbitrability. They come before me all the time making an argument on the merits, and thinking they are making an argument that it is not arbitrable. In other words, the company has a perfect defense in this case: There is nothing arbitrable here. They just confuse the merits with the issue of arbitrability, and if this Uniform Act is passed, instead of coming before the arbitrator and making that argument on the merits, which they think is an argument on arbitrability, they are going to go into court with a motion to stay arbitration, and I can see that there will be a lot of such motions made.

Now, you go into court with a motion for a stay of arbitration, and make that argument, which is really an argument on the merits, and one or the other of two things happens—either the court disposes of it as we arbitrators do, by telling the parties that it is arbitrable, that you are talking about the merits; or the court goes into the merits, as the courts in New York have done a good many times. So it seems to me that whenever you have an encouragement to go into the courts like that, you have also an encouragement to resort to a quickie strike instead of to arbitration.

BERTHOLD W. LEVY: It seems to me, somewhat along the lines that Mr. Simkin just spoke of, perhaps you have not got a rather fundamental point here this morning. We seem to be assuming that the existence of an arbitration statute, even generally like the proposed Uniform Statute, will encourage resort to the courts, where previously there has been none, or has been very little.

Now, of course, New York is an important State, and we are all familiar with the things that have happened to the New York statute and the Arbitration Statute in New York, but I know of several other States, among which Pennsylvania is one, where there are arbitration statutes. The Pennsylvania statute is an imperfect statute, but it is patterned along the general lines of the one now in controversy.

So far as I know, because of that statute, there has not been any incitement to the parties to run to the courts. I think that those of us here who have any familiarity with the Pennsylvania law—and I see quite a few of you who do—will immediately concede that the difficulty with litigating the very rare cases in Pennsylvania which arise as a result of an arbitration award, or of an arbitration clause in the contract,—the difficulty that the lawyer finds is that there aren't any cases. The fact is, in Pennsylvania, at least, and I suspect in those other States where there are arbitration statutes of one kind or another, that they have not, as a matter of fact, incited resort to the courts, and you will find that the overwhelming majority of arbitration cases end with the award, whether or not there is satisfaction with it.

CHAIRMAN SMITH: It would be interesting to have some kind of a study made—maybe one has been made—as to what the impact on that is, whether there is an increasing tendency to resort to the courts in New York.

DEAN PIRSIG: On that specific point, I have it on hearsay, that an intensive study which is being made in the University of Chicago Law School on arbitration, including a study of this very point, to what extent are parties going to court under the New York Act, has shown that just in the most exceptional, infinitesimal portion of the cases, has there been any resort at all. That will tend to verify the point that has been made.

FREDERICK H. BULLEN: We have had an experience during the last year, which I think is directly on this point, which may interest some of you.

We attempted to negotiate a long-term contract with two unions, we representing an association, in a State where there is no arbitration act. We are unable to get a no-strike provision in that contract. They have not had one for many years, never had one, in fact. We were unable to get a no-strike provision in the contract, because the union said they had no other remedy except a strike to enforce an arbitration award. They recognized that they might, through the State courts, attempt to enforce the award through common law processes, but they felt it was too cumbersome for them and they were agreeable to signing a no-strike provision if there was some method in the State courts, some reasonable method of enforcing the award.

This was a peculiar situation, because it involved approximately seventy employers in the association, many of whom were, of course, irresponsible employers, but some of whom were not. The more responsible group within the association was very much in favor of having an act of some type in the State because they felt it would enable the unions to force, through court actions, rather than strike, those employers who did not go along with the procedure to enter into it and to abide by it. I think that in this case the more responsible elements in the association were damaged considerably through their inability to get a long-term contract with a no-strike provision.

A. HOWARD MYERS: It seems to me that all of the discussion and all of the writings on the subject assume that the result of the statute will be solely to provide an instrument whereby management may be able to obstruct arbitration by use of the resources that the statute would provide by way of access to courts.

There is another side to this problem. I find a great many situations where this kind of statute might put some pressure on unions to arbitrate situations where, for instance, the direct action boys who submit themselves to arbitration sometimes, do not want a piece rate set by an arbitrator, because they are happier working under the contract in the absence of a piece rate; or where they don't want to go to arbitration on an employer's request for an increase in work loads, because they are happier with four machines rather than seven; or they don't want to accept the arbitrator's award after he has ruled some change in economic conditions.

It seems to me—I am not making any arguments for or against the statute—but it seems to me our discussion ought to approach it in the broader sense than that this merely provides an instrument whereby employers may obstruct arbitration.

I think, to be perfectly honest about the problem, the unions, too, ought to think a little more about it in this direction. Some of them are supporting statutory action, and they also recognize the fact that it may be used very often by employers to promote arbitration which, in terms of our organization here, is a major consideration that may have been overlooked.

Chapter VII

THE NEXT DECADE

Ralph T. Seward [1]
Washington, D. C.

Ten years is a long time in the life of a man; though some of us are reaching the age where the decades do not stretch out into the long, endless, inviting vistas that we knew in our youth. They begin to go by pretty rapidly and get sort of crowded together these days.

Ten years is a very short time in the life of an organization such as the National Academy of Arbitrators. During these first ten years, I think it is fair to say, we have been shaking down. We have been finding out who we are and what we are as an organization, what we can hope to do and what we cannot hope to do. We have, in a sense, met the issue of the kind of an organization we are in pretty fundamental terms in defining and discussing our membership policy; for one of the keys to the character of an organization is the basis upon which people join it, and are admitted to it. Whom are we looking for, whom will we accept? We all remember the early disputes and arguments and discussions as to whether or not we should try to make ourselves a closely knit group of self-considered elite; or, on the other hand, whether we should open our doors to anybody who ever saw a grievance hearing, and make ourselves primarily an educational organization for people who want to arbitrate.

I think that the manner in which those issues have been resolved—following, in a sense, the approach of which arbitrators are sometimes accused of compromise and cutting the baby in half—has been sound.

I think we do feel and can rightly feel that there is represented in our membership as good or possibly the best that our profession has to offer. And I think that we can also be proud that our membership

---

[1] Editor's note: Mr. Seward was the first President of the Academy. This address was given at the Tenth Anniversary Luncheon, following the talk of the incumbent President, Mr. John Larkin, which serves as the introduction to this volume.

has not only been opened to and has welcomed, but has aided the young blood that is coming into the profession, and that the profession so greatly needs.

With the splendid cooperation of the American Arbitration Association we worked out the basic framework, the basic ground rules of a Code of Ethics.

And I think that we have come to realize that one of our functions in life—and a very necessary function—is that of sheer companionship and friendship. We are one of the lonely professions. Some of our contacts at work involve close and rewarding friendships. Some involve situations in which we must follow the course of Caesar's wife and be above suspicion, alone and aloof from the parties. And when we get down to brass tacks in deciding cases, then, Brother, we are alone!

It is good to get together; it is good to know other people in the same boat. I think that the feelings that some of us sometimes have about ourselves as arbitrators was expressed at a hearing in Lackawanna sometime ago, at a Bethlehem Steel Plant there. It was a merit increase case, and an employee was trying to explain, in the first place, why he deserved a merit increase, and in the second place, why he had not gotten one. He finally turned to me and said, "Mr. Umpire, this is how it is. I have got two bosses. One of them hates me, and the other one doesn't like me at all."

I say, it is good to get together with our friends in the profession. And if the Academy never did anything else, I think that the strength and backing, the emotional release and security that we find with one another, is a contribution to the arbitration process in the United States, as well as to our individual lives and happiness.

Well, we have shaken down. Where do we go from here?

I hope that, in part, the answer to that question will be: more of the same. Because I think that our discussions, our papers, our Regional Meetings (though there ought to be more of them), our consideration of the problems of our profession at these meetings, have been valuable, enriching and rewarding. I hope we keep on doing that sort of thing, studying procedure, how we can improve the arbitration process, how we can learn more about the substantive problems that we face.

I am wondering, though, whether we are doing as much as we can to help one another; whether we are making available to one another, as we might, our experience; whether we are doing what we can to learn from one another.

In a sense, our function as an organization, is to improve the arbitration process, and to help management and labor, in so far as we can. But, basically, you do not improve the arbitration process, except in terms of framework and so forth, by rules, by techniques. Basically, you improve the arbitration process by improving arbitrators, by learning, by growing in the profession.

Of course, in regard to this matter of helping one another, and educating one another, it occurred to me on the train yesterday that possibly the course of instruction in which arbitrators might be most interested would be a course in: "How to Get Hired as an Arbitrator." It occurred to me, also, that possibly such a course might be given by one or another of the young ladies of the country who are so adept at the delicate art of pursuing while still appearing to be pursued. Some might phrase it, thinking of arbitrators: "The Delicate Art of Chasing While Still Appearing to Be Chaste."

But, beyond that, there is gathered in this room, I think, a unique set of experiences.

Bill Simkin, Saul Wallen, Bob Feinberg, Allen Dash, Lew Gill, have sat through a wide variety of humdrum cases, of crises, of disputes of all kinds. Each of them has his unique techniques. Each of them has different ways of meeting problems. We all write our opinions differently. We conduct our hearings differently. We meet crises differently. And all of us run into situations, I am sure, when something happens at a hearing and you know you have to make a decision in five minutes, and you think, "My God, what on earth do I do at this point?" I think some means by which we could make our professional experience, our personal professional experience, more available to one another—some means of sitting at Dave Cole's feet, or John Larkin's or Gabe Alexander's, or Aaron Horvitz's, or Jake Blair's or Bert Luskin's and learning for a couple of days something of their experiences and how they have handled cases—would be a wonderful thing.

I can remember, from the early days, one of the first cases I ever handled for the War Labor Board out in Chicago. The parties came in—it was a discipline case—lined up on each side of the table, greeted me cordially, and we sat down, and that was it. Dead silence.

I said, "Well, gentlemen, who is going to begin?"

The union said, "We think the company should begin."

The company said, "We think the union should begin."

I said, "Well, what have you done in the past?"

"Well, this is our first arbitration case. We haven't done anything in the past."

The company said, "We feel very strongly about this. We think the union should begin. The union is bringing the grievance on behalf of the discharged employee. It ought to present its case."

The union said, "Oh, no, the burden of proof, of making a case against this discharged employee, of proving his guilt, should be on the company. They ought to start off, and our man should not be considered to be guilty until he has been proven so. He shouldn't have to reply to a case which has not yet been made, and Mr. Arbitrator, unless the company goes first, we will walk out of the hearing."

The company said, "Mr. Arbitrator, that goes both ways. Unless the union goes first, we will walk out of the hearing."

At this point I would have loved to have known what in the world some of you would have done. The only thing I could think of to do was to go first myself!

But I do think we are not taking the advantage we could of the opportunity to learn from one another. I suggest, as one thing that we might consider, some way of making available to all of us the individual experience which each of us has, so that we can, not only learn from the process, but contribute what we have learned.

I think that we also have a responsibility—which we have discussed but have not done much about—in regard to this matter of new arbitrators. More arbitrators are needed, more good arbitrators are needed, than there are. People are coming into the profession, and should. What can we do to help them? What can we do to help the men who have not yet had the experience to gain general acceptance, or to qualify for membership in the Academy? What can we do? I believe it is part of our responsibility to the country to make our experience—for what it is worth—available, not only to one another, but to those who really need it, the men who are coming in and who have to learn.

Ultimately we know that we learn our job only by doing it, or primarily by doing it—by trial and error. But learning by making mistakes means that we are learning completely at the expense of management and labor. I do think that we might possibly help management and labor by making our experience available in some way—and I am talking vaguely, because I am trying to think this thing out—in some way to the new men who are arbitrating, not just students in college who are interested in labor relations, but the men who actually need the experience and are starting to get it.

We are not an educational institution ourselves, in the sense of being set up to conduct courses, but I am not sure that there would not be in Chicago, in Cornell, in Berkeley or in various of the other educational institutions, an interest in courses in arbitration for practicing arbitrators, which we might help to organize and with which we might cooperate.

I know the Practicing Law Institute is doing that sort of thing for the benefit of practitioners before arbitrators, and the experience, so far, I think, indicates that it is a rewarding effort.

Finally—and now I am going to get awfully vague and awfully tentative—I am wondering whether we are fulfilling our functions as an organization, when we confine ourselves, as so far we have, merely to the examination of our own professional problems.

We have no right, of course, to claim that we have ultimate wisdom in the field of labor-management relations. It is obvious that with regard to any specific situation, the companies and the unions know more about their problems than we ever will, and they know more about their processes and objectives than we ever will, and any effort by this Academy to set itself up as an instructor of management and labor would, obviously, be laughable.

Yet, in this room, we do have experience which neither management nor labor has. We have among ourselves, for what it is worth, the unique experience of having sat through thousands of cases from the impartial point of view, of having seen both management's side and labor's side, and of having watched in hundreds of different situations the successes which management and labor have achieved, their failures, and their problems.

We have a perspective and a point of view which, for what it is worth, is different, is unique, and I think may be of value.

Are we making our experience as arbitrators available, as we should, to the country, to management, and to labor?

Are we formally called on, as an organization, for our advice or comments on problems touching management-labor relations—touching the very problems which we spend days examining in their most specific details?

Were we called upon, as a matter of fact, when something so vital to the process as the Uniform Arbitration Act was initiated and discussed in its early stages? Did anybody think it natural to turn to the National Academy of Arbitrators at that point for our views and comments?

Do we know, have we studied, and have we cared as an organization, what effect our activities, the endless arbitration of grievances, are having on the collective bargaining process in this country?

Have we fulfilled our responsibility as an organization if we neglect consideration of that effect?

Is our objective merely to decide cases, to be available to help in the decision of cases? Or must we not pay attention in our thinking and discussion to the larger picture?

Do we mean what we say so often, that the objective of an arbitrator should be to put himself out of a job ultimately, to aid the parties, as best we can, to cease using us as a crutch, and to measure up to the responsibility of solving their problems themselves, as they ought to be solved?

Arbitration is an important part of the democratic process, and we are uniquely privileged in functioning professionally in that area, but the democratic process itself, ultimately, in its highest form, is not running to a judge, nor running to somebody else to decide your problems for you. It is the much harder thing of hammering out agreements, of measuring up to the difficult job of relating a contract to life yourselves.

Are we doing anything about the situations—and there are so many of them—where there are endless grievances, case dockets with 500, 1000, 1500 cases awaiting arbitration, because arbitration has become routine, and it is so much easier to come to us than to take the heat yourself, as a union leader or a company representative, of stepping in and solving those questions?

Are we just swimming with the current, or are we doing what we can to foster the process of agreement as opposed to the process of deciding?

Now, in so far as we raise our sights, we run into dangerous territory. We have been cautious—and I think that looking carefully at the problem is wise—cautious as an organization in taking positions on public issues involving management and labor.

It is not only a matter, I hope, of personal protection. The usefulness of arbitrators can be prejudiced if they take too clear positions on certain issues. But have we been too cautious? Have we been too afraid? Have we been too willing just to drift and get the jobs and decide the cases and not make our experience and our points of view— our varied points of view—on the questions facing management and labor in this country available to management and labor and the country?

I suggest that, in thinking of this sort of thing, we look before we leap, but I suggest also, that an organization which merely sits forever examining its own navel will sooner or later shrivel up; that the only way an organization can grow is always to look beyond what it is doing now; and that the real measure of an organization is not only its past accomplishments and its present activities, but its aspirations.

CHAPTER VIII

THE EFFECTUATION OF ARBITRATION BY COLLECTIVE BARGAINING*

GEORGE W. TAYLOR
Wharton School, University of Pennsylvania

The collective bargaining orientation of the labor movement in the United States is in marked contrast to other democratic countries where, to a far greater degree than here, organized labor emphasizes political methods and objectives. And, nowhere as in the United States is the voluntary arbitration of employee grievances so extensively utilized by unions and managements.

These institutions—collective bargaining and arbitration—have been and are being developed as a part of a uniquely American program of industrial self-government. A union and a management work out the arrangements for their joint dealings which seem to be best adapted to their particular needs. Policies and practices as respects both collective bargaining and arbitration vary, therefore, "all over the lot." Nor is this a weakness. It provides strength to our way of living and working together.

However, it is not easy to generalize about, or neatly to define policies and practices which are so diverse. Maybe that is one reason why empirical studies typify industrial relations research. Without any disparagement of them, it can be observed that definitive studies of arbitration, particularly of its functions and of its connection with collective bargaining, have yet to be made. Difficulties in the way of making such definitive analyses were underlined, or so it seemed to me, by the discussion of "Management's Reserved Rights," at last year's meeting of this Academy.[1] The union representative there claimed far broader collective bargaining rights of participation in decision-making than

---

* Dinner Address.

[1] EDITOR'S NOTE: See *Management Rights and the Arbitration Process* (Washington, BNA Incorporated, 1956), Chapter VIII.

151

the management representative was willing to concede. In other words, there were some basic conceptual differences about the very nature of collective bargaining. Such attempts at generalization, however, often generate far greater differences than exist in actual practice where a working arrangement has evolved. Nevertheless, the divergent expressions would be, one might think, a matter of considerable interest, if not concern, to the members of this Academy. What is the significance to those interested in arbitration of the sharp conceptual differences about the nature of collective bargaining?

In considering this question, it seems necessary to start with a clear recognition that voluntary labor arbitration is concomitant, or perhaps subordinate, to collective bargaining. But, what—just what is the relationship? Sometimes it is said that a submission to arbitration represents (1) a final conclusion of negotiators that collective bargaining has failed, i.e., no agreement is possible and (2) mutual acceptance of a procedure to provide for an imposed answer by a third person. There are many situations in which the submission is so conceived but this is far from universal. Who would say that cases go to arbitration only after a failure of assiduous and purposeful bargaining? The really pertinent facts in a case are occasionally produced for the first time at an arbitration hearing and, not infrequently, only then does the real issue emerge. The best arguments may be "saved for the hearing" for maximum tactical effect. Should arbitrators simply refer issues "back to the parties" in such cases to insure the "proper" use of collective bargaining? There is much to be said for this kind of action. But, that would not be at all what some parties expect or want. Much could also be said about whether an imposed decision is really contemplated by either party except in the expectation that the "other party" will be "imposed upon." But, the matter about the degree of emphasis upon gaining a meeting of minds in arbitration has already been extensively discussed and need not be considered here.

The fact of the matter is that arbitration reflects the nature of each joint relationship of which it is a part. Arm's length bargaining begets arm's length arbitration. Highly cooperative relationships tend to produce a problem-solving concept of arbitration. How could it be otherwise? There is, however, an important common denominator. To have continuing usefulness, the arbitration procedure must be so developed as to be preferable to strikes and lockouts. The kind of arbitration that will meet this criterion is, itself, a bargainable subject. As experience is gained, changes in the arbitration arrangements are made in collective bargaining. Such adjustments have been particularly marked in the past several years. This, it seems to me, is a sign of vitality and strengthens arbitration.

The current proposal for a Uniform Arbitration Act might well be considered against this background. It is pertinent to inquire: will such legislation assist or hinder unions and managements in working out their own particular arbitration arrangements? To be sure, there are frustrations, and even inequities, created by a refusal to arbitrate when clearly required by an agreement, or by some farfetched challenges to an arbitrator's jurisdiction, or by an arbitrary refusal to carry out an arbitrator's award. These actions constitute, in reality, a breakdown of collective bargaining. Of this breakdown, the failure of arbitration is but a symptom. I am skeptical about the usefulness of the proposed legislation in meeting the real problem in the situations referred to. It takes the will of the parties—their agreement—to make arbitration work in a collective bargaining system. After all, it is *voluntary* arbitration which we are talking about and that means mutual acceptability.

There are some risks, moreover, that legislation could induce the modification of established arbitration clauses or conceivably even their elimination. In this connection, it will be recalled that one result of Section 301 of the Taft-Hartley Act, which spells out a litigation route for alleged labor agreement violations, was a new clause in the coal industry agreement under which miners obligated themselves to work only when they were "able and willing" to do so. Immunity against possible damage suits arising out of wildcat strikes was easily gained by deleting the no-strike clause. An arbitration clause, and the closely associated no-strike clause, is not mandatory in labor agreements.

This kind of extreme reaction is doubtless not a matter of great present concern. More careful thought might be given, however, to the risk that modifications of established arbitration clauses might be induced by a Uniform Arbitration Act.[2] Even now, when the risks of arbitration are generally preferred to the risks of work stoppages, there are some notable exceptions. In a number of agreements, grievances on particular subjects are excluded from an arbitrator's jurisdic-

---

[2] EDITOR'S NOTE: For text of this proposed act see Appendix B of this volume.

tion and specifically made subject to ultimate settlement by work stoppage. Piece-rate disputes in some branches of the needle trades and work standards grievances in many parts of the automobile industry are notable examples. In a sense, arbitration is in competition with the strike or lockout as alternate processes of grievance settlement. If the objective is constructively to develop arbitration, legislation should not be merely punitive for that could affect the competitive balance. Certainly no one wants to require, by legislation, a neat, orderly arbitration procedure which will make arbitration itself less acceptable. I am not at all asserting that this would inevitably happen under the Uniform Act as it is now proposed. I am suggesting an important criterion for appraising that proposal.

I ask your indulgence to make one other comment about the proposed legislation. There are joint relationships—many of them—where the problems of the arbitrator's jurisdiction have been rather well worked out and where the finality of an arbitrator's decision has been firmly established. Concern has been expressed in those quarters that any new emphasis upon court review might be disruptive because of the possibility that an additional procedural step can be interpreted as making a "fourth strike" available. Even the stanchest proponents of the Uniform Act would doubtless want to guard very carefully against that contingency. It is their responsibility, it seems to me, to say how this will be done.

I hold the view that voluntary arbitration will inevitably be fashioned by the collective bargaining relationship and not by legislation. In this connection, it is of more than casual interest to note the varying extent of resort to arbitration under different relationships. A steady stream of cases might indicate easy access to arbitration and a disposition of the parties to put off their negotiating responsibilities. Give-and-take negotiations are then sometimes not earnestly undertaken until an arbitration hearing is scheduled. Shortly before the hearing, the arbitrator is notified that the case is "withdrawn" either because it has been settled or is in the process of settlement. Arbitration then serves what might be termed a bogy-man function. It is hard on arbitrators, but that is how some parties seem to conceive the process.

The large volume of arbitration cases more typically occurs, however, when clauses in the basic labor agreement do not actually reflect a meeting-of-minds or when some of the conceptual differences about collective bargaining mentioned at the outset of this paper are vigorously present in practice. Vague or contradictory clauses may be accepted to avoid a strike over agreement renewal but they do not represent a real settlement. Or, for various reasons, a big subject is briefly dealt with, leaving the details to be worked out later. Unresolved fundamental differences are likely to crop up as grievance disputes. Or, each side presses through grievance settlements for ends it could not specifically achieve in contract negotiations. There are probably exceptions, but it generally follows that much arbitration is not wholly unsatisfactory arbitration. The reason is simple. The parties— or one of them—seek to use arbitration as a substitute for fundamental collective bargaining. When the shortcomings of using arbitration in this way are recognized, a permanent arbitrator has sometimes been requested, in cases submitted to him, to suggest guideposts or to "lay down some general rules," for the use of the parties in bargaining out those issues which give rise to a heavy case load. They then seek to develop what might be termed a consultative function of arbitration. Of course, this function cannot be assumed by an arbitrator in the absence of an explicit request from both parties. But, it is a thoroughly legitimate function if that is what the parties want.

I do not imply that arbitration lacks usefulness where there is a flood of cases and where attention is not given by the parties to stemming the tide. Arbitration may still be deemed preferable to work stoppages under which the legitimacy of the same kind of discharge, for example, will vary with seasonal fluctuations of the business. A sort of "traffic cop" function is assigned to arbitration when hundreds of cases arise every year. While head-on collisions may be avoided, the traffic load can get so heavy as to impress the parties with the need for devising ways and means to get it into manageable proportions. This is, of course, no responsibility of the arbitrator. Arbitration is a tool of industrial self-government for unions and companies. It should be developed by them to meet their needs.

Under some collective bargaining relationships, then, arbitration is big business. This is not at all typical. There are some—most of the joint dealings, I venture to guess—in which very few grievances ever have to be arbitrated. Collective bargaining is often carried out, over a long period of years, without a single resort to arbitration. Such a record may reflect either appeasement by the company or enervated unionism, but neither explanation seems to be very important. In more collective bargaining relationships than get into the headlines, unions and managements have worked out mutually satisfactory bases for settling their day-by-day operating problems.

The quite limited dependence upon arbitration in many, or most, situations is one indication, I would like to think, of the long-sought-for maturity in industrial relations. Lest some of you need assurance that I am not subversive of the arbitrators, let me hasten to add that arbitration still has an extremely important function to perform when such collective bargaining maturity obtains. There is, then, an awareness of the possibility that an exceptional case may arise at any time in which a difference of opinion cannot be directly resolved. At the same time, the limitations of a work stoppage are clearly recognized. In several relationships of this kind, in which I serve as "permanent" arbitrator or impartial chairman, the parties themselves talk of the "insurance function" of their arbitration clause. They say, "We carry fire insurance on our buildings which we hope never to collect. We also provide for arbitration to settle unresolved grievances, even though we hope never to resort to it."

I might add that under some arrangements of this type, while a very broad jurisdiction is assigned to the arbitrator, the maturity of the bargaining results in a narrower practical limitation of his authority than under any other approach. As respects the relatively few but important cases that must be arbitrated, the parties agree on as many facets as they can, submitting for decision only the unresolved parts of the issue. They want only such imposition of terms by an outsider as cannot be avoided. In critical cases, the arbitrator or impartial chairman may decide only 10 percent or 20 percent of the original total issue. Both the risk of arbitration and the role of the impartial chairman are limited. This stands in marked contrast to some other relationships where the grievance assumes bigger and bigger proportions as it moves along until the issue submitted to the arbitrator is 150 percent or 200 percent of the original grievance. The relatively long tenure of a number of so-called impartial chairmen is not so much a tribute to their arbitrating abilities as it is a reflection of the kind of arbitration which the parties have evolved.

It does seem that an understanding of labor arbitration has to be grounded upon an understanding of collective bargaining and its diverse manifestations. The marked differences in particular relationships, which have just been referred to, are pertinent. So are the conceptual differences alluded to at the outset. The genesis of these differences is interesting.

Because of its collective bargaining orientation, carrying acceptance of the private enterprise system and profit economy, our labor movement has had, it is often said, a "limited objective." Even without reference to an expansion of objectives in recent years beyond "pure and simple unionism," the collective bargaining objective has not seemed to be very limited to most employers. They just did not see how business managers could perform their functions—or how operating efficiency could be achieved—if decision-making had to be shared with union representatives or abdicated to an arbitrator. The development of union strength and the advent of legally required collective bargaining, however, meant that managements had to share decision-making as respects conditions of employment.

I have never seen "shared authority with the union" on the organizational chart of a business, and maybe this concept defies this kind of representation, but controls and directional authority are certainly involved in collective bargaining. They are variously asserted. Some union representatives actively seek a voice in making decisions which management feels must be excluded from the joint relationship. Other unions are satisfied to leave a large measure of administrative initiative to management. There are companies which apparently seek to hold the administrative initiative so firmly as to severely exclude the union from participation in decision-making. Some unions, possessing a relatively great economic power, have apparently been able, unilaterally, to exercise considerable directional authority. Within these extremes, many kinds of accommodations have been and are being worked out.

Lack of confidence in the idea that decision-making could be shared at all was one reason for widespread employer opposition to collective bargaining. Now, however, most unions express the view that there are limitations to the subject-matters which can be dealt with by collective bargaining. And, many companies have learned to live with joint decision-making in some areas. The line of demarcation is still controversial. When the Wagner Act was passed, it seemed urgent to management to limit, as far as possible, the scope of collective bargaining and to retain "management's right to manage." To this end, a particular theory of collective bargaining was advanced. It went like this: (1) in the absence of collective bargaining, management possesses exclusive directional rights; (2) through collective bargaining, management shares decision-making with the union but only as clearly and specifically expressed in the labor agreement; (3) management retains all directional rights except as so conceded. For reasons not entirely clear to me, this was frequently called "the common law theory of collective bargaining."

As an illustration of the theory in practice—perhaps an extreme example—consider the more or less standard clause in which management agrees that any discipline imposed must be "for cause." It was reasoned that management ceded but one part of its disciplinary power—the right to make capricious discharges, or those without any cause. If there was a cause for discipline, then the nature and degree of the discipline imposed would be solely a matter of management decision. Only if there was no cause at all would a right for reinstatement accrue to the employee.

The theory was widely asserted, but it was not widely effectuated. Employees could and did strike if they believed the discipline in a case was inequitable, even though there was some cause for its imposition. In order to avoid or to terminate a work stoppage, management frequently negotiated with the union about the equity of the discipline imposed and often modified an action taken. In other words, the practice of collective bargaining did not conform to the so-called common-law theory.

The extensive use of strikes to settle grievances, however, was soon found detrimental to everybody concerned. The no-strike no-lockout clause and the related arbitration clause came into being. Reassertion of the previously mentioned concept of collective bargaining was again possible. At least, the ban on strikes during the term of the agreement tended to remove one inhibition. Whether or not the particular concept of collective bargaining just noted should prevail emerged as a problem of arbitration. If the unions and the employees had accepted the concept to a greater extent than they did, the development of arbitration would have been a rather simple undertaking and its role would have been minor.

Not very long ago, I saw an arbitrator's decision in a discharge case which squarely upheld the retained rights doctrine of the common law approach. The arbitrator said he merely gave a strict interpretation of the agreement; it seemed to me he "added" a great deal in imposing a theory of collective bargaining. I refer to the "addition" because the issue about what collective bargaining entails has changed its form owing to that more or less standard clause which prohibits an arbitrator from "changing, modifying, or adding to" the expressed terms of an agreement. It is sometimes argued, in effect, that the inclusion of this clause in a labor agreement constitutes an adoption of the common law theory of collective bargaining. There is no problem at all if there really is a mutual agreement to this effect but, on such an important point, more than inference dialectics seems called for. One obstacle to the clarification of the parties' intent in agreeing to the clause under discussion is that, under a few relationships, a "strict" construction may help, or has helped, either party in a particular case. At any event, positions respecting the application of this clause have been known to shift.

A brief reference to how the clause in question first came into being may be of some interest. Whenever arbitration was evaluated as a substitute for strikes over grievances, in the 1920's, the jurisdiction of the arbitrator was sure to receive careful consideration. It was usually agreed very quickly that the arbitrator was not a "substitute" for collective bargaining and so he could not change or modify what the parties had clearly agreed to, even if an error had admittedly been made. But, what about the great number of terms and conditions of employment which are not covered by the agreement? They were, it was generally concluded, neither bargainable nor arbitrable during the agreement term.[3] To effect this understanding, the arbitrator was denied the right to "add to" the labor agreement. In other words, an issue over whether or not new subjects were to be encompassed by collective bargaining could be raised only in contract negotiations. The scope of the agreement could not be extended by the arbitrator or, indeed, was not a bargainable issue during the agreement term. Certain actions of the N.L.R.B., such as in the precedent-making Allied Mills and Tidewater Oil cases, are of a contrary nature. These deci-

---

[3] A very difficult subsidiary problem arose. Should the past practices as respects excluded matters be continued during the term of the agreement except as changed in negotiations? Or, did management retain the right unilaterally to change such practices? These questions were variously answered.

sions seemingly support the negotiability of excluded subjects at any time during the term of an agreement.

It now appears that in early bargaining on the arbitrator's jurisdiction, the parties would have more clearly expressed their intent had they denied an arbitrator the right to "add terms to the labor agreement." At that time, however, any notion that the arbitrator could perform his function without ever adding any substance to those clauses which were a part of the agreement would have seemed quite far-fetched. The parties were seeking an acceptable substitute for the strike and would not have seriously thought that end could be achieved by an agreed-upon adoption of the so-called common law theory of collective bargaining. The manner in which that clause has been "interpreted" in recent times does make one wonder about whether clauses do have clear and unmistakable meanings.

It has been my purpose to touch upon some of the basic questions which must be grappled with in arriving at a better understanding of labor arbitration. I recognize that some controversial matters have been touched upon. I hope we have not become so conformist as to make them unmentionable.

One conclusion stands out—arbitrators have a difficult role. Working in a new field, where basic concepts are often cloudy and controversial, an arbitrator's usefulness is, nevertheless, dependent upon his mutual acceptability to unions and to companies. All the more significant, then, is the fact that there are arbitrators in number who are regularly called upon by unions and management to assume certain assigned responsibilities in the joint relationship. Much of the credit goes, I think, to the unions and to the managements who persist in their endeavors to perfect collective bargaining and arbitration. It has been said that America has a genius for government. That extends, it seems to me, to the industrial self-government which is slowly but surely being developed under collective bargaining. The record of achievement gives the lie, I submit, to that doctrine which is based on the premise that the differences between employers and employees are irreconcilable.

Chapter IX

THE JOHN DEERE-UAW PERMANENT ARBITRATION SYSTEM

Harold W. Davey
Professor of Economics
Iowa State College

1. Early History

Permanent arbitration of the judicial type with a single umpire has been an integral part of contract administration in the John Deere chain of farm equipment companies since 1946. The United Automobile, Aircraft and Agricultural Implement Workers of America, AFL-CIO, is the Union concerned.[1]

This chapter describes and evaluates the permanent arbitration system of John Deere and UAW at eight of the company's plants in Iowa and Illinois.[2] Although Deere has seven other factories,[3] the eight

---

[1] Formerly, the Farm Equipment and Metal Workers (Ind.) held bargaining rights at the Dubuque plant and the Deere Planter Works, now under contract with UAW.

[2] The eight plants with their products and approximate number of employees in UAW bargaining units are set forth below:

John Deere Des Moines Works, Des Moines, Iowa, employs approximately 1300 production and maintenance employees represented by UAW. The IAM represents employees in the machine shop and tool room. The Des Moines plant makes corn and cotton pickers, cotton harvesters, row-crop and tool-bar cultivators, and sulky rakes. This plant began operations in 1948.

John Deere Dubuque Tractor Works, Dubuque, Iowa, employs approximately 1,380 in the production and maintenance unit. Farm tractors and stationary engines are made at Dubuque. This is also a new plant which began operations in 1947. The first contract was with FE, but the employees switched to UAW in 1948.

John Deere Ottumwa Works, Ottumwa, Iowa, employs approximately 946 in the production and maintenance unit. Ottumwa products include side-delivery rakes, automatic pickup hay balers, forage choppers, ensilage harvesters, and blowers.

John Deere Waterloo Tractor Works, Waterloo, Iowa, is the largest plant in the chain. The Waterloo plant makes farm tractors and employs aproximately 5,000 in the production and maintenance unit. (Footnote continued bottom of page 162)

plants bargaining with UAW locals form the heart of the company's manufacturing operations.

John Deere ranks second to International Harvester in the farm equipment field. Deere produces a full line of tractors and agricultural implements. Unlike Harvester, Deere has always confined its operations exclusively to farm equipment. However, in 1954 Deere began operating a urea and anhydrous ammonia plant at Pryor, Oklahoma. This new plant bargains with the Oil, Chemical and Atomic Workers Union and has an ad hoc arbitration system at the present time.

Deere and UAW negotiated their first contracts in 1943. These early contracts did not provide for arbitration. The 1945 contracts introduced grievance arbitration for the first time on an ad hoc basis. The switch to permanent arbitration was made by contract amendment in 1946, applying at that time to five of the eight plants covered in the present analysis.[4]

From the inception of the permanent arbitrator system, both the company and the union have agreed on the type of arbitration they want. Both parties firmly support judicial arbitration. Neither party wishes the permanent arbitrator to act as a mediator at any time. Cases arriving at arbitration are jointly presumed to be incapable of informal

---

John Deere Harvester Works, East Moline, Illinois, makes combines, mowers, windrowers and pickups. Approximately 2,010 employees comprise the production and maintenance unit at the Harvester plant.

John Deere Spreader Works, East Moline, Illinois, employs approximately 570 in the "p and m" unit. The Spreader plant makes manure spreaders and loaders, corn shellers, hammer mills, portable elevators, blades, loaders, bulldozers, and scoops.

John Deere Malleable Works, East Moline, Illinois, is a foundry making malleable iron and pearlitic malleable iron castings for other Deere plants. The UAW bargaining unit at Malleable includes approximately 524 employees.

John Deere Planter Works, Moline, Illinois, makes disk harrows, corn planters, and cotton planters. UAW defeated FE in a schism election in 1954. The bargaining unit includes approximately 460 employees.

[3] The non-UAW plants in addition to the Oklahoma area plant include the Vermillion Works at Hoopeston, Illinois; the Van Brunt Works at Horicon, Wisconsin; the Killefer Works at Los Angeles, California; the Plow Works and the Wagon Works in Moline, Illinois; and the Welland Works in Welland, Ontario, Canada.

[4] The five plants originally covered included the Iowa plants at Ottumwa and Waterloo and the three East Moline, Illinois, plants. See note 2 *supra*. The Des Moines plant was covered from the time it began operations in 1948. Dubuque was included when UAW took over from FE in 1948. The Planter Works became the eighth plant in the system when UAW defeated FE in 1954.

resolution. The arbitrator is expected to make a clear-cut decision based on interpretation and application of contract language.

The permanent arbitrator's authority and jurisdiction have always been carefully defined. No contract has ever provided for unlimited arbitration. However, there has been some variation in the scope of the arbitrator's jurisdiction. In early contracts, the arbitrator had authority to rule on issues over the propriety of piece rates and rates on new hourly or incentive jobs. The permanent arbitrator's authority was made congruent with a comprehensive no strike-no lockout clause in these contracts.

In the 1950-55 contracts, however, the arbitrator was specifically precluded from ruling on piece rates and rates on new jobs. In the 1955-1958 contracts, the arbitrator's authority is expanded to cover certain incentive grievances alleging improper standards. However, his new authority is strictly circumscribed as follows:

> The jurisdiction of the Arbitrator is specifically limited and restricted to the sole determination of the following questions:
> 1. Was there a clerical error in the computation of the Incentive Standard, or
> 2. Was there a change in design, equipment, material specifications or manufacturing methods, and/or
> 3. If there was a change in design, equipment, material specifications or manufacturing methods, what elements were changed?

In addition to the foregoing narrow questions, the arbitrator can also hear grievances on incentive standards which question whether the standard was established in conformance with the Standard Hour Incentive Plan or which raise the question "of the adequacy or inadequacy of the standard". In the first year under the 1955-1958 contracts, no disputes have reached arbitration under these headings.

The 1955-1958 contracts specifically exclude four categories of grievances from the arbitrator's jurisdiction. These same categories are not covered by the contracts' no strike-no lockout clauses. The four excluded categories are: 1) changes in existing incentive standards, except for disputes of the type just described, 2) establishment of new incentive standards, 3) rate ranges for new hourly paid job classifications, and 4) occupational rates for new incentive work job classifications.

Deere-UAW contracts have always combined an open grievance procedure with a tightly defined arbitration step. The earlier steps in grievance machinery admit all grievances, whether or not they relate to matters covered by contract. However, the arbitration step is limited to disputes concerning the interpretation or application of contract provisions.

The record of Deere and UAW on tenure of permanent arbitrators is excellent. Since permanent arbitration was first introduced in 1946, the parties have been served by only three permanent arbitrators. Professor Charles Updegraff served as sole arbitrator from August, 1946 until 1950. Five year contracts were negotiated at all plants in 1950. From December, 1950 until March, 1952 the case load was handled by several arbitrators selected on an ad hoc basis utilizing the services of the Federal Mediation and Conciliation Service. Eleven different arbitrators handled cases on an ad hoc basis during this period. Most of the cases were heard by Updegraff, Kelliher, and the present arbitrator. The other eight arbitrators heard only one or two cases each. In March, 1952, Peter Kelliher was named as permanent arbitrator under the 1950-1955 contracts. Kelliher served from March until July, 1952.

Effective August 15, 1952, I was named as permanent arbitrator and have served in that capacity up to the present time.

2. Operations of the Umpire System

A. Grievance Procedure

Deere and UAW employ a five-step grievance procedure in all plants. This procedure is substantially the same for all contracts and is carefully articulated.

Unless otherwise noted, all direct contract quotations are taken from one of the 1955-1958 contracts. Although each plant and local union have their own contract, negotiations for the eight plants are conducted simultaneously in Moline, Illinois. The resultant contracts are substantially uniform on most important subject matter areas.

Step A is between the aggrieved employee, his departmental steward and his immediate foreman. The grievance is to be reduced to writing and signed by the employee and his steward at this first step.

The written grievance must be presented to the employee's foreman "within five (5) working days from the date on which the act or condition complained of last occurred." The foreman's answer must be given within one (1) working day following receipt of the written grievance. As might be expected, many grievances are discussed informally with the foreman either by the individual employee or his steward without being reduced to writing. Many are settled at this stage.

If the foreman's answer at Step A is deemed unsatisfactory, the appeal to Step B must be filed within three (3) working days after receipt. Otherwise the grievance is deemed settled on the basis of the foreman's written answer.

The second step involves the divisional steward and the plant's director of industrial relations. The latter must answer in writing to the divisional steward and the aggrieved employee "as soon as possible" and in any event within four (4) working days after receiving the grievance.

General grievances are entered at Step B. A general grievance is defined by contract as one affecting all employees in the bargaining unit or one involving a matter outside the jurisdiction of the departmental foreman.

The written answer of the director of industrial relations will settle the grievance unless appealed to Step C at the second regular shop committee meeting following his answer in Step B.

The third step (Step C) involves the local union shop committee and the plant manager or other representative designated by him. However, the contracts provide that one of the company representatives shall not have participated in any previous step.

Company representatives and the union shop committee have regular weekly meetings on grievances appealed from Step B. The shop committee must furnish in writing the day before the weekly grievance meeting a list of all grievances to be discussed at this meeting, together with a brief statement of the shop committee's position on each grievance.

If a grievance is not settled informally at Step C, the director of industrial relations must give his written answer not later than three (3) working days following the regular weekly meeting at which discussion of the particular grievance was concluded. If the union is not satisfied with the company's Step C answer, the grievance must be appealed to Step D within ten (10) working days from the date of said answer.

Discipline grievances enter the procedure at Step C. The contracts provide a special procedure for handling all discipline cases, including a disciplinary action hearing in the plant, following which the actual decision as to whether to discipline is made. This procedure serves in lieu of Steps A and B on other types of grievances. A discipline grievance must be filed within three (3) working days following the disciplinary action hearing.

Step D, the step immediately prior to arbitration, involves the local union president, chairman of the shop committee, and an international union representative meeting with designated company representatives. Again, at least one of the company's representatives shall not have participated in any previous step. The union's international representative makes his first appearance at the Step D meeting.

As in prior steps, the time limits for appeal and answer are carefully spelled out in the contracts. The present 1955-1958 contracts also contain new language designed to insure that the nature of each party's position will be more precisely spelled out in the event the grievance should go to arbitration.

Deere and UAW have never used submission agreements. The issue has heretofore been framed by the grievance and the company's answer. Where the parties came to arbitration in disagreement as to the framing of the issue, the arbitrator's first duty was to formulate the issue as it appeared to him from argument of the parties after noting the progress of the grievance in pre-arbitration steps.

Under the current contracts, the union in its appeal to Step D is required to ". . . set out the alleged contract violation, if any, the Section or Sections of the contract violated, and the specific relief sought thereunder." If a dispute should arise as to whether the union's appeal conforms to the foregoing requirements, the contract provides that the appeal may be amended to conform at the Step D hearing.

If the union refuses to amend its appeal and the company still considers the appeal defective, the issue is arbitrable as to whether the written appeal conforms if the case is carried to Step E. To date, no issues have arisen in arbitration over these new requirements.

The union's appeal to Step D must be filed within ten (10) days after receiving the company's Step C answer. The written Step D appeal must be presented at least three (3) workiug days prior to the Step D meeting at which it is to be discussed and such meeting must be held within fifteen (15) days after receipt of the company's Step C answer.

Any grievance submitted to Step D must be answered in writing within ten (10) working days following the meeting at which discussion of the grievance was concluded. If the grievance is denied or remains unsettled, the company's answer shall state that ". . . the contract provisions cited by the union are not violated or that other contract provisions govern the subject matter of the grievance or that no contract provision is involved in the grievance or any combination of these positions."

Any grievance not appealed to Step E within fifteen (15) working days from the date of the company's written answer in Step D is deemed settled on the basis of the company's answer.

Step E, the arbitration step, is strictly limited to grievances involving the interpretation and application of contract provisions. Furthermore, as already noted, four types of contract issues are specifically excluded from the arbitrator's jurisdiction under the 1955-1958 agreements pursuant to the parties' joint thinking that arbitration should be limited to issues amenable to judicial treatment.

Such disputes are excluded from the coverage of the no-strike, no-lockout clause and may become the basis for a legal strike during the life of the contract. Four of the eight plants were on strike for over four months in 1956 over a dispute on changed incentive standards. The permanent arbitrator took no part in this dispute in keeping with the joint desire of the parties to exclude such matters from arbitration.

At the time the union appeals a grievance to arbitration, it may, if it wishes, amend the language of its Step D appeal ". . . to cite additional or substitute contract provisions allegedly violated and to amend the relief sought." If the union takes advantage of this option, the contract gives the company an additional five days to amend its own Step D answer.

The Step D appeal and answer, or as amended in Step E, constitute the issue for determination by the arbitrator. The new language on Step D and Step E as described is designed to improve the framing of the issue for arbitration and to serve in lieu of the formal submission agreement.

The present arbitrator has a strong personal preference for submission agreements. It is curious that parties devoted to the judicial type of arbitration do not employ this familiar device for framing issues in arbitration.

The current 1955-1958 contracts involve a change in practice on requesting a hearing date from the arbitrator. The former contracts involved a "joint request" to the arbitrator within five (5) days following the filing of the Step E appeal. However, the new contracts provide that ". . . either the company or the union shall submit a request to the arbitrator that he set a date for a hearing on the disputed issue."

This change in practice on arbitrator notification resulted from a union demand in the 1955 negotiations, apparently motivated by the practice of some of the plants of refusing to join in request for arbitration on issues that management felt were not arbitrable. Deere at first resisted and then agreed to abandoning joint referral. Apparently, the *quid pro quo* for the change in referral procedure was the revision of the Step D appeal language described above.

Contract language on grievance and arbitration procedure is notable for its clarity of expression and lack of ambiguity. No disputes have arisen during my tenure over its interpretation or application.

B. Arbitration Procedures

The nature and limits of the arbitrator's authority are carefully defined. He is empowered to determine the relevancy of the evidence presented and his decision shall be "final and binding" upon the parties. Standard language is employed to make clear that the arbitrator shall have no power to "alter, change, detract from or add to" the provisions of the contract.

Not more than three grievances covering different subject matters may be heard at any one arbitration hearing. Unlike many contracts, the Deere-UAW contracts do not impose limits upon the arbitrator for handing down his decisions. However, the great majority of decisions reach the parties within two to four weeks after the cases are heard.

Many cases appealed to Step E are not actually arbitrated. If the union is not satisfied with the company's Step D answer, the grievance is usually appealed to Step E in order to "save" it in terms of the contract's time limits. However, the union has a reasonably effective screening procedure that serves to eliminate a great many cases. The screening is now done at a two-day meeting held each month attended by local shop committee chairmen for the eight plants and international representatives servicing the eight locals.

The arbitrator has no precise information as to what percentage of cases are screened out at these monthly meetings. My impression is that the number eliminated at this stage is considerable. Occasionally, a local union may carry a case to arbitration on its own against the recommendation that it be dropped.

Cases appealed to Step E and not screened out at the monthly meeting are set down for hearing. However, not all of these are actually heard. Not infrequently the international representative assigned to present the case in arbitration will drop cases after consultation with local union officials just prior to the hearing.

In recent months, there have been a number of cases withdrawn or settled after the hearing has actually begun. In June, 1956, two days of hearing were scheduled at Waterloo for seven cases. One case was heard on the morning of the first day, followed by a long lunch hour during which the parties disposed of five of the remaining six disputes. There appears to be little doubt that the parties are intensifying their efforts to reduce still further the number of cases actually going to arbitration.

The company has never objected formally to withdrawal of cases by the union at the last minute. However, company representatives charged with the task of preparing for arbitration have expressed annoyance at having cases dropped by the union just prior to the actual hearing. Their argument is that they have to prepare on the assumption that the union will press all cases assigned for hearing at a particular session, only to find that the union is dropping several.

Company screening procedures are informal. They hinge upon a tangible yet flexible relationship between local plant management and industrial relations staff personnel of Deere & Company in Moline. Each of the eight plants is a separate operating entity. The local director of industrial relations has authority to proceed as he sees fit. However, my impression is that close liaison is maintained between local and central office industrial relations personnel.

Industrial relations directors of the eight plants meet at least once a month with Deere & Company industrial relations personnel in Moline to confer on common problems. Incentives for uniform contract interpretation and application in all eight plans operate upon management as well as upon the union.

The company's decision as to whether to arbitrate or settle a grievance appears to be conclusively determined in most instances by the time of the Step D meeting. However, there have been cases in which the company has granted grievances between the time of the Step D answer and the arbitration hearing.

In recent months, the Union in particular is showing interest in more thorough screening of grievances. The suggestion has been made that both parties write up in some detail a justification of their positions prior to the Step D meeting. If this were done, it might serve to wash out more cases at the Step D level and would furnish a more substantial basis for action at the Union's official monthly screening session. Furthermore, such Step D write-ups could serve as pre-hearing briefs on those cases going to arbitration.

The contracts do not specify at what stage in the procedure the introduction of new evidence is to be foreclosed. In practice, it is rare for either party to introduce new evidence or testimony at the arbitration step unless it is "fresh" evidence that has come to light since the Step D meeting.

There have been a few occasions where one party or the other has attempted to "spring" new evidence or introduce a surprise witness at the arbitration hearing. In such cases, where the objecting party can show that the evidence could have been presented earlier in the grievance procedure, its tardy introduction for strategic reasons is likely to boomerang.

On this matter, as on many other procedural questions, both parties are reasonable and flexible. The great majority of cases are heard on their merits, even where one party or the other might stand to gain by insisting on a procedural technicality. Once in arbitration, however, no new evidence may be introduced after a party has completed presentation of its direct case. Use of rebuttal witnesses is strictly limited to rebuttal.

Grievances appealed to arbitration are heard in the order of their referral to the arbitrator as a general rule. An exception to this policy is occasionally made on discipline cases. These are always heard as promptly as possible. The arbitrator retains the initiative in setting hearing dates.

The arbitrator has no assistance other than secretarial. All cases are heard personally by the arbitrator who takes his own hearing notes on most cases. In a minority of cases, a court reporter is employed to take a verbatim record of the proceedings. The arbitrator has encouraged the parties to obtain a court reporter when it is anticipated that the case will involve complex technical questions or possible conflicts in testimony requiring determinations as to credibility.

Case presentation follows the same general pattern in all plants. Both parties make brief opening statements setting forth their contentions as to the grievance at issue and what they expect to prove. The Union then presents its direct case through witnesses and exhibits, with the Company cross-examning.

Objections as to materiality or relevancy of testimony or evidence are occasionally made. However, the rules of evidence are not followed. Seldom has either party pressed the arbitrator for an on-the-spot ruling as to admissibility. The contracts permit considerable freedom in presentation. All provide that "either party shall be entitled to present its claims to the Arbitrator in such manner as the party may desire, provided that the Arbitrator may determine the relevancy of the evidence presented."

The Company's direct case is put in following the Union's presentation, with the Union exercising cross examination privileges. An opportunity is then afforded each party for rebuttal testimony or evidence. The Union then presents its summation and final argument, followed by the Company. In only one case in five years have post-hearing briefs been submitted. In all other cases, the record was closed at the completion of oral argument.

Conduct of hearings is greatly facilitated in the Deere-UAW relationship by the fact that representatives of both parties are experienced and knowledgeable in case presentation. In my five years' experience, only two cases have required more than one day's hearing time. Frequently, two or three cases are presented in a single day's hearing.

Both the Company and the Union maintain centralized control at the arbitration stage. The management case is presented in all eight plants by an attorney from the central industrial relations staff of Deere & Company in Moline. The Union case is always presented by an international representative rather than by local union personnel. The quality of presentation on both sides is generally excellent.

The centralized management presentation appears to have been instituted in response to a prior centralization on the Union side. Early in my tenure as arbitrator, the industrial relations directors for the four Iowa plants presented their own cases whereas the Illinois plants had their cases presented by an attorney for Deere & Company. However, for the past three years all management presentations have been made by a staff attorney for Deere & Company specializing in industrial relations.

Orderly informality is characteristic of most hearings. Little time is wasted in procedural arguments or extensive digressions from the point at issue. Duplicatory testimony is usually avoided. The average case takes about two to three hours to present.

The basic hearing pattern as described above has not changed during my tenure. From an arbitrator's standpoint, there is little to criticize. However, it would be inaccurate to conclude that there is no room for improvement.

In November, 1954 the writer met with Company and Union representatives to discuss techniques for shortening case presentations without loss of clarity. The conference was prompted by a common awareness that hearings had been tending to lengthen out unnecessarily. An informal understanding was reached on a number of points with beneficial results.

Greater use is now being made of informal stipulations as to facts. This saves a great deal of time. Also, the arbitrator has become less tolerant than he used to be whenever either party shows a tendency to mix argument in with direct case presentation. In recent months, hearings have run more smoothly and economically.

In keeping with my own beliefs and the desires of the parties, I have never attempted to settle a dispute during the course of a hearing, even when it seemed obvious that a particular grievance should have been granted or withdrawn. Once a case actually goes to arbitration, both parties expect the arbitrator to hear it and hand down a decision on the merits.

If during the course of a hearing the parties wish to confer informally as to a possible settlement, as occasionally happens, it is understood that the arbitrator will leave the hearing room until the conference is concluded. This prevents either the arbitrator or the parties from being embarrassed by an off-the-record discussion if the settlement fails to materialize and the dispute remains to be adjudicated.

Deere-UAW hearings have been free in my experience from "excessive legalism." [5] Motions, counter-motions, objections, and quibbling over questions of materiality and relevancy are seldom encountered. There is a minimum of procedural formalism. Participants know one another well and respect each other's abilities. Much time is saved by elimination of post-hearing briefs. Each party makes a careful summation of his position and analysis of the evidence and contract at the conclusion of the hearing. The record is then closed.

The experience, integrity and ability of the participants have facilitated the arbitrator's task of running an orderly hearing. Occasionally, tempers flare momentarily. From time to time, it has been necessary to caution an inexperienced witness about the rules of the game. In general, however, it has not been difficult to maintain a pattern of orderly informality.

One index of a sound relationship is the attitude of the parties toward social contact with the arbitrator before and after hearings. I have stressed already the importance placed by Deere and UAW on having the arbitrator function in a strictly judicial capacity. From this it might be inferred that the parties prefer the arbitrator to have no personal contact with either side outside the hearing room. Nothing could be farther from the truth.

I have always felt free to dine or "fraternize" with Union and Company representatives separately or jointly. A firm understanding exists that during any social contact neither party will discuss with the arbitrator any case that is awaiting hearing or one which has been heard but not yet decided.

This ethical understanding was abused only once early in my tenure as permanent arbitrator when I was approached with a plea for leniency on a discipline case that had not yet been heard. This contact was reported by me to representatives of both parties at the hearings on the

---

[5] See my article, "Labor Arbitration: A Current Appraisal" in Vol. 9, No. 1, *Industrial and Labor Relations Review* (Oct. 1955), pp. 85-94, where "excessive legalism" is defined to include: 1) overtechnical presentation, principally in such matters as strict adherence to the rules of evidence and rigid formality in the examination of witnesses; and 2) insistence upon prehearing and/or posthearing briefs.

case in question. The understanding stated above was articulated at that time. It was agreed that if either party ever violated this understanding the arbitrator was to report this promptly to the other party. Since then the unwritten law barring discussion of an undecided case or a case awaiting hearing has never been broken.

The contract requires that the permanent arbitrator's decision be reduced to writing and each party furnished with a signed copy thereof. Complete opinions are written on all cases and are mailed to the parties. Only two memorandum opinions have been issued during the writer's tenure as arbitrator. One of these incorporated the terms of a settlement reached by the parties during a hearing. The other involved a "directed verdict" when it developed during the hearing that the Union's case was founded on an erroneous factual premise. No awards have ever been issued without opinions in my experience. Both parties prefer a complete opinion containing a full statement of the arbitrator's reasoning in arriving at his decision.

At least three sound reasons support this joint desire for full-bodied opinions. In the first place, the great majority of disputes arriving in arbitration are bona fide cases involving basic differences of opinion as to the interpretation or application of contract provisions. A final and binding decision of such disputes under long-term contracts is of critical importance to both parties. They have a right to expect the arbitrator to accompany his awards with carefully reasoned opinions.

A second consideration is the precedential impact of awards in one plant on the other seven. Although each plant and local union have their own contract, the eight contracts are nearly uniform in all important substantive areas. Thus, where identical language is involved, a decision in one plant—while technically applicable only under the contract between that particular plant and particular local—has strong precedential value in the other seven plants with UAW contracts.

A third factor favoring complete opinions is more effective utilization of arbitration decisions in contract administration. All decisions are carefully studied by management and union representatives. They furnish a basis for training foremen and stewards in improved handling of grievances. Thorough knowledge of decisions is also imperative for both parties as preparation for contract negotiations.

Both Deere and UAW endorse the educational value of arbitration opinions. Neither objects to their publication. A considerable number of decisions by Updegraff and myself have been published, principally in BNA's LABOR ARBITRATION REPORTS.

Each plant and each local union has a complete file of all arbitration decisions arranged by subject matter. So do the international union and Deere & Company. The present arbitrator's decision files are arranged chronologically and are not indexed by subject matter.

C. Substantive Issues Brought to Arbitration

1. *The Case Load:* From August, 1952 through 1956, the arbitration case load has been relatively stable at a considerably lower level than prior to 1952. Table 1 indicates the number of decisions involving UAW plants by calendar years covering my service as permanent arbitrator since August, 1952.

TABLE 1

Year	No. of Decisions
1952 (Aug.-Dec.)	3
1953	24
1954	33
1955	23
1956	24

As used in Table 1 and as defined by both the parties and the arbitrator, a case or decision refers to any disputed issue requiring the writing of a separate opinion and award. Not infrequently, a large number of grievances involving a similar issue have been consolidated by agreement for purposes of hearing and decision. These are counted as one case, even though a much larger number of grievances are actually disposed of by the decision. Similarly, the parties may stipulate that the arbitrator's award in a particular dispute will be decisive in disposing of a number of related or companion grievances. Again, only one case or decision is counted.

The great majority of cases involve only a single disputed issue submitted for determination. However, a minority of cases may involve two or more substantive issues of interpretation or application. Again, somewhat arbitrarily, these have been counted as one decision or case.

The case load was considerably heavier during Updegraff's tenure as permanent arbitrator. He became permanent arbitrator for five plants and five locals on August 8, 1946. During the balance of 1946, Updegraff heard and decided only six cases. However, the load increased sharply in the four subsequent years as indicated in Table 2.

TABLE 2

Year	No. of Decisions
1947	35
1948	41
1949	60
1950	55

No analysis has been made of the issues involved in cases heard by Updegraff. However, it is reasonable to infer that the heavy load in 1949 and 1950 might have been due in part to the broader jurisdiction of the arbitrator over incentive pay cases than has been true since 1950. Also, prior to 1950, there was considerably more diversity in contract language from one plant to another. Case presentation had not been centralized to its present extent. Screening procedures were probably less effective than at present. Finally, a number of issues were definitely laid to rest by decisions during the earlier years.

The 1950-1955 contracts were signed in December, 1950 following a strike lasting over 100 days. A new permanent arbitrator could not be agreed upon at that time. The parties decided to operate ad hoc until a new permanent arbitrator was selected. Use of ad hoc arbitrators covered a period of appproximately fifteen months until March, 1952 when Peter Kelliher was appointed permanent arbitrator.

The ad hoc period was an active one for at least three reasons: 1) the parties were testing a number of different arbitrators; 2) the contracts, patterned after the historic General Motors-UAW five year pact, contained a great deal of new language requiring interpretation; and 3) instability and friction existed at some plants as an aftermath of the long strike.

Over 50 cases were heard on an ad hoc basis in 1951. Thirty-three decisions were handed down between January, 1952 and my appointment in August, 1952. Fourteen of these were decided by Kelliher, most if not all of them during his period as permanent arbitrator between March and July, 1952.

New three-year contracts were negotiated in the summer of 1955 running until August, 1958. These contracts contain considerable new language and involve a new incentive system for six of the eight plants. It was anticipated that new contracts with new language might well produce a flood of arbitration cases comparable to that experienced during the first fifteen months of the 1950-1955 contracts. However, the case load has continued at approximately the same level as during the latter years of the 1950-1955 agreements. According to present indications, it is probable that the recent average of two cases per month will continue.

2. *Important Substantive Issues:* Quantitatively speaking, the four most important areas of dispute are 1) incentive pay grievances, 2) seniority issues, 3) discipline cases, and 4) job classification disputes. Table 3 below gives a breakdown on the basis of the issues involved in 105 cases decided by the present arbitrator from August, 1952 through December, 1956.

TABLE 3*

Issues Involved	*Number of Cases*
"Average earnings" and other incentive pay issues	21
Seniority, involving layoff and recall and job bidding provisions	21
Discipline	16
Job classification issues	13
Overtime work assignments	8
Rate of pay or rate reduction	4
Report-in pay	3
Holiday pay	2
Vacation pay	2
Inventory pay	2
Method of payment	2
Merit rating	1
Unexcused absence	1
Foreman doing production work	1
Union membership in good standing	1
Responsibility for scrap	1
Probationary period	1
Job delay factor	1
Shift preference	1

* 105 out of 107 decisions made by the writer between August, 1952, and December, 1956, are covered. Two cases in which there was "no winner" are not included in the foregoing analysis.

TABLE 3 (Continued)

Issues Involved	Number of Cases
Arbitrability	1
Steward seniority	1
Down time	1
Total	105

From the arbitrator's standpoint, the most difficult type of case is the so-called "average earnings" dispute. Deere and UAW for many years have incorporated in their contracts language detailing certain "special cases" where an incentive worker will receive his average straight-time hourly earnings, although not engaged in direct incentive production work.

Language governing the circumstances when average earnings will be paid is now substantially uniform in all eight UAW contracts, although some variation still remains. The average earnings provisions from the current Waterloo plant contract are set forth below:

> Section 15. In the following special cases, incentive workers will be paid at an hourly rate equal to their average straight-time hourly earnings. The method of computing the incentive employee's average straight-time hourly earnings shall be as follows: Divide the sum of the money paid for all hours worked (excluding the shift differential premium and overtime penalty pay) during the two (2) previous computed work weeks by the sum of the hours worked during such period.
>
> A. When an employee experiences excess stock or hard stock which is outside the material specification, either of which makes it impossible to run an operation at machine speeds and/or feeds used in determining the incentive standard, and his Foreman having been notified, directs the employee to continue at work.
>
> B. When an employee is directed to reclaim his own work when such defective work is because of improper blueprints of operations or wrong instructions by the Foreman or other authorized instructor or to rework returned material.
>
> C. When an employee is taken away from his regular incentive work when such work is available, scheduled and can be performed, and is directed to rework another employee's defective work where circumstances prevent the rework operation from being performed by the original workman.

D. When at the request of Management an employee is temporarily taken off his regular incentive work, when such work is available, scheduled and can be performed to take care of an emergency, to do maintenance work or to do work of an experimental nature on a new or basically modified product. An "emergency" as applying to work assignments for incentive workers may be created by the development of an unforeseen situation, such as power, water, or electric trouble, heavy snowfall or rainfall, fire or explosion, that requires immediate additional help at a given location by an employee or employees from a different work classification.

E. When an employee is taken from his regular incentive work when such work is available, scheduled and can be performed, to do the work of an absent employee.

F. When at the request of Management an employee is temporarily taken from his regular incentive work, when such work is available, scheduled and can be performed, to perform work of a trial nature to try out jigs, dies, and tools for a new product, job or process; the length of time spent or number of pieces to be run on a trial basis to be pre-determined by the Foreman.

G. When an operation is performed at the direction of the Foreman on a machine other than the one on which the standard was established and it is impossible to run the operation at machine speeds and/or feeds established in the standard.

H. When an employee is required to serve as an instructor.

I. If, due to failure of equipment, an operator is unable to continue his work and is not assigned to other incentive work, but is directed by his Foreman to repair the equipment.

J. An incentive standard covering the temporary conditions enumerated in paragraphs A, B, C, and G above may be established provided the conditions so enumerated last for at least eight (8) hours.

"Scheduled" is assumed to mean that the work is or would be normally machined, made, or used, as the case may be, and is required for use in succeeding operations within the current week, provided, however, that in all circumstances in which an employee's job is in operation during his absence or when he resumes his regular job immediately following a temporary assignment, his job will be considered as scheduled.

"Such work is available and can be performed" is assumed to mean that the material is at hand, in position and condition to be worked upon and it is physically practical to perform the operations listed on regular machines. In the Foundry not "physically practical" would mean that it would not be practical to charge the material in the cupola not required by the Foundry; that the cores not be made unless required by the molding department for the current day's operation. Since the Foundry operates on a daily schedule, it is not practical to store hot metal or cores for but a very short time.

K. In all cases where a condition arises which calls for payment of average straight time hourly earnings, the employee will notify the Foreman imediately. If the Foreman authorizes the employee to perform such work, the time of starting such work and the time of stopping such work shall be shown on the back of the employee's Daily Time Report and approved by the Foreman.

Most students of incentive systems would agree in principle with the policies expressed in the foregoing language. The Deere-UAW provisions on average earnings are explicit and concrete. Notwithstanding this careful effort to articulate precisely each "special" case, these paragraphs have proved over the years to be a productive source of disputes reaching arbitration. The reason appears to be a basic conflict in philosophical approach to incentive payments that finds expression in cases under this language.

Broadly speaking, the company starts from the proposition that an incentive worker should normally be paid incentive earnings only when he is directly engaged in productive incentive work.

The union, on the other hand, starts from the proposition that an incentive worker should have a normal expectation of being able to earn incentive earnings eight hours a day, 40 hours a week.

The company is understandably interested in having the contract language strictly and narrowly interpreted. The union is understandably interested in bringing as many situations as possible under the rubric of average earnings.

The typical average earnings case is one wherein the union maintains that *all* the contract conditions of one of the "special cases" are met by a given factual situation, with the Company arguing that one or more of the conditions essential to applying the clause is not fulfilled.

The parties agree in principle that average earnings is not due unless all the conditions set forth in the particular "special case" are satisfied by the factual circumstances involved. Thus, in disputed cases, this prerequisite for payment of average earnings stands in the company's favor. In each case, the union always must assume the burden of proving that all conditions are met.

Over the years, many key words and phrases in these paragraphs have had their meaning definitely settled by arbitration decisions. For example, a key requirement in a number of the special cases is that an employee be taken from his regular incentive work when such work is "available, scheduled and can be performed." These words are defined in the contract, but their meaning has been further clarified by a series of decisions. Also, such questions as what constitutes an "absent employee", and what constitutes "work of a trial nature" or "work of an experimental nature on a new or basically modified product" have been reasonably well answered by decisions in recent years.

A continuing basis for conflict exists, however, because new or modified factual situations are constantly developing. Many grievances of this type carry considerable "heat". An adverse decision is not always well received.

Not infrequently, cases have arisen where in my judgment equitable considerations dictated payment of average earnings, but where contractually one or more of the requisite conditions had not been satisfied. Such decisions are difficult to make and even more difficult to accept. However, in terms of the judicial theory of arbitration, the contract itself must always be the touchstone. If contract requirements and equity do not appear to coincide, the contract governs.

As in most other union-management relationships, seniority is a frequent source of grievances arriving in arbitration. However, when one considers the many layoffs and recalls that have occurred within the farm equipment industry in recent years, it is surprising that seniority cases have not made up the lion's share of the arbitration load.

An important factor here is the careful drafting and administering of the seniority articles in the eight contracts. Although there are some variations from plant to plant, in each case a careful compromise is articulated between the union's interest in straight seniority and the company's interest in insuring that those remaining at work and recalled from layoff are qualified to do the available work.

At each layoff or recall the company may designate certain individuals "whose services are required under the special circumstances then existing." Employees so designated may be retained or recalled to service regardless of their seniority while the "special reasons" exist.

The upper limit of such "deviates" from natural seniority is five percent of the plant-wide seniority list. Such an option, of course, gives the company considerable flexibility in retaining key skilled employees who may be "young" in terms of natural seniority.

Deere-UAW contracts are designed to avoid multiple bumping during layoffs. Two key arbitration decisions at the Waterloo plant in 1953 (when major layoffs were in process) firmly established the proposition that a senior employee whose work has run out during a reduction in force in his department or seniority unit bumps the "youngest" man in the department or seniority unit whose work the senior man is qualified to perform. Since 1953, although there have been a considerable number of layoffs and recalls at the various plants, comparatively few cases have come to arbitration under the seniority article.

All the contracts provide for a system of vacancy posting and job bidding. The basic principle here is that the vacancy is assigned to the "senior qualified applicant." This potentially troublesome area has produced only four arbitration cases over four years. An early decision defined conclusively what was meant by a "vacancy in the working force" and no subsequent disputes on this point have arisen. Also, the principles have been firmly established that the company prescribes qualifications for the vacancy and that management's determinations as to which applicants are qualified shall not be disturbed unless shown to have been arbitrary, capricious or discriminatory. Acceptance of these principles has doubtless reduced the number of disputes in this area.

In many union-management relationships, discipline cases account for one third or more of the arbitrator's case load. In the Deere-UAW relationship during my service as permanent arbitrator, discipline cases have accounted for approximately fifteen percent of the total case load. Only 16 out of 107 cases in approximately four and one-half years have involved discipline issues.

An important factor contributing to the comparatively small number of discipline cases reaching arbitration is the special procedure provided for in the contracts for handling discipline cases in the plant. Before an employee is sent out of the plant as a result of an incident calling for disciplinary action, the contracts provide that the employee's divisional steward, if in the plant, or another union representative must be notified and have an opportunity to hear the employee's statement.

Within a "reasonable time" after the employee has been sent out of the plant, a so-called disciplinary action hearing is held at which the employee is entitled to be present and to be represented by his divisional steward. Both parties may call witnesses and introduce evidence at this hearing before the actual decision on discipline is made. Written minutes of the disciplinary action hearing must be furnished to the chairman of the shop committee.

This uniform procedure for handling discipline cases, supplemented by certain principles established in a number of key arbitrations, has reduced the number going to arbitration. Among the more important of these principles are 1) the burden of proving "good and just cause" for discipline rests on on management; 2) if cause has been proved, a penalty imposed will not be modified unless shown to have been clearly arbitrary, excessive, capricious or discriminatory in relation to the offense; 3) discipline for going outside the grievance procedure will be sustained, notwithstanding the substantive merits of the employee's complaint.

It is difficult, if not misleading, to single out one or more decisions as being of particular significance in highlighting the relationship between Deere and UAW. The great majority of the 107 decisions in the period covered by this analysis have involved grievances of considerable general significance beyond the immediate dispute. Many have involved policy grievances where new language was being tested or a governing principle sought. In this connection, it is well to keep in mind that the eight contracts are substantially uniform, if not identical, on most subjects. A decision in one plant is not technically binding on the other seven. Realistically, however, especially where identical language is involved, a decision in one plant is followed in the other seven.

The general significance of most of the cases reaching arbitration is attested to by the fact that most of the key substantive sections of the contracts have been involved in at least one arbitration case. A complete itemized breakdown of arbitrated issues would show over thirty separate and distinct areas of controversy. The duplication of issues occurs primarily where one might expect on discipline cases, protested overtime assignments, job classification controversies and job bidding disputes. In such areas, the general principles may be clear, but the factual circumstances and thus the proper application may vary from case to case.

3. Reasons Why Cases Reach the Arbitrator: In analyzing why cases reach arbitration, it is important to discover if possible whether either or both parties really trusts the arbitrator to decide critically important questions. In some relationships, it is obvious that the only cases going to arbitration are "dogs" where neither party really cares about the outcome. In other relationships, it is equally obvious that the parties are delegating too much of their own work to the arbitrator.

Deere and UAW have not been afraid to trust the permanent arbitrator with some fairly critical decisions. However, a number of potentially explosive issues have been settled by agreement rather than by arbitration. In these cases, the motives for settlement may well have been complex and do not necessarily reflect lack of faith in the arbitrator or the arbitrator process. Furthermore, it appears to be axiomatic that a settlement on any disputed issue is by definition preferable in most cases to an imposed award.

In a mature relationship, both parties are cautious about taking to arbitration disputes whose decision may kill off the arbitrator's future usefulness. This should be a factor in withholding certain types of cases from arbitration in a relationship where the parties believe in the arbitration process.

Subject to the foregoing qualifications, I have never observed any tendency on the part of either Deere or the UAW to withhold a dispute on the basis of lack of confidence in either the process or the individual arbitrator. An arbitrator whose official contacts with the parties are formal in keeping with the judicial approach is not in a position to be too accurate on appraising why cases reach him. However, I would venture the opinion that a minimum of cases in this relationship are traceable to internal union or company politics or to inadequate factual investigation of the grievance at earlier steps.

When major layoffs began to hit the farm equipment industry in 1952 and 1953, some key grievances were taken to arbitration testing out the meaning of the layoff and recall sections of the seniority article. However, with this exception, few grievances carried to arbitration could be directly attributed to unanticipated economic conditions or basic technological change.

The majority of disputes concern application of contract language to particular factual situations rather than interpretation issues as such. The contracts are clearly written and contain few surface ambiguities.

4. The Umpire's Philosophy of Arbitration: My approach has always been that of adjudication rather than mediation.[6] Deere and UAW do not wish the arbitrator to attempt to mediate or to settle disputes submitted to him. In fact, I believe that one of the principal considerations in my original appointment was my known adherence to the "judicial school" of arbitration.

The company appears to feel somewhat more strongly on this point than does the union. The latter has been critical of several decisions for being overly strict in contract construction to the point of being unrealistic and inequitable. However, at no time has the union ever sought to invoke the arbitrator's office as a mediator of a case actually in arbitration. Nor has the union ever used a straight box score approach as a method for evaluating the arbitrator's services. As a matter of fact, had the union been so disposed, my tenure would have long since ended since the quantitative box score has been substantially in management's favor on an over-all basis.

Arbitrators should never keep box scores since this is a practice that we all condemn. However, I could not resist the temptation in preparing this paper. I found out that out of 107 decisions, management had "won" 63, the union had "won" 42, and two cases had no winner, for technical reasons. The win-loss breakdown by individual plants reveals some interesting differences that would warrant some tentative hypotheses as to the relative abilities of local union leaders in selecting cases to push in arbitration.

The contracts themselves are an excellent index to the parties' joint expectations from arbitration. The line between the arbitrable and non-arbitrable grievances is carefully spelled out. At no time during the more than four-month strike in 1956 over changed incentive standards did either party ever suggest utilizing the permanent arbitrator as a mediatory aid to settlement. Many companies and unions might disagree with this approach. They would prefer to make all grievances subject to arbitration or, at least, any grievances arising under the contract. Deere and UAW, however, have chosen to exclude grievances not susceptible of judicial solution from the arbitrator's jurisdiction. It is possible that the long and costly 1956 strike over changed incen-

---

[6] See my article cited in note 5, *supra*, and an earlier article entitled "Hazards in Labor Arbitration" in Vol. 1, No. 3, *Industrial and Labor Relations Review* (April, 1948), pp. 386-405. See also Chapter 12 of my *Contemporary Collective Bargaining*, New York: Prentice-Hall, Inc., 1951.

tive standards may prompt the parties to modify their position that such disputes should be subject to strike action rather than arbitration. The disadvantages in using arbitration for such disputes may come to be regarded as a lesser evil than the possibility of prolonged strikes during the life of a contract.

Disputes over arbitrability have been comparatively rare. Only one out of 107 decisions covered by this analysis dealt solely with an arbitrability issue.[7] In a few other cases, the company raised a contention as to non-arbitrability that was rejected by the arbitrator before proceeding to a decision on the merits.

Rarely do the parties cite decisions involving other companies and unions. However, rather extensive use is made of prior arbitration decisions within the Deere chain. Prior awards are relied upon or distinguished as the case may be. This is entirely proper. I can recall comparatively few cases that appeared to be on all fours with a prior decision. However, a number have arisen where earlier decisions involving similar language or similar circumstances were helpful in clarifying the argument in the contemporary dispute.

I can recall only a few cases in which one party or the other has attempted to escape the consequences of an unpalatable award by seeking a different ruling through what might be termed a flanking operation on a very similar case. In a sophisticated relationship such as this one, such efforts do not go undetected by the opposing party.

Only one dispute was returned to the parties for negotiation. This was a recent case in which the arbitrator found that a particular job fell between two existing job classifications and, in keeping with the contract, awarded that he was without power to establish a classification or rate for the duties in question. All other cases finally submitted to arbitration have resulted in decisions on the merits, with three exceptions. In one case I ruled that the dispute was not arbitrable.[8] Another involved a memorandum opinion and award when during the hearing it developed that the Union's case had been founded on an erroneous

---

[7] This decision is reported at 22 LA 143. A survey of recent literature on arbitrability prompts the conclusion that the Deere-UAW experience is somewhat unusual in its comparative freedom from issues of this sort. See the scholarly paper by Jules J. Justin and my comments thereon in *Management Rights and the Arbitration Process*, Washington: BNA Incorporated, 1956.

[8] See note 7, *supra*.

factual premise. The third exception was a case where, by agreement reached during the hearing, the terms of settlement were incorporated in the award.

3. Summary Evaluation of the Deere-UAW Umpire System

Even in a permanent arbitration system where the arbitrator is reasonably well-acquainted with the parties, it is difficult for an arbitrator to assess the impact of arbitration upon labor relations at the plant level. One of the frustrating aspects of arbitration is that the arbitrator, curious though he may be, seldom learns very much about the postoperative effects of his decisions. Occasionally, he may hear by chance how John Doe made out on a higher-rated job to which the arbitrator had ruled he was entitled in rejecting a management contention that John Doe was not qualified. The arbitrator may also hear indirectly of the whereabouts of Richard Roe whose discharge for cause the arbitrator had upheld. In a few cases, the arbitrator may be reasonably sure that certain changes in contract languages are linked to earlier decisions. As a general rule, however, the arbitrator's direct knowledge of the impact of decisions upon relationships between the parties is meager and fragmentary. This is perhaps particularly true in a system of grievance arbitration of the judicial type.

With the foregoing qualifications in mind, it is possible to draw certain broad conclusions as to the impact of the arbitration system described in this chapter on union-management relations generally and on contract administration in particular. The ensuing analysis divides into three parts, 1) an appraisal of the positive accomplishments of the system described, 2) an appraisal of remaining flaws in the system viewed from the arbitrator's standpoint, and 3) a summary of certain distinctive characteristics of the Deere-UAW system that may have application value in other relationships.

Positive Accomplishments

The most fundamental affirmative conclusion that can be drawn is that the permanent arbitration machinery described in this chapter appears to have satisfied the expectations of the parties in establishing the system. To my knowledge, neither party has seriously considered abandoning the permanent arbitration mechanism since it was first introduced in 1946. The 1950-1955 contracts, signed at a time when the parties were unable to agree on a new permanent arbitrator, contemplated a return to permanent arbitration from ad hoc as soon as a mutually acceptable individual could be found. At present writing, the conclusion appears warranted that both parties have a solid preference for permanent arbitration over ad hoc arrangements.

A second conclusion that appears to be justified by the record is that permanent arbitration has encouraged the parties to settle a greater percentage of grievances short of arbitration, particularly in recent years. The annual average of cases heard by me in the period 1952-1956 is considerably lower than during the four-year period 1946-1950 when Professor Updegraff was the permanent arbitrator. As I have already noted, there are a number of factors contributing to the reduced arbitration load in recent years. In my judgment, the most important are 1) the increased uniformity in language among the eight contracts, 2) the increased centralization in the pre-arbitration and arbitration stages on both sides of the table, and 3) the impressive body of common law built up since 1946 that has clearly operated to reduce grievances going to arbitration in recent years.

It is also safe to conclude that a better understanding of the principles of contract administration has been achieved in recent years by both foremen and stewards. I can recall no case in recent years of an employee or group of employees attempting to short-circuit the contract's grievance machinery or of a foreman's ignoring or flanking of contract provisions.

There appears to have been a marked reduction of wildcat stoppages in recent years. It would be presumptuous to attribute such improvements entirely to the presence of an effective arbitration system. However, it is probable that the impact of certain key discipline decisions growing out of earlier wildcats contributed substantially to their diminution.

Another indication of more effective contract administration is the comparatively light load in the first year under the 1955-1958 contracts in contrast with the first year of operation under the 1950-1955 agreements.

Present indications are that this trend will continue. There is evidence in recent months of a marked reduction in the total of grievances filed at the various plants and a clear decline in the ratio of cases arbitrated.

Judged by my own standards, another positive accomplishment of the Deere-UAW system has been the continuing adherence to the judicial approach to arbitration. The great majority of cases have been bona fide disputes over contract interpretation or application. Seldom have I enjoyed the experience of working on a case that was "easy" to decide.

Directly related to this joint faith in the judicial approach is the record of the parties on acceptance of awards. To my knowledge, there has never been an instance of failure to put an award into effect. No arbitration decision has been contested in the courts by either party. Nor has either party ever attempted to secure a motion to stay arbitration. As already noted, issues as to arbitrability rarely arise. To my mind, these factors are indicative of a stable, mature use of permanent arbitration machinery.

Unsettled Problems

The Deere-UAW arbitration is not without its flaws. The principal areas where improvement is needed include the following: 1) better referral procedures, 2) better case preparation in some instances, 3) greater use of stipulations as to facts, 4) adoption of submission agreements, and 5) more liberal use of transcripts in complex factual disputes. Each of these problems deserves brief comment.

No uniform procedure exists for referral of cases to the arbitrator. Each local union follows its own inclinations on this matter. Only three of the eight locals submit copies of the written allegations and answers at the various steps prior to arbitration. In most cases, the arbitrator has no idea prior to the hearing what cases he is to hear and what they involve. Various abortive efforts have been made to improve the referral procedure without success. There is some indication currently that the problem may be solved by the suggestion that each party write up its case rather fully at the Step D level. If this should be agreed upon, the arbitrator would have the equivalent of pre-hearing briefs which might facilitate greatly the actual presentation of cases. As matters now stand, on each case the arbitrator starts absolutely from scratch. Of course, this is less disadvantageous in a permanent umpire set-up where the arbitrator is familiar with the contract and with the basic presentation techniques of the parties.

A second problem arises from rather considerable differences in the ability and efficiency of local union personnel in preparing cases for arbitration. Although all cases are argued by an international representative, the latter must depend necessarily on local union officials for development of the evidential basis of his case. Inadequate or incomplete preparation handicaps the international representative rather seriously in some cases. I have had the impression on some occasions that the international representative was "playing it by ear" at the hearing because of inadequacies in case preparation. There are indications also that the attorney for Deere & Company who makes all the management presentations in arbitration has encountered this same problem, although in lesser degree than his Union opposite number.

The third criticism relates to techniques in presentation of direct evidence. Both parties still rely primarily on witnesses for presentation of factual evidence. I would personally prefer greater use of stipulations on factual material. Extensive use of witnesses may sometimes tend to cloud rather than to clarify the factual picture in the arbitrator's mind. It is my impression that in some cases more thoroughgoing investigation in pre-arbitration steps would result in expanded possibilities for stipulations as to facts. Whenever stipulations can be agreed upon, there is a clear gain in economy of case presentation and probably fuller understanding on the arbitrator's part. Also, when witnesses are used this serves not infrequently to encourage the tendency to mix argument with proof.

From the arbitrator's standpoint, it would be preferable to have a submission agreement on the issue to be decided in each case. As already noted, a step in this direction has been taken under the current agreements with the issue being framed by the Step D appeal and the company's Step D answer. However, there seems to be no valid reason for continuing to avoid the use of the submission agreement. Although I am critical of this omission, fairness compels noting at this point that the actual case presentation seldom leaves the arbitrator in any doubt as to the correct phrasing of the actual issue before him.

As a final criticism, I feel compelled to comment on the infrequent use of a court reporter in Deere-UAW hearings. A transcript is not necessary in cases where the facts are not disputed and the issue is a pure question of what clause X means or whether clause Y applies to an agreed set of circumstances. However, in a case involving credibility of testimony (discipline cases, for example) or in a case raising complex technical questions (e.g., job classification disputes and incentive pay cases), a verbatim transcript is a tremendous aid to an arbitrator in reaching an informed, accurate and correct decision. In my opinion, the advantages of having a transcript in such cases far outweigh the disadvantages of added expense and time lag between the hearing and receipt of the decision.

Distinctive Aspects of the Deere-UAW System

Perhaps the primary justification for a full description of a particular arbitration system is its possible value in application to other arbitration relationships. The Deere-UAW system has a number of distinctive characteristics that make it worthy of emulation by any company and union involved in a multi-plant bargaining set-up with a comparable case load.

In the first place, ten years' experience has demonstrated the viability of the judicial approach in the use of arbitration as an instrument for improved administration of contracts. Secondly, the experience of Deere and UAW shows the value of professionalizing the presentation function in arbitration.

Both the company and the union employ "specialists" in presenting their cases. The beneficial consequences are apparent. Screening of grievances is more effective on both sides, as a result of informal advice by the "professionals" who ultimately have to present the cases going to arbitration. At the hearing stage, case presentation is more economical and more effective by virtue of the specialized talent involved on both sides of the table. Skilled oral presentation of cases serves to eliminate the need for briefs.

The absence of briefs is one of the truly distinctive characteristics of the Deere-UAW system. Briefs have been filed in only one out of 107 cases heard during the more than four years covered by this analysis. Elimination of briefs entails substantial savings in expense and time. My experience with Deere and UAW leads me to conclude that briefs are generally an expendable luxury that can be eliminated in the great majority of cases by intelligent, professional case presentation.

On the substantive side, the principal distinctive characteristic of the Deere-UAW set-up is the comparatively small number of discipline and seniority disputes reaching arbitration. The reasons for this have been dealt with earlier. Also, the exclusion of disputes over revised incentive standards and rates on new hourly or piecework jobs from the arbitrator's jurisdiction is sufficiently unusual today to warrant being labeled distinctive. Whether to continue excluding such disputes from arbitration and the coverage of the no strike-no lockout clause is probably the most serious unsettled question facing the parties at present.

It is necessarily hazardous to predict the future course of any dynamic relationship. Present indications are that Deere and UAW will maintain the arbitration techniques and procedures described in this paper. Both parties regard arbitration of the judicial type as a logical terminal step for resolution of grievances concerning contract interpretation or application. Their estimate of its importance in contract administration is measured by the increasing attention given in recent years to improving the effectiveness of screening and to raising the level of case preparation and presentation.

Basic to the general success of the Deere-UAW system of permanent arbitration is the fact that the parties understand and agree upon the role of grievance arbitration in contract administration. The system has proven itself over a period of ten years and several contracts. It is an excellent working model of grievance arbitration of the judicial type.

PROGRAM

National Academy of Arbitrators Annual Meeting

JANUARY 31, FEBRUARY 1 and 2, 1957

BELLEVUE-STRATFORD HOTEL

PHILADELPHIA, PENNSYLVANIA

THURSDAY, JANUARY 31—Burgundy Room (All Sessions)

9:00 A.M.—10:00 A.M.....Registration

10:00 A.M.—11:00 A.M.....Business Session and Committee Reports

11:00 A.M.—12:15 P.M.....*Chairman:* LLOYD H. BAILER

"Halting the Drift Toward Technicalities in Arbitration"

Speaker: JOHN F. SEMBOWER

Discussant: G. ALLAN DASH, JR.

12:15 P.M.— 2:00 P.M.....Luncheon Recess

2:00 P.M.............................*Chairman:* NATHAN P. FEINSINGER

"Arbitration Awards and Just Cause"

Speaker: J. FRED HOLLY

Discussant: BENJAMIN AARON

"What Happens After Reinstatement?"

Speaker: ARTHUR M. ROSS

Discussant: SIDNEY A. WOLFF

FRIDAY, FEBRUARY 1

10:00 A.M.—12:15 P.M.....*Chairman:* RUSSELL SMITH
Burgundy Room   Panel Discussion: "Proposed Uniform Arbitration Act"

Speakers: DEAN MAYNARD E. PIRSIG, ROBERT L. HOWARD, WHITLEY P. MCCOY

12:15 P.M...........................Luncheon Meeting Session in Recognition of
Clover Room   the 10th Anniversary of the Academy

Speakers: PRESIDENT JOHN DAY LARKIN (Presidential Paper); RALPH T. SEWARD, First President of the Academy

2:15 P.M............................*Chairman:* SYLVESTER GARRETT
Burgundy Room   "Arbitration of Disputes Involving Incentive Problems"

Speakers:

OWEN FAIRWEATHER, an Industry View
WILLIAM GOMBERG, a Labor View

Discussants:
Mr. Fairweather's Paper—PEARCE DAVIS

Mr. Gomberg's Paper—RONALD W. HAUGHTON

6:30 P.M............................Reception—Cocktails
North Garden

7:30 P.M............................Annual Dinner
Rose Garden   *Presiding:* PRESIDENT JOHN DAY LARKIN

Speaker: DR. GEORGE W. TAYLOR

SATURDAY, FEBRUARY 2

9:30 A.M. ....Business Session—Committee Reports

11:30 A.M. ....Election of Officers

Noon ....Adjournment
Burgundy Room

PROPOSED UNIFORM ARBITRATION ACT

Act Relating to Arbitration and to Make Uniform
the Law with Reference Thereto *

SECTION 1. (*Validity of Arbitration Agreement.*) A written agreement to submit any existing controversy to arbitration or a provision in a written contract to submit to arbitration any controversy thereafter arising between the parties is valid, enforceable and irrevocable, save upon such grounds as exist at law or in equity for the revocation of any contract. The act also applies to arbitration agreements between employers and employees or between their respective representatives (unless otherwise provided in the agreement.)

SECTION 2. (*Proceedings to Compel or Stay Arbitration.*)

(a) On application of a party showing an agreement described in Section 1, and the opposing party's refusal to arbitrate, the Court shall order the parties to proceed with arbitration, but if the opposing party denies the existence of the agreement to arbitrate, the Court shall proceed summarily to the determination of the issue so raised and shall order arbitration if found for the moving party, otherwise, the application shall be denied.

(b) On application, the court may stay an arbitration proceeding commenced or threatened on a showing that there is no agreement to arbitrate. Such an issue, when in substantial and bona fide dispute, shall be forthwith and summarily tried and the stay ordered if found for the moving party. If found for the opposing party, the court shall order the parties to proceed to arbitration.

(c) If an issue referable to arbitration under the alleged agreement is involved in an action or proceeding pending in a court having jurisdiction to hear applications under subdivision (a) of this Section, the application shall be made therein. Otherwise and subject to Section 18, the application may be made in any court of competent jurisdiction.

(d) Any action or proceeding involving an issue subject to arbitration shall be stayed if an order for arbitration or an application therefor has been made under this section or, if the issue is severable, the stay may be with respect thereto only. When the application is made in such action or proceeding, the order for arbitration shall include such stay.

* *Adopted by the* National Conference of the Commissioners on Uniform State Laws, August 20, 1955, as amended August 24, 1956. *Approved by the* House of Delegates of the American Bar Association, August 26, 1955, and August 30, 1956.

(e) An order for arbitration shall not be refused on the ground that the claim in issue lacks merit or bona fides or because any fault or grounds for the claim sought to be arbitrated have not been shown.

SECTION 3. (*Appointment of Arbitrators by Court.*) If the arbitration agreement provides a method of appointment of arbitrators, this method shall be followed. In the absence thereof, or if the agreed method fails or for any reason cannot be followed, or when an arbitrator appointed fails or is unable to act and his successor has not been duly appointed, the court on application of a party shall appoint one or more arbitrators. An arbitrator so appointed has all the powers of one specifically named in the agreement.

SECTION 4. (*Majority Action by Arbitrators.*) The powers of the arbitrators may be exercised by a majority unless otherwise provided by the agreement or by this act.

SECTION 5. (*Hearing.*) Unless otherwise provided by the agreement:

(a) The arbitrators shall appoint a time and place for the hearing and cause notification to the parties to be served personally or by registered mail not less than five days before the hearing. Appearance at the hearing waives such notice. The arbitrators may adjourn the hearing from time to time as necessary and, on request of a party and for good cause, or upon their own motion may postpone the hearing to a time not later than the date fixed by the agreement for making the award unless the parties consent to a later date. The arbitrators may hear and determine the controversy upon the evidence produced notwithstanding the failure of a party duly notified to appear. The court on application may direct the arbitrators to proceed promptly with the hearing and determination of the controversy.

(b) The parties are entitled to be heard, to present evidence material to the controversy and to cross-examine witnesses appearing at the hearing.

(c) The hearing shall be conducted by all the arbitrators but a majority may determine any question and render a final award. If, during the course of the hearing, an arbitrator for any reason ceases to act, the remaining arbitrator or arbitrators appointed to act as neutrals may continue with the hearing and determination of the controversy.

SECTION 6. (*Representation by Attorney.*) A party has the right to be represented by an attorney at any proceeding or hearing under this act. A waiver thereof prior to the proceeding or hearing is ineffective.

SECTION 7. (*Witnesses, Subpoenas, Depositions.*)

(a) The arbitrators may issue (cause to be issued) subpoenas for the attendance of witnesses and for the production of books, records, documents and other evidence, and shall have the power to administer oaths. Subpoenas so issued shall be served, and upon application to the Court by a party or the arbitrators, enforced, in the manner provided by law for the service and enforcement of subpoenas in a civil action.

(b) On application of a party and for use as evidence, the arbitrators may permit a deposition to be taken, in the manner and upon the terms designated by the arbitrators, of a witness who cannot be subpoenaed or is unable to attend the hearing.

(c) All provisions of law compelling a person under subpoena to testify are applicable.

(d) Fees for attendance as a witness shall be the same as for a witness in the ....Court.

SECTION 8. (*Award.*)

(a) The award shall be in writing and signed by the arbitrators joining in the award. The arbitrators shall deliver a copy to each party personally or by registered mail, or as provided in the agreement.

(b) An award shall be made within the time fixed therefor by the agreement or, if not so fixed, within such time as the court orders on application of a party. The parties may extend the time in writing either before or after the expiration thereof. A party waives the objection that an award was not made within the time required unless he notifies the arbitrators of his objection prior to the delivery of the award to him.

SECTION 9. (*Change of Award by Arbitrators.*) On application of a party or, if an application to the court is pending under Sections 11, 12 or 13, on submission to the arbitrators by the court under such conditions as the court may order, the arbitrators may modify or correct the award upon the grounds stated in paragraphs (1) and (3) of subdivision (a) of Section 13, or for the purpose of clarifying the award. The application shall be made within twenty days after delivery of the award to the applicant. Written notice thereof shall be given forthwith to the opposing party, stating he must serve his objections thereto, if any, within ten days from the notice. The award so modified or corrected is subject to the provisions of Sections 11, 12 and 13.

SECTION 10. (*Fees and Expenses of Arbitration.*) Unless otherwise provided in the agreement to arbitrate, the arbitrators' expenses and fees, together with other expenses, not including counsel fees, incurred in the conduct of the arbitration, shall be paid as provided in the award.

SECTION 11. (*Confirmation of an Award.*) Upon application of a party, the Court shall confirm an award, unless within the time limits hereinafter imposed grounds are urged for vacating or modifying or correcting the award, in which case the court shall proceed as provided in Sections 12 and 13.

SECTION 12. (*Vacating an Award.*)

(a) Upon application of a party, the court shall vacate an award where:

(1) The award was procured by corruption, fraud or other undue means;

(2) There was evident partiality by an arbitrator appointed as a neutral or corruption in any of the arbitrators or misconduct prejudicing the rights of any party;

(3) The arbitrators exceeded their powers;

(4) The arbitrators refused to postpone the hearing upon sufficient cause being shown therefor or refused to hear evidence material to the controversy or otherwise so conducted the hearing, contrary to the provisions of Section 5, as to prejudice substantially the rights of a party; or

(5) There was no arbitration agreement and the issue was not adversely determined in proceedings under Section 2 and the party did not participate in the arbitra-

tion hearing without raising the objection;

But the fact that the relief was such that it could not or would not be granted by a court of law or equity is not ground for vacating or refusing to confirm the award.

(b) An application under this Section shall be made within ninety days after delivery of a copy of the award to the applicant, except that, if predicated upon corruption, fraud or other undue means, it shall be made within ninety days after such grounds are known or should have been known.

(c) In vacating the award on grounds other than stated in clause (5) of Subsection (a) the court may order a rehearing before new arbitrators chosen as provided in the agreement, or in the absence thereof, by the court in accordance with Section 3, or, if the award is vacated on grounds set forth in clauses (3), and (4) of Subsection (a) the court may order a rehearing before the arbitrators who made the award or their successors appointed in accordance with Section 3. The time within which the agreement requires the award to be made is applicable to the rehearing and commences from the date of the order.

(d) If the application to vacate is denied and no motion to modify or correct the award is pending, the court shall confirm the award.

SECTION 13. (*Modification or Correction of Award.*)

(a) Upon application made within ninety days after delivery of a copy of the award to the applicant, the court shall modify or correct the award where:

(1) There was an evident miscalculation of figures or an evident mistake in the description of any person, thing or property referred to in the award;

(2) The arbitrators have awarded upon a matter not submitted to them and the award may be corrected without affecting the merits of the decision upon the issues submitted; or

(3) The award is imperfect in a matter of form, not affecting the merits of the controversy.

(b) If the application is granted, the court shall modify and correct the award so as to effect its intent and shall confirm the award as so modified and corrected. Otherwise, the court shall confirm the award as made.

(c) An application to modify or correct an award may be joined in the alternative with an application to vacate the award.

SECTION 14. (*Judgment or Decree on Award.*) Upon the granting of an order confirming, modifying or correcting an award, judgment or decree shall be entered in conformity therewith and be enforced as any other judgment or decree. Costs of the application and of the proceedings subsequent thereto, and disbursements may be awarded by the court.

[SECTION 15. (*Judgment Roll, Docketing.*)

(a) On entry of judgment or decree, the clerk shall prepare the judgment roll consisting, to the extent filed, of the following:

(1) The agreement and each written extension of the time

within which to make the award;

(2) The award;

(3) A copy of the order confirming, modifying or correcting the award; and

(4) A copy of the judgment or decree.

(b) The judgment or decree may be docketed as if rendered in an action.]

SECTION 16. (*Applications to Court.*) Except as otherwise provided, an application to the court under this act shall be by motion and shall be heard in the manner and upon the notice provided by law or rule of court for the making and hearing of motions. Unless the parties have agreed otherwise, notice of an initial application for an order shall be served in the manner provided by law for the service of a summons in an action.

SECTION 17. (*Court, Jurisdiction.*) The term "court" means any court of competent jurisdiction of this State. The making of an agreement described in Section 1 providing for arbitration in this State confers jurisdiction on the court to enforce the agreement under this Act and to enter judgment on an award thereunder.

SECTION 18. (*Venue.*) An initial application shall be made to the court of the (county) in which the agreement provides the arbitration hearing shall be held or, if the hearing has been held, in the county in which it was held. Otherwise the application shall be made in the (county) where the adverse party resides or has a place of business or, if he has no residence or place of business in this State, to the court of any (county).

All subsequent applications shall be made to the court hearing the initial application unless the court otherwise directs.

SECTION 19. (*Appeals.*)

(a) An appeal may be taken from:

(1) An order denying an application to compel arbitration made under Section 2;

(2) An order granting an application to stay arbitration made under Section 2 (b);

(3) An order confirming or denying confirmation of an award;

(4) An order modifying or correcting an award;

(5) An order vacating an award with directing a rehearing; or

(6) A judgment or decree entered pursuant to the provisions of this act.

(b) The appeal shall be taken in the manner and to the same extent as from orders or judgments in a civil action.

SECTION 20. (*Act Not Retroactive.*) This act applies only to agreements made subsequent to the taking effect of this act.

SECTION 21. (*Uniformity of Interpretation.*) This act shall be so construed as to effectuate its general purpose to make uniform the law of those states which enact it.

SECTION 22. (*Constitutionality.*) If any provision of this act or the application thereof to any person or circumstance is held invalid, the invalidity shall not affect other provisions or applications of the act which can be given without the invalid provision or application, and to this end the provisions of this act are severable.

SECTION 23. (*Short Title.*) This act may be cited as the Uniform Arbitration Act.

SECTION 24. (*Repeal.*) All acts or parts of acts which are inconsistent with the provisions of this act are hereby repealed.

SECTION 25. (*Time of Taking Effect.*) This act shall take effect ....

Brackets and parenthesis enclose language which the Commissioners suggest may be used by those States desiring to do so.

NATIONAL ACADEMY OF ARBITRATORS

REPORT OF COMMITTEE ON LAW
AND LEGISLATION

January 18, 1957

Arbitration Legislation: Uniform Act

On August 20, 1955, the National Conference of the Commissioners on Uniform State Laws adopted a draft "Act Relating to Arbitration and to Make Uniform the law with Reference Thereto", covering, in a single proposed statute, both commercial and labor dispute arbitration. This Act was approved by the House of Delegates of the American Bar Association on August 30, 1955.

At the January, 1956 Annual Meeting of the National Academy of Arbitrators, a Report of the Committee on Law and Legislation, headed by Russell A. Smith as Chairman was read and approved. The general conclusion of the Committee was that the Draft Act had many good features, but it was subject to serious objections as a statute covering labor dispute arbitration, primarily in its failure to restrict judicial review of Awards to the extent which is desirable.

A resolution was thereupon passed at the said Annual Meeting which read as follows:

NATIONAL ACADEMY OF ARBITRATORS
RESOLUTION PASSED AT 1956 ANNUAL MEETING

At the January, 1955 Annual Meeting it was resolved that the Academy should refrain from taking any official position on the question of whether there should or should not be statutory regulation of voluntary labor dispute arbitration, but that the Academy could, consistently with this policy, indicate its judgment as to the desirable content of regulatory statutes. Since then the proposed Uniform Arbitration Act, covering both labor dispute and commercial arbitration, has been promulgated. An analysis of this proposed Act by our Legislative Committee and certain of our regional groups shows that it contains certain deficiencies and defects insofar as it would apply to labor dispute arbitration. It is therefore the judgment of the Academy that the widespread adoption of the proposed Act in its present form would be a disservice to labor-management relations.

RESOLVED, therefore, that the Academy oppose the enactment of the proposed Uniform Arbitration Act in its present form insofar as it would apply to labor dispute arbitration;

RESOLVED, further, that the Board of Governors of the Academy; in consultation with the Academy's Committee on Law and Legislation, prepare a formal statement of the position of the Academy concerning the proposed Uniform Act, such statement to include specific proposals of changes deemed necessary to make the proposed Act acceptable;

RESOLVED, further, that the Board of Governors take appropriate action to make known the position of the Academy on the proposed Uniform Act.

At a meeting of the Board of Governors held in Chicago on April 28, 1956, the following resolutions were adopted:

1. All Regional Chairmen shall be requested to notify the Chairman of the Committee on Law and Legislation of the introduction of any legislation in the geographical area covered in their respective regions relating to the Uniform Arbitration Act.

2. The Chairman shall be notified of any commissions or committees appointed by the respective legislatures for the purpose of conducting any hearings relating to the Uniform Arbitration Act.

3. The Academy desires the opportunity to be heard at local levels in the event that legislative hearings are held on the Uniform Arbitration Act.

4. The Chairman shall distribute the Russell Smith Report accompanied by a copy of the resolution passed by the Academy concerning its policy relating to the Act to all interested parties, legislators, state commissioners, labor organizations and management organizations which evince interest in the Uniform Arbitration Act.

5. The Chairman of the Committee shall advise the Regional Chairman of any pending legislation concerning the Uniform

Arbitration Act in the respective geographical areas which may be brought to the attention of the Chairman.

6. The Chairman shall distribute any and all reports, articles or other publications relating to the Uniform Arbitration Act which in his opinion would be of interest to members of the Academy or other interested parties.

7. The President of the Academy is authorized to make any and all expenditures necessary to implement the above resolutions, and to appear at hearings or authorize appearances of Academy Members at such hearings at Academy expense.

In accordance with the resolution of the Board of Governors, all Regional Chairmen were advised of the Act of the Board and the Russell Smith Report of the Committee on Law and Legislation dated January 26, 1956 was sent to everyone listed by a member.

In accordance with the said resolutions of the Board of Governors, a letter was sent to all the members of this Committee asking them to advise the Chairman of the introduction of any legislation that may be introduced in their Region or any hearings that may be set relating to the Uniform Arbitration Act; also requesting that they mail to the Chairman of this Committee the names and addresses of leaders of Unions and Companies and other organizations that should be advised of the action taken by the National Academy of Arbitrators. A copy of the Russell Smith Report was mailed to each person named by the Members of this Committee.

On August 30, 1956, the House of Delegates of the American Bar Association approved the following amendments in the Uniform Arbitration Act which were adopted by the National Conference of the Commissioners on Uniform State Laws on August 24, 1956:

Section 12 (Vacating an Award)

> *Sub-section (a) (3)* which read, "The Arbitrators exceeded their powers or rendered an Award contrary to public policy" was amended to read: "The Arbitrators exceeded their powers."
>
> *Sub-section (a) (4)* which read, "The Award is so indefinite or incomplete that it cannot be performed" was stricken.
>
> *Sub-section (a) (5)* was changed to sub-section (4) and the word, "or" was inserted at the end of the paragraph marked "(4)."

Sub-section (a) (6) which read "The Award is so grossly erroneous as to imply bad faith on the part of the Arbitrators, or" was stricken.

Paragraph (7) was re-numbered "(5)" and *Sentences in Section 12 (c)* were re-numbered.

The members of this Committee were advised of the changes made in the Uniform Arbitration Act, and the view of each member as to the Amended Uniform Arbitration Act was requested.

* * *

In accordance with the Report of the American Bar Association at its 1956 Meeting, it was stated that the Uniform Arbitration Act as now approved by the American Bar Association will be presented to the Legislature of each State by the American Bar Association Standing Committee of State Legislation.

It should now be up to the members of the National Academy of Arbitrators to notify the Chairman of the Committee on Law and Legislation of the introduction of any such legislation in their State, and their approval or disapproval of it. The Russell Smith Report, as approved by the National Academy of Arbitrators at its 1956 Convention, should be used as a means of analyzing such legislation for the good of labor arbitration.

Harry Abrahams, Chairman of the
Committee on Law and Legislation

Members of the Committee: George E. Bowles, Archibald Cox, Frank Elkouri, Robert Feinberg, William Forrester, Alexander H. Frey, Sylvester Garrett, Walter Gellhorn, Robert Howard, Robert E. Matthews, Russell A. Smith, Clarence M. Updegraff.

NATIONAL ACADEMY OF ARBITRATORS

CONSTITUTION AND BY-LAWS

CONSTITUTION

ARTICLE I

Section 1. The name of this association shall be National Academy of Arbitrators.

Section 2. The principal office and headquarters of the Academy shall be located in such place as shall be designated by the Board of Governors.

ARTICLE II

Section 1. The purposes for which the Academy is formed are: To establish and foster the highest standards of integrity, competence, honor, and character among those engaged in the arbitration of industrial disputes on a professional basis; to adopt and encourage the acceptance of and adherence to canons of ethics to govern the conduct of arbitrators; to promote the study and understanding of the arbitration of industrial disputes; to encourage friendly association among the members of the profession; to cooperate with other organizations, institutions, and learned societies interested in industrial relations, and to do any and all things which shall be appropriate in the furtherance of these purposes.

Section 2. The Academy shall not recommend, designate or appoint arbitrators.

ARTICLE III

Section 1. The Academy is a non-profit, professional and honorary association of arbitrators, open to membership without regard to politics, race, creed, color or sex; its membership shall be composed of those who have hereby associated themselves together in furtherance of the objects and purposes here set forth and such other persons as may from time to time be elected to membership as hereinafter provided.

ARTICLE IV

Section 1. "The government and management of the Academy shall be vested in a Board of Governors consisting of twelve (12) members in addition to the ex-officio members hereinafter provided for. At the annual meeting in January, 1957, four (4) shall be elected for a three year term, and one (1) for a two year term, and one (1) for a one year term. At each annual meeting thereafter four (4) members shall be elected for a three year term. After the election to be held January 20, 1950, no member of the Board shall be eligible for two (2) successive three year terms." (As amended February 2, 1957.)

ARTICLE V

Section 1. Members shall be participating, contributing and sustaining members.

Section 2. Members shall be elected by the Board of Governors in the manner provided in the By-Laws (As amended)

ARTICLE VI

Section 1. The officers of the Academy shall consist of a President, four Vice Presidents, an Executive Secretary, and a Treasurer, who shall be elected at the annual meeting for one year terms and who shall serve as ex officio members of the Board of Governors with the right to vote.

Section 2. The President and Vice Presidents shall be eligible for no more than 2 successive terms in the same office. Upon the expiration of his term of office the retiring President shall serve as ex officio member of the Board of Governors for one year with the right to vote.

ARTICLE VII

"Amendments to the Constitution or By-Laws shall be made by affirmative vote of two thirds (2/3) of those voting at any membership meeting: Provided, however, that after February 2, 1957 no proposed amendment shall be adopted unless it has been (a) approved by a majority vote of the Board of Governors, or (b) signed by ten (10) members of the Academy; and thereafter filed in writing with the Secretary at least ninety (90) days prior to the membership meeting, and distributed by mail to the entire membership at least forty five (45) days prior to the meeting. (This proviso shall not be construed to prevent the making of germane amendments to such provision at the time of the membership meeting)." (As amended February 2, 1957.)

BY-LAWS

ARTICLE I

Duties of Officers

Section 1. President

The president, or in his absence, one of the Vice Presidents, shall preside at all meetings of the Academy. At the Annual Meeting the President shall present a report of the general affairs of the Academy.

Section 2. Secretary

The Secretary, under the direction of the President and the Board of Governors, shall perform the customary duties of such office. He shall conduct the correspondence of the Academy; record the proceedings of all meetings of the Academy and the proceedings of the meetings of the

Board of Governors. He shall issue all notices and other documents requiring verification; make at each Annual Meeting a report of the membership of the Academy and all other matters pertaining to the conduct of his office; and perform such other duties as may be assigned to him by the President and by the Board of Governors.

Section 3. Treasurer

The Treasurer, under the direction of the President and the Board of Governors, shall collect and deposit all moneys due the Academy; verify all bills and pay them when approved by the President or the Board of Governors; and make at each annual meeting, or more often if required by the Board of Governors, a report of the accounts of the Academy.

ARTICLE II

Annual Meeting

Section 1. The Annual Meeting of the Academy shall be held on the third Friday in January of each year at such place as shall be designated by the Board of Governors.

ARTICLE III

Board of Governors

Section 1. The Board of Governors shall be the governing body of this Academy.

Section 2. The Board of Governors shall be elected by the members, as provided in the Constitution, and shall hold office for the term elected or until successors are elected and qualified.

Section 3. Vacancies on the Board of Governors occasioned by death, resignation, or other reason, shall be filled by appointment by the President, and Governors so appointed shall serve until the next Annual Meeting of membership.

Section 4. The Annual Meeting of the Board of Governors shall be held immediately following the Annual Meeting of the membership for the purpose of considering such matters as may be properly brought to its attention.

Section 5. Regular meetings of the Board of Governors shall be held semi-annually at such time and place as the President shall designate.

Section 6. Special meetings of the Board of Governors of this Academy may be called by the President or upon formal request in writing by a majority of its members. Such notice shall specify the objects and purposes of such special meeting and no other business shall be transacted except by unanimous consent of those present.

Section 7. Notice of all meetings of the Board of Governors stating time and place of the meetings shall be forwarded by the Secretary to each member of the Board at least ten days prior to any such meetings.

Section 8. Five or more members of the Board of Governors shall constitute a quorum.

ARTICLE IV

Committees

Section 1. The President shall appoint the following standing Committees:

    a—Membership Committee

    b—Committee on Ethics

    c—Committee on Research and Education

    d—Committee on Legislation

    e—Auditing Committee

Section 2. The President shall appoint such Special Committees as he may from time to time deem necessary and advisable in the furtherance of the objects and purposes of this Academy or as voted by the membership at any Annual Meeting. Nothing herein contained shall be so construed as to limit the power of the Board of Governors to appoint such sub-committees as it may deem necessary in the furtherance of the powers conferred upon it under the Constitution.

ARTICLE V

Dues

Section 1. The annual dues for participation membership shall be $10 per year.

Section 2. The annual dues for contributing members shall be $25 per year.

Section 3. The annual dues for sustaining members shall be $100 per year.

Section 4. Each year each member shall choose the class of membership which he desires to hold during the year giving consideration to the importance of arbitration and to its importance to him as a source of income. The class of membership so adopted by each member shall not be shown in the public roster of Academy Membership.

Section 5. The dues of members elected to membership after July 1 of any year shall be one half the amount of annual dues for that year.

Section 6. Dues statements shall be distributed to the members as of the first of the month following the annual meeting and shall be paid by the tenth of the following month. Members who have not paid as of such date shall be notified that they are in arrears and unless payment is made within sixty days thereafter, they shall be subject to suspension by the Board of Governors. Any member suspended by the Board of Governors for the nonpayment of dues shall be automatically reinstated upon payment of all arrears within thirty days of notice of such suspension. After the lapse of such thirty days, reinstatement may be made only by vote of the Board of Governors. (As amended January, 1955.)

ARTICLE VI

Membership

Section 1. Application for membership shall be filed on an approved form with the Secretary of the Membership Committee.

Section 2. At least forty-five days prior to the approval or disapproval of an application by the Membership Committee, the Committee shall send to each member a statement of the qualifications of the applicant.

Section 3. Upon completion of the review of an application and following a majority vote of those present at a meeting called for the consideration of such application, the Membership Committee shall submit its recommendations to the Board of Governors.

Section 4. The Board of Governors shall act on the recommendations of the Membership Committee at each semi-annual meeting, or at any special meeting called for that purpose, and applicants shall be admitted to membership by a two-thirds vote of those present.

INDEX